K

D1256692

MAPPING THE FIRST WORLD WAR

BATTLEFIELDS OF THE GREAT CONFLICT FROM ABOVE

SIMON FORTY

CONWAY

NOTE ON THE MAPS

All the maps illustrated in this book have been drawn from the large collection held by the National Archives (formerly the Public Record Office [PRO]) at Kew in west London. This is the major holding of all public documents in the United Kingdom. The maps are derived from a number of government departments and reflect the interests and concerns at the time they were compiled. The maps incorporated in this selection are drawn primarily from contemporary World War I sources and many of them have been annotated by the commanders or operational staff who used them. This additional information adds greatly to their value as historical documents. The contemporary annotation by commanders or other operational staff helps to provide a fascinating insight to concerns at the time and into the minds of the leading British military figures of the war. All the maps have their PRO reference number at the end of the caption to facilitate further research.

ACKNOWLEDGEMENTS

This book combines the work of a number of writers and researchers. I'd like to thank for their major written contributions Sandra Forty, Ian Westwell, and Michael Swift; and for their assistance in the PRO archives Paul Johnson and Hugh Alexander.

PHOTO CREDITS

All the maps and other images in this book, including those on the front and back covers, have been reproduced by courtesy of the National Archives. Crown Copyright material in the National Archives is reproduced by permission of the Controller of Her Majesty's Stationery Office.

This edition published in Great Britain in 2013 by
Conway
A Division of Anova Books Ltd
10 Southcombe Street
London W14 0RA
www.anovabooks.com
www.conwaypublishing.com
Twitter: @conwaybooks

© PRC Publishing 2002

Distributed in the US and Canada by Sterling Publishing Co. Ltd
387 Park Avenue South, New York, NY 100016-8810

All rights reserved. No part of this publication may be reproduced, stored in a retrieval system, or transmitted in any form or by any means electronic, mechanical, photocopying, recording or otherwise, without the prior written permission of the copyright owner.

British Library Cataloguing in Publication Data:
A catalogue record for this book is available from the British Library.

ISBN 9781844862184
Printed by 1010 Printing International Ltd, China.

To receive regular email updates on forthcoming Conway titles, email conway@anovabooks.com with Conway Update in the subject field.

CONTENTS

INTRODUCTION

From our perspective, of a hundred years on, World War I has become the forerunner to World War II—the first half of a conflict that spanned half a century. But in the immediate aftermath of the war it was not seen like this at all. It was the 'Great War,' and people confidently expected to have seen the end of war forever. The 'war to end wars' had been such a long drawn out and bloody affair – with such colossal numbers of dead and wounded on both sides – that the utter futility of war was apparent to everyone who lived through the nightmare. Indeed, this view became so deeply ingrained that many hid their heads in the sands during the rise of Hitler and National Socialism in Germany in the 1930s. Appeasement in the face of German expansion was not spineless or neo-fascist: most appeasers simply could not stomach the thought of a second conflict.

The assassin's bullet in Sarajevo has been recorded as the opening shot, literally, of World War I, but it takes more than the death of an important man for a local conflict to develop into worldwide war. Europe was ready for war; Sarajevo was just the excuse. International relations were already hostile: battle lines had already been drawn up. The British, French, German, and Belgian crowns and governments were all anxious to expand and consolidate their foreign holdings – many of which were in Africa – and almost always at the expense of each other. The opinions of the natives of the countries in question were irrelevant to the ambitious Western politicians and empire builders. A lot was at stake; land brought political clout and prestige, but more importantly, mineral and agricultural wealth.

The British Empire was unquestionably the wealthiest and most important global power and worked hard to keep the *status quo* because conflict could only disrupt trade and government. Satisfied and complaisant, Britain tried to keep out of European disputes. This, however, was to prove increasingly difficult, particularly as German aggression and acquisitiveness came further to the fore.

France and Germany shared a mutual historic resentment and suspicion of each other, not least because of Napoleon's endeavors to conquer Europe. As Germany became a nation it was the Prussians that ran it. Prussian success against Napoleon and Prussian military ethics and attitudes pervaded wealthy German society. The Franco-Prussian war of 1870 saw France crushed again, Paris besieged, and the disputed French provinces of Alsace and Lorraine taken. In the process the German border moved southward and left the French simmering with resentment. The French army and French foreign policy became dominated by the desire to retake their lands and arm themselves to the teeth in order to defend themselves from further aggressive incursions.

Germany needed friends and in 1882 formed the Triple Alliance with the Habsburg Empire (Austria-Hungary) and Italy. The former joined hoping the alliance would shore up its crumbling empire; the latter hoped to benefit financially and territorially from German expansionism. On the eastern fringe of Europe Turkey, too, was sympathetic to the German cause, if only because they had enemies in common (France, Russia, and Britain). Turkey – the 'sick man of Europe' – also needed a powerful friend to help stave off the collapse of an empire that had been in place for nearly 500 years. The links between France and Russia showed how refined and subtle diplomacy had become. The alliance—declared in 1892—between France and Russia can only be called unexpected. The two countries still remembered the last major European war, Napoleon's invasion of Russia, and the slaughter of his retreating army. For Kaiser Wilhelm II and his cabinet it was tangible proof of their fear that Germany would be encircled and then attacked by her enemies.

Despite being the only genuine global power, Britain, too, was worried about the security of her land and home waters, and so another unlikely pairing took place. The 'Entente Cordiale' with France of 1904 was not so much an alliance as an 'understanding,' that allowed various colonial disputes to be settled and their navies redeployed—the French mainly to the Mediterranean, the British primarily around the British Isles. In further diplomatic moves Britain and Russia rationalized their disputes in Persia in 1907 with another 'understanding' that created the 'Triple Entente.'

In a flanking movement Germany endeavored to expand overseas, including an attempt in 1910 to acquire Morocco, but French opposition blocked the way. Frustrated in North Africa as well as elsewhere, Germany returned attention to central Europe and worked at creating a closer diplomatic alliance with the ethnically similar Habsburg Empire and Emperor Franz-Josef I. It was an empire (like Turkey) that needed friends. Deluding themselves with memories of past glories, the Habsburgs were no longer the military or political force they had been in the 18th and 19th centuries. And as the Habsburg and Ottoman empires crumbled, so the nationalist movements of the peoples they controlled came to the fore, and the ambitions of other powers in the Balkans – such as Greece, Serbia, and Bulgaria – were increased.

The First Balkan War broke out in 1912–13 between Ottoman Turkey and the allied forces of Serbia, Bulgaria, Greece, and Montenegro. The Turks lost heavily and had their western border pushed back almost to the walls of Constantinople. But the allies fell out after the division of the spoils. Bulgaria attacked her former allies, Greece and Serbia, in the short-lived Second Balkan War of summer 1913. However, while Bulgarian attention was diverted, Romania attacked and occupied the northeast border region of Bulgaria. By the time a quasi-peace settled, Serbia had almost doubled in size.

Nobody was fooled by the peace. Russia and France supported Serbia, and the Habsburg Empire was openly ready to fight to support her provinces in Slovenia,

Croatia, and Bosnia-Herzegovina. Countries around Europe responded by gearing up for war and rearming; conscription was used to train young men for a war that was seen as inevitable by their political masters. Detailed plans and in some cases defensive works were carried out; armies and navies expanded in anticipation. The western colonial empires relied on their navies to guard the shipping lanes and enforce their will on distant countries. Great economic damage would ensue should these navies fail in their enforcement role, so new ships were hastily built and commissioned.

The rivalry to build the biggest and best navy was intense, particularly between Britain and Germany. Apart from colonial patrolling, their mutual challenge was domination of the Baltic sea lanes. The Royal Navy was the prime instrument of British economic muscle around the world, but was suffering from a lack of investment by the turn of the 20th century. In stark contrast the German Navy was being built up, driven by the enthusiastic support of navy minister Tirpitz who announced his ambitious building program in 1898. Britain was forced to respond and, after the cessation of the Boer War in South Africa, embarked on a modernization and rebuilding program for both the army and navy.

There was a strong antiwar movement, especially among the poor and oppressed, the women's emancipation movement, and among unionized labor. International Socialism was the most potent antiwar instrument, as it identified war between capitalist states as a conspiracy to break the power of the workers by making them fight against each other. The workers held few illusions that they would be the ones sent into battle to die, not the wealthy bankers, businessmen, and politicians who could remain safe at home sitting in luxury.

All the political intrigue and diplomacy working to keep the peace was shattered by an assassin's bullets in Sarajevo, Bosnia, on June 28, 1914, when Archduke Franz Ferdinand (heir to the throne of the Habsburg Empire) was murdered alongside his wife by a Serbian nationalist, Gavrilo Princip. Suddenly, the system of European alliances, which had seemed to underpin the late 19th century, proved to be disastrous. The Habsburgs demanded restitution from the Serbs; the French and Russians – both of whom had guaranteed Serbian independence – vowed to defend the Serbs; the Germans, allies of the Austrians, reiterated their support for the Habsburg Empire and thus, in effect, declared war. Furthermore, Germany prepared to invade France in order to pre-empt the French from honoring their alliance with Russia and so joining the conflict.

Following an ultimatum, on July 28, 1914 the Austrians declared war on Serbia. The Russians mobilized their forces along the German and Austrian borders on July 29 and Germany then declared war on Russia (August 1) and on France (August 3). However, German strategy was to strike first. Realizing that the invasion of France through the Ardennes was impractical, the German high command, under the leadership of Kaiser Wilhelm II, had evolved a plan to invade France from the north. This route, however, involved the invasion of Belgium, a country whose neutrality and independence had been guaranteed since 1839 by the most powerful nation in Europe – Great Britain – through the Treaty of London.

On the same day as war was declared against France, German forces invaded neutral Belgium. The next day Britain declared war on Germany. The German and Austrian alliance was to be supported during the war by Bulgaria and Turkey, while Britain, France and Russia were ultimately to be supported by some 18 other states around the world, including Italy, the United States, and Japan. Italy, allied to Germany prewar, intervened on the side of the British and French from May 1915. The Triple Alliance had stated that Italy would support Germany if France attacked; however, because Italy perceived that Germany was the aggressor, the country did not feel bound by the treaty.

Surprisingly, given the loud pacifist outpourings, patriotic fever swept like wildfire through Europe as eager young men signed up to fight for their countries. Flags were waved and great cheers went up as the tension was at last burst by the promise of imminent action – action that would, of course, ensure the war was over by Christmas.

The Main Nations at the Outbreak of War

1—The Western Allies

BELGIUM

Historically Belgium has suffered through most European conflicts because of geography. Sandwiched between two major European powers, France and Germany, and its one-time overlord The Netherlands, with the sea as its western frontier, the country was divided internally into the provinces of Wallonia and Flanders, different in language and customs. Belgium had remained carefully neutral since 1831 and the successful revolution for independence from The Netherlands. This neutrality was endorsed by every important European power as a vital element in the balance of power in Europe.

In 1910 Belgium was a prosperous country of some 7.5 million people ruled by a constitutional monarchy in the person of King Albert I. On August 2, the king and government received a German ultimatum: fight or accept German rule. Confident of support from the other European nations, Belgium rejected Germany's offer and King Albert took command of the military. This was his constitutional right in wartime and he deployed his wildly outnumbered armed forces on Belgium's borders. In August 1914 the Belgian Army consisted of some 40,000 men and around 115,000 reserves. Most of the officers had been trained in France and the majority of the military equipment was of obsolete German stock. Their numbers were insufficient to garrison their defensive lines and the Belgian Army was quickly swept aside by the advancing Germans. Albert I and his remaining troops retreated, initially northwest to Antwerp then to Ysers, then finally to Le Havre from where Albert governed Allied-controlled Flanders. Throughout the war Albert protected his men by refusing to allow his Belgian forces to be part of the offenses on the Western Front.

BRAZIL

The largest and most populous republic in South America, Brazil had overthrown its monarchy in 1891. Its principal exports were rubber and coffee, but also minerals and meat. Her main trading partner in 1914 was the United States, but Brazil also had important economic ties across the Atlantic with Great Britain and Germany. At the start of the war Brazil was officially neutral although Brazilians generally supported the Allied cause. But the German sinking of two Brazilian ships in April and May 1917 brought a declaration of war against Germany on October 26, 1917.

Brazil's main contribution to the Allied war effort concerned her navy which worked the South Atlantic on trade protection patrols.

CHINA

China was a vast and still largely unknown quantity in 1914, an alluring market for traders but largely impenetrable. Traditionally isolationist and hostile to foreigners, China had a population of about 420 million and growing in 1911. The centuries-long rule of the emperors had been overthrown in October 1911 in a republican revolution, but Chinese industry, such as it was, continued to be controlled by Europeans with cotton and opium being the main revenue earners. The newly installed Kuomintang government only controlled some parts of China, with the Japanese having effective control over Manchuria. Japanese expansionist policies threatened Chinese rule and the outbreak of war in Europe meant that China was more exposed to Japanese aggression, hitherto tempered by the presence of the European powers.

Despite its political fragility in the new era of the republic, China was too big and important for Britain and Germany to ignore: both tried to rally Chinese support. For most of the period of the war China was too busy fighting internally to pay attention to foreign affairs, but on August 14, 1917, China declared war on Germany although it took no actual part in the fighting. From 1914 some 320,000 Chinese were recruited to work for the Allies, mostly as laborers but some in the medical units. About 100,000 worked for the British Expeditionary Force in France, another 100,000 for the French Army, and a further 100,000 with the American Expeditionary Force.

FRANCE

Prewar France had a population of around 40 million and was still predominantly agricultural with little modern manufacturing industry. The few heavy industries lay in the north and east, but these were not as advanced as in neighboring Germany or Britain. France had established the Third Republic in 1870 following the fall of Napoleon III after defeat by the Prussians. French politics were as highly volatile as ever and broadly center-left but with enough right-wing royalists to complicate matters; furthermore politics was even more convoluted by intense regional interests and political alliances. However, France was comfortably prosperous and had important overseas interests in the Far Eastern colonies of Indo-China and in Africa.

In the front line of World War I from the beginning, the French Army had undergone a complete revision after the devastating loss of the Franco-Prussian war of 1870. All the restructuring was planned in the expectation of a forthcoming war against Germany, and in 1872 short-service mass conscription was introduced to produce a wartime mobilization force of three million. The field army before war broke out consisted of 823,000 men, of which 46,000 were colonial troops. These were split between 47 divisions in 21 regional corps and mostly deployed in France. Overseas forces added a further 75,000 men in North Africa, 32,000 men in Indo-China, and 3,000 men in Madagascar. About 60 percent of these were native troops. A difficult problem for politicians and army alike was the length of the French borders and the difficulty of protecting them. The French Navy operated mostly in the Mediterranean after the Entente Cordiale with Britain freed their responsibility from the Atlantic, North Sea, and Channel waters.

An immediate program of mass conscription followed Germany's occupation of Alsace and Lorraine and produced almost three million men within a few weeks. Another mass call-up in June the following year signed up a further 2.7 million men by extending the age limit to 45. The knock-on effect of this was to produce a manpower crisis in agriculture and industry prompting the alternative employment of women and teenagers too young to fight.

GREAT BRITAIN

During the 19th and early 20th century Great Britain was the most powerful and wealthy country in the world, with an empire that stretched around the globe and enjoyed unprecedented access and influence in most countries. The empire comprised the dominions of Canada, South Africa, Australia, and New Zealand, the subcontinent of India, large areas of Africa, numerous islands around the world including the West Indies, and numerous colonies and protectorates, including Hong Kong on mainland China.

The British economy was bolstered by colossal world trading via a merchant marine of more than 9,000 vessels. Their passage was guarded and guaranteed by the Royal Navy. Agriculture was still the biggest industry in Britain but the government relied heavily on foreign food imports – almost entirely from the colonies – to feed a population of some 45 million. Although Britain led the world in shipbuilding, her coal and iron production was inferior to that of Germany.

In 1910 a new constitutional monarch, George V, came to the throne. British society was secure and there was little fear of revolution despite the unusually high number of strikes as workers fought for union representation and better working conditions. The womens' suffrage campaign was vocal and fervent but regarded as a side issue by parliamentarians. Of more immediate consequence was the continuing unrest in Ireland about Irish home rule. In early July 1914 this erupted in mutiny against home rule by British officers serving in Ireland. Civil War in Ireland looked increasingly likely.

British foreign policy – of necessity – was global in nature and tended to encourage existing practices as being to Britain's advantage; Britain lived by trade and anything that would disrupt the world economy would be more likely to damage Britain than anyone else. British diplomats worked to maintain the status quo. A number of important alliances or ententes were ratified in the early 20th century; in 1902 with Japan, 1904 with France, and in 1907 with Russia – in addition Britain was bound by treaty to uphold Belgian neutrality. Britain's relations with Germany became more hostile and suspicious as German expansionist policies became increasingly obvious. The German Navy was undergoing rapid expansion and the Royal Navy rather belatedly started to build up in response.

The July crisis in 1914, after the assassination of Archduke Ferdinand, was a period of escalating tension. Britain had to decide whether to honor her agreement with France and support her militarily if she was attacked. The British cabinet was split and the public undecided. However, when Germany attacked Belgium the matter was resolved and Britain declared war on Germany on August 4. The British, in common with other governments, expected a war of short duration and planned accordingly. The Defence of the Realm Act was passed on August 8, giving government control of the railways and scarce supplies.

The British standing army was a relatively small force of volunteer regulars, very much second in importance to the considerably larger Royal Navy. Both government and army traditionally rejected bolstering the numbers of servicemen with unwilling conscripts, a policy of volunteer professionals was much preferred. After the grueling Boer War in South Africa, the army had undertaken an extensive program of reform with one of the chief aspects being the improved command structure and communications between politicians and senior soldiers. The emphasis was put on modernizing the army and professional training.

Home defense comprised one cavalry and six infantry divisions which could, when necessary, be quickly mobilized as a British Expeditionary Force for service abroad. In addition there were 14 Territorial volunteer reserve divisions organized by region. Other British Army forces were garrisoned around the world as well as in North Africa, South Africa, and the Middle East. In 1914 all these overseas forces were underresourced in men and materials and were issued with obsolete equipment.

In August 1914 the British Army mustered 247,432 regular troops of which 120,000 were based in Britain. In the BEF, there were 224,223 reservists and 268,777 Territorials. Initial mobilization of the land forces assembled 750,000 men including volunteer reserves.

There was no conscription before the start of war but recruitment posters went up on August 6, with the intention of creating a large volunteer army. Appointed in August 1914 the war minister – Horatio Herbert Kitchener of Khartoum and of Broome – was almost alone in his analysis that the country was embarking on a long, drawn-out war of attrition. By the end of August he had raised six new divisions of regular troops. In September 33,000 men a day were joining up. By the end of 1915, 2,6 million recruits had joined up. This sudden increase in the army resulted in chronic shortages of equipment and problems with training all the volunteers adequately, it also badly drained the industrial labor force of the country.

The Royal Navy had been the most powerful navy in the world since the early 19th century, and in 1914 only the German Navy challenged it for supremacy of the seas. The Royal Navy was the government's designated weapon of choice (rather than the army) and would be used to blockade enemy trade routes – consequently most available financial resources went to the 'Senior Service' rather than the army. The Royal Navy's job was to protect British home waters and coastline, guard the trade and shipping lanes, and police the colonies.

In early 1914 the navy had 10 battlecruisers, 18 dreadnoughts (with another six by December), another 29 pre-dreadnoughts, around 40 fast cruisers plus over 150 pre-1907 cruisers (all used for long-range trade protection), 25 fast modern destroyers and 150 older destroyers. Until the German naval expansion rang alarm bells in the government, the Royal Navy budget had been falling for some time. Under the aegis of Admiral Fisher spending was increased enormously.

The British public as a whole was delighted at the outbreak of war after a period of almost unbearable tension. Extreme patriotism and xenophobia were rife.

THE BRITISH EMPIRE

Australia

Since 1901 Australia had been a self-governing dominion of the British Empire. The largest island in the world, its population of some five million lived predominantly around the coast while the native Aborigines (numbering somewhere around 200,000) lived in the hostile interior. Both the Australian Labour and Liberal parties were in complete agreement about dispatching Australian forces to Europe to aid Britain in the war and on August 3, 1914 offered to provide 20,000 troops.

The small regular Australian army was assembled entirely for home defense until 1914. They were backed up by a part-time volunteer militia that numbered 45,000 at the outbreak of war. However, because all Australian males were required by law to undergo regular military training, trained volunteers were quick to assemble. At the outbreak of war a new volunteer force – the Australian Imperial Force – was created for overseas service and the ranks were quickly filled with enthusiastic volunteers. The first AIF troopships left Western Australia on November 7, 1914.

Canada

Canada was a British dominion with a population of 7.2 million in 1911. Of these, some 22 percent belonged to Quebec province, the French-influenced and French-speaking region of Canada—a legacy of French colonial ambitions in North America. In 1914 the regular peacetime Canadian force consisted of around 3,100 troops. Most of these were local militia volunteers and men who garrisoned harbor fortifications.

By constitution Canada was automatically included in Britain's declaration of war against Germany; there was no murmur of dissent from Canadians. The Canadian government immediately offered any available assistance to Britain and quickly started gathering together volunteers for a Canadian Expeditionary Force. Volunteer forces started gathering immediately and reached Britain for training in mid-October. The First Canadian Division was one of the first groups to reach the Western Front in February 1915, in time to participate in the Second Battle of Ypres in April.

Canadian volunteers were so numerous that the Second Division was able to join the First in France in September.

India

Britain acquired its empire by ruling India, the sheer size and diversity of the vast subcontinent added enormously to British prestige. The British Raj operated over a vast and multiethnic selection of peoples, regions, and religions and was the most important outpost of the British Empire. It cast a blanket government over the pre-existing political structures and made English the language of government, diplomacy, and administration. British rule and exploitation was accepted by Indians in return for economic and social stability, investment in infrastructure (in particular the building of the railways), coupled with modern developments such as medicines and health, as well as the benefits a strong and important ally and protector could provide.

In 1914 India was split into 13 major provinces and about 700 autonomous states and contained some 320 million people, of which Hindus were in the majority. Indians were employed in government and administration but were anxious to participate in important decision making.

The peacetime Indian Army ranks were composed mainly of Indian volunteers, while the officers were mostly British. They were controlled by the Indian government on home territory but automatically came under the command of the most senior British officer when they left India and joined British troops. The army was used for internal policing and quelling local violence between communities, also for defending India's northwest frontier with Afghanistan.

Reforms in the early 20th century had reorganized the army into a national field army of 155,000 men serving in 10 divisions, and an internal security force of about 80,000. About half the troops were Muslim Punjabis from the northwest frontier and there was also a high proportion of Sikhs, while Gurkha units from Nepal were the fighting elite. Indian troops were among the earliest British Empire troops to join the war, fighting on the Western Front from September 1914.

The Indian National Congress (founded in 1885), if not exactly enthusiastic in its support of the British war effort, was by no means against it. Interestingly, much of the notorious unrest between ethnic groups calmed down considerably during the period of the war, and even German attempts to foster trouble by supplying revolutionary Bengali Muslims with arms got nowhere.

New Zealand

In 1914 New Zealand and its outlying dependant islands were an autonomous dominion of the British Empire. In 1916 the population totaled just over 1.1 million, including 50,000 Maoris. The majority of the population was of recent British descent and identified closely with the war in Europe. Both political parties supported Great Britain in the war effort and were anxious to contribute; there was no contention about sending troops to fight alongside the Allies.

New Zealand was well-prepared to muster troops for the conflict: from the age of 12 all able-bodied male New Zealanders received some military training, and adults under 25 joined the Territorial Army, a part-time national militia. In peacetime this was a volunteer force of 25,000 part-timers led by a full-time staff of 600. At the outbreak of war in August 1914 the Territorial Army became the basis of the new volunteer regiments raised for the war in Europe. The very first New Zealand troops set off straight away for the German Pacific islands of Western Samoa, which they took without resistance.

The New Zealand Expeditionary Force was raised to fight in Europe and left with the Australian Imperial Force. A Maori contingent was also formed in 1914 and went into action as the New Zealand (Maori) Pioneer Battalion. By the war's end almost 10 percent of the population of New Zealand had served in Europe.

South Africa

After the Boer War (1899–1902) fought against Britain, the four South African colonies of Transvaal, Natal, Cape Colony, and Orange Free State united in 1910 to form the Union of South Africa, a self-governing dominion within the British Empire. Natal and Cape Colony were occupied by British settlers and Transvaal and Orange Free State by Dutch Huguenot Boers (Afrikaners). South Africa possessed rich mineral resources, especially gold and diamonds, but little industry – almost all manufactured goods had to be imported. Cape Colony was important for international shipping but this declined during the war as world trade declined.

The peacetime South African Army was formed out of police units from the four states and consisted of five regular mounted regiments and a small artillery unit. In mid-1913 the Active Citizen Force was created as South Africa's part-time national guard. The ACF mustered about 50,000 men and incorporated the volunteer state militias, but to make up the numbers young men aged between 16 and 25 were conscripted by lottery. A number of African tribes offered assistance but were prohibited from combat service and turned down by the South African government. Many, however, served in labor battalions and as support services.

In 1914 the country was led by General Botha, who immediately offered the assistance of South African troops to the war effort. British South Africans volunteered in numbers to serve in the armed forces and moderate Afrikaners enlisted as well. The more radical Boers opposed getting involved and wanted a policy of neutrality. The South African offer of help was accepted, and they were ordered to invade German-held Southwest Africa but were delayed from going by internal troubles. The Boers were not at all happy about supporting Britain – their very recent enemies – and instigated a major revolt against the war effort in late 1914. After the military suppression of the revolt the invasion of Southwest Africa resumed and the colony fell in mid-1915.

In World War I most South Africans saw military service in German East Africa but a number joined British units and served in Europe.

GREECE

Greek politics at the beginning of the 20th century were as ever dominated by hostile relations with Turkey. Greece and the Aegean had been governed for centuries by the Ottoman Empire until a popular revolt in 1829 overthrew the Ottoman yoke and established a constitutional monarchy. Throughout the later 19th century Greece had expanded her territories and in the Balkan Wars of 1912–13 acquired Turkish Macedonia and Thrace. Greece had a small population of some 4.8 million people at the start of the war, most of them engaged in not much more than subsistence agriculture. However about 50,000 men were employed in heavy industry, primarily shipbuilding, for the large Greek mercantile marine.

In 1914 Greece was ruled by Constantine I who was strongly pro-German, as were many of the important army officers. However, the government was forced to accept neutrality for fear of Bulgaria and Turkey invading the Greek mainland. Despite the Greek Army's support for the German cause, the Greeks declined a German offer of alliance on August 4, 1914, nor could they come to any accord with the western allies.

The Greek peacetime army consisted of around 32,000 conscripts organized into three divisions. Many of these were veterans thanks to the recent Balkan wars, but they were equipped with heavy, out-dated equipment.

ITALY

The Kingdom of Italy was founded in 1848 after a long struggle to unite the many city-states, principalities, and kingdoms of the Italian peninsula and surrounding islands. By 1914 only the Vatican and San Marino remained aloof. Italy was a constitutional monarchy with Victor Emmanuel III ruling through a national assembly. Italian politics was debated along regional political rather than national party lines. At the start of the war the population of Italy was some 35 million, mostly concentrated in the industrial north. The south remained largely agricultural, although Italy was not self-sufficient for food. Italy's main aggressor was the Austro-Hungarian Empire to the north, which still controlled many putative Italian lands and people. Another factor in Italian politics was the security of the Mediterranean and the volatile Balkans just across the Adriatic. Italy wanted to acquire lands in the Balkans but could not compete against all the other ambitious nations that were scheming to control the Adriatic.

The Italian Army only developed properly with the introduction of conscription in 1907, but it suffered so badly from lack of funds that only a quarter of conscripts received training and every winter the entire army more or less shut down. By the time the 1911 war with Turkey was over, Italian Army resources were at rock bottom; there were few trained officers and NCOs and the theoretical peacetime strength of 300,000 men was nowhere near the actual number. The government called for the army to be rebuilt and resourced, but was unable to provide the funds. This underfunding had dramatic ramifications – for example, the officer corps was nearly 15,000 men below the stated requirements by the middle of 1914.

In 1882 Italy had joined Germany and the Habsburg Empire in the Triple Alliance. German investment in northern Italian industry was crucial to the well-being of the economy but the possession by the Austro-Hungarians of large tracts of 'Italian' lands was a continuing irritation. In common with the other European nations, Italy had designs on building foreign colonies for the economic potential they offered. In September 1911 this ambition led to open war with Turkey over control of Tripoli and Benghazi. There were no winners at this juncture but after Turkey became involved in war against the Balkan states, the Turks sought peace with Italy and ceded Libya, Rhodes, and the Dodecanese islands. But the war had cost the economy deeply, so much so that in 1914 Italy was economically unstable.

Despite being a member of the Triple Alliance (with Germany and Austria-Hungary), Italy declared neutrality at the beginning of the war, then quietly tried to build up the army's strength acknowledging inevitable involvement in the conflict.

JAPAN

Traditionally more isolationist than China, Japan was even more estranged from the Western world than her massive neighbor. A new emperor, Yoshihito, had ascended the throne in 1912 and ruled with absolute authority over a technologically astute country with a population of over 50 million that had enjoyed rapid economic development in the last half century or so. The emperor was treated as a god and Japanese nationalism was rife. Society as a whole was heavily influenced by the military so that soldiering values and ethics pervaded virtually all levels of society and the ruling elite in particular. Japan specialized in heavy industry – shipbuilding, iron, and steel – and in addition enjoyed a thriving textile industry.

However, Japan, felt constrained by her island territories and cast envious eyes over mainland China and Russia. This took shape in the 1890s when Japan invaded and went to war against China. The more technological Japanese overwhelmed the Chinese forces and annexed southern Manchuria, Korea, Taiwan, and a number of Pacific islands. As a reflection of her new international awareness, Japan contracted an alliance with Britain in 1902. This, however, did not stop Japan attacking Russia in the Russo-Japanese War of 1904–5 and defeating the Russian Navy. Japan declared war on Germany on August 23, 1914, citing the terms of its treaty with Britain. This actually served Japan's expansionist desires very nicely as it could now, quasi-legally, occupy German-held Pacific islands and concessions on mainland China.

PORTUGAL

Portugal became a republic after the revolution of 1910 but remained a deeply divided country, with many activists wanting a return to the monarchy. The economy was fragile and relied heavily on trade with the Portuguese colonies in Africa. Despite continuous political upheaval there was never any doubt that Portugal would declare for the Allies. Portugal and Great Britain had been allies in war and peace through history since the Middle Ages. On the other hand, with Germany, Portugal was at odds over colonial and trading interests in Africa. In fact the two countries were already involved in local skirmishes in German East Africa (Kenya, Tanganiyka, and Uganda) and on the Mozambique frontier of Portuguese East Africa. Furthermore German infiltrators were encouraging tribal unrest in Portuguese Angola. Portugal declared support for the Allies against Germany on August 7, 1914, but did not actually declare war until March 1916.

The Portuguese Army was raised by conscription and mustered about 33,000 men in 1914. These numbers rose rapidly as soldiers were recruited to protect the Portuguese African colonies when their trade was threatened by increasing enemy activity. After Portugal came into the war about 100,000, Portuguese soldiers saw action on the Western Front and in Mozambique.

RUSSIA

The vast Russian Empire was creaking into its final years at the start of World War I. The czar ruled over some 170 million people across lands that stretched from the Baltic in the West to the Bering Sea in the East. Most Russians were poverty-stricken, illiterate peasants involved in agriculture, about 27 million in European Russia alone. Russia as a whole was still a very rural economy but the cheap and abundant labor force provided the manpower to start Russia's own industrial revolution, and industry was expanding in the west employing some three million people and growing by 1914. Big industries were starting to develop, in particular the metalurgical industry in the Ukraine and the textile industry in Moscow and St Petersburg. Cities were starting to grow rapidly; the urban population in 1914 being around 18.6 million as poor agricultural workers moved to the towns to find work. This was not as rapid as it could have been, as across Russia generally transport communications were still very poor.

At the start of the war Russia also controlled Poland, Finland, the whole of northern Asia up to the great natural boundaries created by the mountain chains – Carpathians, Caucasus, Himalayas – Siberia, and much of Transcaucasia. Expansion eastward during the 19th century almost went unchecked, but Russia still had ambition to grow southward, especially in the Balkans which would give the Russian Navy direct access to the Mediterranean – long a territorial dream of the Russian czars.

Russia had even invaded the Balkans in 1877 after a local revolt against the Turks, but was unsuccessful and was forced to withdraw.

A complete autocrat like his ancestors, Czar Nicholas II had been compelled to accept a form of constitutional monarchy following a revolution in St Petersburg after Russia's defeat by Japan in the war of 1904–5. Russian politics were as factional and complicated as ever but for a few years following enjoyed a relatively quiescent period. By 1914, however, revolution was in the air and industrial unrest in the early months involved almost half the industrial workforce of Russia.

The Japanese defeat also forced a general reassessment of policies, in 1905 the government embarked on rearming the army and navy and brought about a fresh view on foreign relations. The entente with Great Britain in 1907 accorded with the existing entente with France (1892). The protection of Slavic peoples was a high priority, especially those in the Balkans, Russia supported Serbia and encouraged the Serbs to mobilize against threatening Austro-Hungarian incursions. Ambitious to control the Dardanelles, Russia consequently was at loggerheads with Turkey and Austria-Hungary.

Russia's standing army included more than 25 million men just two years before the outbreak of war. But her huge population had convinced many foreign observers that Russia could win any conflict on sheer manpower alone. In fact the army had its problems: money was always lacking and exemptions from conscription considerably limited the intake, and people from the further reaches of empire were rarely reached by bureaucracy. Modernization of the organization and armaments was badly needed as much of the equipment was obsolete. Furthermore officers were only taken from a narrow social elite which left a chronic shortage of competent leaders.

The Russian Navy, following defeat by the Japanese, was poorly resourced and deeply demoralized as evinced when the Baltic and Black Sea fleets mutinied leaving the Russian Navy in complete disarray. The government ordered a massive reconstruction program but morale was still very low in 1914. In common with the army, lack of money lay at the root of the problem. What the navy did have were good new officers after the loss of the old elite during the war, plenty of weapons, ammunition, and fuel, but the lack of the newly ordered ships meant that obsolete vessels were pressed into service for the first three years of the war. The Russian Navy's main priority was guarding the Baltic shipping lines and keeping the German Navy at bay. However the Black Sea was also of vital strategic significance and the fleet there reflected its importance. After 1912 the navy was engaged in blockading the Dardanelles to prevent the Turkish Navy from operating in the Black Sea.

Russians in general welcomed the war, talk of revolution died down and the crippling industrial strikes initially ceased. In August 1914 the Russian Army mustered 11 armies and 37 corps organized into 12 military districts. The navy in the Baltic had 85 assorted ships and 11 submarines; the Black Sea Fleet comprised around 50 assorted vessels; the Siberian flotilla was a small selection of cruisers and torpedo boats.

SERBIA

Serbia was a newly freed state granted independence in 1878 by the Ottoman Empire, of which it had been a part since the 14th century. The Russian Empire was quick to support their fellow Slavs and gave Serbia its most powerful diplomatic muscle. In 1903 a military coup led to the constitutional monarch, King Alexander, being assassinated and the crowning of the military's favorite, King Peter. Serbia had territorial ambitions to break out of its mountainous, land-locked country; the long northern border adjoined the avaricious Austro-Hungarian Empire, the northeast met Romania, the east hostile Bulgaria, the south Greece, and to the west Montenegro and Albania.

Serbia wanted and needed access to the Adriatic and thus the Mediterranean, but Albania blocked the way. She also wanted to unite the Slav peoples of the Balkans under one rule – namely her own. The Balkan wars in 1912–13 left Serbia much the winner, with almost double her prewar territory and a proportionately increased population. But the Serbs continued to conspire to unite the Slav peoples in the region as a whole and encouraged unrest in Croatia and Bosnia-Herzegovina. In 1908 Austria-Hungary seized Bosnia outraging Serbian feelings in the process: war was imminent.

Economically Serbia relied heavily on agriculture and had few mineral or industrial resources to provide fiscal stability. What little manufacture there was employed 10,000 people in and around Belgrade. Serbia only just survived by supplying food and hides to Germany, Turkey and Austria-Hungary; in addition Serbia had to import almost everything else, including fuel, all military equipment, armament and ordnance.

The Serbian Army at the time of the First Balkan War in 1912 mustered about 260,000 men, almost 10 percent of the population. The army consisted of male citizens aged between 21 and 46 who were drafted for compulsory military service. Men served 10 years in the army or on active reserve and then a further eight years in the territorial militia. After their successful war and territorial expansion the Serbian Army increased significantly so that when war was declared in July 1914 against Austria-Hungary there were 360,000 men ready for mobilization, many of them in the four field armies and many of them veterans. The experienced front-line troops were mostly well-equipped with modern weapons but the reserve units had much older and often obsolete equipment and uniform.

Constant internal unrest as well as intense suspicion of foreigners made Serbia a very volatile place. In July 1914 disputes between the civil and military authorities broke into all out crisis as to how to deal with the recently occupied Macedonian territories. The extreme nationalist Black Hand society forced the king to abdicate in favor of his second son, Alexander. While this constitutional upheaval was ongoing, the Black Hand planned and carried out the murder of Austrian Archduke Franz Ferdinand in Sarajevo. The outraged Austro-Hungarian government suspected the Serbians were responsible for the assassination and demanded to send their army into Serbia to search for the terrorists. The government, with the full backing of the Serbian people, refused and instead declared war on Austria-Hungary. Wider conflict was inevitable given the complicated alliances of the involved parties.

UNITED STATES OF AMERICA

The United States was traditionally isolationist and fundamentally unwilling to get drawn into any Eurocentric conflict. In the early 20th century the population was growing fast to over 100 million, and more arrived every day on the immigration ships. America was a rich country with vast mineral wealth and industrial output. Heavy industry was concentrated in the industrial northeast but good infrastructure in the railroads and rivers enabled quick and reliable distribution. Exports were buoyant: oil, cotton, and wheat accounted for over a third of gross earnings.

The only American interest in European war lay in its effects on the United States world position and that meant mainly trade: the markets and opportunities it would present. When war broke out the Democrat Woodrow Wilson was president after winning the 1912 election with a landslide. He ruled a still very divided country with loyalties split between North and South, employers and unions, industry and agriculture, black and white. Economic depression and unemployment hit the US in 1913–14 coupled with the struggle for union recognition, but unlike in Europe there was no call for revolution.

On August 19, 1914, when war was declared in Europe, President Woodrow Wilson, with the full support of Congress, declared the United States neutral. This did not just reflect US isolationism, but also the fact that, with the mass immigration of Europeans as new US citizens, internal feelings between ex-British, Irish, French, German, Polish, Russian, Greek, Austrians, Armenian, Hungarians, and various other European citizens could easily spark into internal conflict if favor was declared for one side against the other.

Consequently the US could supply both sides with food, armaments, and materials with impunity. In 1914 after the outbreak of war the US exported goods worth $825 million to the Allied countries (this increased to a massive $3.2 billion in 1916) and American businessmen got wealthy on the process. Furthermore US businessmen and banks were loaning money to the Allies so that they could buy US goods.

Among Americans most sympathies lay with the Allied cause, as Germany was seen as the prime aggressor. The US government also suspected that German spies were operating in America's backyard of Mexico and Central America, and they were thought to be responsible for industrial sabotage within the United States itself.

In 1914 the US Army mustered 98,000 men, of which 29,000 were designated for home defense and 45,000 already served at overseas bases such as the Philippines. Wilson's 'limited preparedness' in 1915 increased the army to more than 140,000 men and made provision for a volunteer trained reserve of 400,000 men. On declaration of war the Selective Service Act in April 1917 introduced conscription, conscripts were sent to the new national army in Europe, they did not join the regulars but were deployed alongside them.

The US Navy was in better state than the army in the period leading up to the war. Shipping had been invested in as a way of protecting US trade interests abroad; it also suited American expansionist aims. In 1914 only the Royal Navy and the German Navy were bigger than the US Navy, which had 300 warships of varying classes. In August 1915 a major expansion program started a massive shipbuilding effort, mostly of merchant ships and light craft. By mid-1918 the US yards were producing over 100 ships a month.

As the war progressed and German submarine warfare increased, popular opinion in the US swung against the Central Powers. The sinking of the 32,000-ton *Lusitania* on May 7, 1915, by German *U20* and the death of 1,198 passengers turned popular opinion against Germany. The further sinking of the French cross-Channel ferry Sussex on March 26, 1916, with the loss of life of 50 civilians, including a number of US citizens, was the final straw. President Wilson demanded an immediate halt to unrestricted attacks on shipping. Anxious to recover lost ground, the German government issued orders to their U-boat commanders to leave passenger ships alone and search merchantmen before sinking them.

Despite these measures the tension increased. An anxious President Wilson announced 'limited preparedness' in September 1915 which included a limited expansion of the army, navy, and merchant marine. This was paid for by a new tax on high income, so was only funded by the wealthy. The US still had no conscription.

After a successful re-election President Wilson issued a Peace Note to all the combatants asking for a statement of their war aims and ambitions. Seeing the way the wind was blowing the Germans recommenced unrestricted U-boat operations against all ocean traffic. Angered by the sinkings on February 4, 1917, the US broke diplomatic relations with Germany. On April 2, 1917, Wilson petitioned the Senate for permission to go to war. Having got its assent, the United States joined the conflict as an 'Associated Power' and declared war against the German government (not the people) on April 6. War was not declared against Austria-Hungary until December 7.

2—The Central Powers

AUSTRO-HUNGARY

The Austro-Hungarian Empire emerged from the ashes of the old Habsburg Empire when Austria and Hungary partially united by agreement in 1867 to form the second largest European country after Russia. The empire covered a vast area of central and southern Europe and included Germans, Hungarians, Poles, Czechs, Romanians, Italians, Croats, Serbs, Bosnians, and Ruthenes (from Russia) within its boundaries. Ruled by Franz Josef I, Emperor of Austria and King of Hungary, each country was technically a constitutional monarchy with two houses of parliament. Each national government controlled its own home army and peoples but they shared an imperial army, currency, and customs. This cumbersome construct inevitably floundered in political and regional divisions and overwhelming bureaucracy, and the empire as a whole suffered from lack of stimulation and political development.

Austria contained some 30 million people, over one third of them ethnic Germans. In the Austrian parliament and administration there was a large conservative pro-German lobby. Economically stable, Austria had a successful heavy industry including armaments manufacture but needed to import food and raw materials. Much of the produce came from Hungary.

Hungary was much more agricultural and rural than her partner and although territorially larger had a smaller population at around 20 million, of these about nine million were Hungarians. The Hungarian parliament was dominated by wealthy conservative landowners. Hungarians were not as pro-German as Austrians and instead their political ambitions looked eastward toward their prime enemy, Romania, with whom they had a dispute over Transylvania. Indeed, Hungarians resented Austrian exploitation, as they saw it, of their resources and continually blocked and obstructed modernization initiatives. As Austria tried to increase their joint military strength, time and again the Hungarian government blocked the effort.

Control of the Balkans and Adriatic was one of the prime motivators of the empire's policies. The empire already controlled the northern Adriatic but saw Serbia plotting to control the lower eastern Adriatic coast. The danger was that Serbia was growing bigger and stronger with the collapse of the Ottoman Empire, and was being encouraged by Russia to contest for control of this vital stretch of land. In order to thwart Serbia, Austria-Hungary annexed Bosnia-Herzegovina in 1908, an action that only caused Serbs living under the empire's jurisdiction in the Balkans to agitate even more for unity with Serbia. A strong military faction of mostly Austrian politicians agitated for pre-emptive war against Italy and Serbia, but were suppressed by successive foreign ministers. However, when Archduke Franz Ferdinand was assassinated in Sarajevo the perfect excuse had arrived and the military demands for action could no longer be ignored. Other ministers insisted on waiting for German assurance of support before committing to war and furthermore were only convinced of the necessity when Russia mobilized in support of Serbia.

The Austro-Hungarian Army was an exotic collection of disparate elements that reflected the diverse nature of the empire. The army consisted of three basic armies: the Imperial and Royal Army was under the emperor's direct personal control and was sanctioned to serve abroad. Its peacetime strength of 325,000 soldiers were conscripts from all over the empire. Austria's land army for home defense held some 40,000 men conscripted from Austrian domains and Hungary's home army of about 30,000 was recruited from Hungarian domains. The officer corps of the army was 80 percent German-speaking but the other ranks were only 30 percent German speakers. This presented difficulties, particularly for the minority language speakers, in command and control. The misunderstandings and confusions only further engendered suspicion about the reliability and loyalty of the minority elements in the army.

Like the parliament, the army was fractured by widely differing opinions and aims. Austrians wanted to enlarge and modernize the army while the Hungarian parliament blocked such attempts and worked to keep it the same size, in particular they continually cut costs and provided extensive exemptions to the draft. In August 1914, despite Austria's attempts to make it bigger, the army numbered just over 2.25 million.

The Imperial and Royal Navy of Austria and Hungary underwent expansion in 1904, mostly to compete with the Italian Navy in the Adriatic. In 1914 the navy could put to sea some 42 assorted ships and about 90 torpedo boats.

War united the empire and people mobilized enthusiastically; the army was the one thing that united the Empire despite the fact that it operated in 15 different languages! Only the Bosnians declined to support the war. Emperor Franz Josef took control as commander in chief and had many of his near relatives in the officers' ranks.

Expecting (as did its allies the Germans) a war of short sharp duration, Austria-Hungary switched all possible manufacturing and effort to its military factories and production lines. All civilian-owned military factories and war-related businesses immediately came under direct imperial command. This also meant that the War Ministry fixed the prices of goods and services and commandeered all output. In late 1914 this military control was extended to cover the distribution of all vital materials. Hungary provided the food for much of this endeavor but there was a particularly poor harvest in 1914 and this, coupled with the devastation of the grain belts on the Eastern Front, contributed to early food shortages.

BULGARIA

Until a nationalist revolution in 1878 won them independence, Bulgaria had been a province of the once powerful Ottoman Empire since the 14th century. On release from Turkey Bulgaria became an autonomous principality and a fully independent kingdom under Czar (formerly Prince) Ferdinand in 1908. The country occupied strategically important territory with a long border on the western side of the Black Sea, and to the south a border along the Aegean. By no means a rich country, agriculture occupied the vast majority of Bulgarians. Foreign investors owned the railways and coal mines and all raw materials, metals and manufactured goods were imported, principally from Germany and Austria-Hungary.

Once independent of the Ottomans, the Bulgarian ruling elite pursued a long-held desire to restore the boundaries of medieval Greater Bulgaria, which meant reclaiming Macedonia from the Turks. Alongside allies and neighbors Montenegro, Greece, and Serbia, Bulgaria engaged in the First Balkan War in 1912 against the remnants of the Ottoman Empire. Although on the victorious side, Bulgaria did not receive the lands she wanted in the peace settlement as Serbia acquired much of the territory. Outraged at the inequity, Bulgaria suddenly attacked her former allies in summer 1913 in the Second Balkan War. At the same time Romania unexpectedly launched an attack from the north, and soon Bulgaria was fighting a losing battle on two fronts. She was defeated within six weeks and lost the Bulgarian-speaking regions of Macedonia and the Black Sea coastal region of Dobrudja.

The armed forces in Bulgaria were raised by the conscription of males aged between 20 and 46. Initially trained by Russia, after independence soldiers still carried a lot of old Russian equipment. The peacetime standing army comprised about 85,000 troops and had the reputation of being the best soldiers in the Balkans. During the Balkan Wars troop numbers were increased considerably and even more so during the period of World War I. By 1918 Bulgaria mustered over 850,000 troops. The Bulgarian Navy consisted of small coastal and river boats divided into small flotillas on the Black Sea and on the Danube River.

Not an obvious ally of either side in World War I, both the Allies and Central Powers tried to tempt Bulgaria with territorial offers in return for support. Britain and France promised captured Turkish lands while Germany and Austria offered Serbian Macedonia. Ferdinand would not commit to either side, but neither did he refuse. He kept both sides uncertain until he eventually committed to the Central Powers in September 1915.

GERMANY

After centuries of regional conflicts and political and religious divisions Germany was unified in 1871 to become a federation of 22 kingdoms and principalities and three independent Hanseatic cities (Hamburg, Lübeck, and Bremen). The largest and most important state was Prussia, which comprised 64 percent of Germany; furthermore the German kaiser, Wilhelm II, was also King of Prussia. He held virtually complete power with the aid of a wealthy aristocratic elite.

On paper the kaiser ruled through two constitutional bodies, the Bundesrat and the Reichstag, but in practice they did as they were ordered. The Bundesrat (the upper house) used a block vote system based on the size of the represented land, in effect giving Prussia absolute control over every decision. Otherwise the parliament split between religious and regional lines but the political parties differed widely in aspect and influence, some wanting reform, others regression and by 1914 constitutional conflict was coming to a head.

Many wealthy influential aristocratic businessmen lobbied for military expansion and an aggressive foreign policy, taxes were hiked and social tension stretched. The workers on the other hand were more concerned about long working hours and social inequality. Socialist ideas were gaining widespread support in Germany especially among the industrial workers; strikes were called and tempers flared. The army was on constant standby to step in should trouble openly break out. Revolution was expected imminently.

The German economy at the turn of the 20th century was one of the strongest in the world with strong international trade with her colonies and other countries while her industry was growing at the fastest rate in the world. Germany had vast coal reserves and mineral wealth as well as important chemical, engineering, and armament industries, many of them based in the Ruhr region. The population was healthy enough to grow quickly and kept pace with demand. By 1914 up to 40 percent of the labor force worked in industry. In addition Germany was virtually self-sufficient in agriculture, which employed a reduced, but important, 35 percent of the labor force. Good internal infrastructure aided the easy movement of goods and people to and from the cities and centers of manufacture and industry.

Despite all this wealth, Germany felt threatened by her near neighbors France, Russia, and Britain. The arms race and 'entente' alliances they formed together gave the Germans a genuine paranoia about the country's very survival. In response, the German Army devised the Schlieffen Plan, a template for quick military victory. This had many vociferous supporters among the Prussian elite. The kaiser and his advisors expected a quick resolution to the war, which they confidently expected would take no longer than nine months.

In 1914 the German Army was considered to be the most efficient in the world, thanks to the Prussian domination with its systems of training and combat. All the German states contributed to its strength and armament with the exception of Bavaria, which retained an autonomous military administration. The army was raised by conscription for short-term military service finished by a longer period serving as a reserve. Unprecedented value was put on training and adherence to orders. Officers were invariably aristocrats. The army could mobilize, maneuver, and operate quicker, better, and more efficiently than any other army in the world. In August 1914 the army mustered 700,000 men split between 25 corps. Each corps was responsible for a region in which a reserve corps could simultaneously mobilize. Within a week 3.8 million men were ready to fight.

Under the aegis of Admiral Tirpitz the German Navy had been undergoing considerable changes designed to turn it into the most powerful navy in the world. The German Navy was needed to secure German overseas colonies and trade and protect the German coastline and waters from hostile incursions. The most immediate foe was the enormous neighboring Royal Navy on which Tirpitz modeled his own High Seas Fleet. Change started in 1898 with the Navy Laws. A dangerous arms and shipbuilding race ensued between the two great powers, in the process worsening already poor relations between the Britain and Germany. The Royal Navy had greater resources to call on and German shipbuilding yards fell behind Tirpitz's ambitious schedule; costs also spiraled out of control. However by August 1914 the German Navy was probably the most advanced technically and the second largest navy in the world with only the Royal Navy bigger.

Germans responded to war against Russia and France with enthusiasm and there was complete national unity to defend Germany against her aggressors. Under the Prussian Siege Law which pertained in time of national crisis the army took control over much civil administration giving the military enormous power and momentum.

TURKEY

The once virtually unbeatable Ottoman Empire was in serious decline by the turn of the 20th century. She had lost most of her lands which, at their peak, had controlled much of the Middle East as far as the Persian Gulf as well as Egypt in North Africa. Internal politics had forced the autocratic sultan to accept a constitution and an elected representative assembly in 1908. However Turkey remained in turmoil; there were supply shortages and communications were breaking down around the remnants of empire. To get out of the crisis the government decided on a course of rapid industrialization and expansion as well as a total military reorganization after the defeats in wars against Austria-Hungary, Italy, and in the Balkans. In 1914 the empire contained an estimated 25 million people, a high proportion of them refugees fleeing back to Turkey after their lands had been seized; the Turks numbered about 14 million.

The Turkish Army was filled with conscripts and included peoples from the empire, especially Arabs, Kurds, Armenians, and Syrians and in peacetime numbered about 75,000 men instead of the 250,000 it should have been. The army was technically weak and over bureaucratic and this inefficiency showed during the Balkan wars in 1912–13. New incentives in 1913 were designed to sharpen up the Turkish Army. These were devised and executed by a German military mission from December 1913.

By August 1914 Turkey possessed three armies containing 36 active divisions between them. But shortages of equipment, food and clothing and lack of trained officers and medical services limited their effectiveness. The Turkish Army was notorious for desertions and units were rarely if ever at full strength. The Turkish Navy suffered from similar liabilities, but it too was restructured specifically in response to the threat of the Russian Black Sea Fleet and the growing strength of the Greek Navy. Old ships were bought and new ships ordered – including two from Britain which were impounded in August 1914 before the declaration of war against the Allies.

Economically vulnerable and territorially threatened, Turkey needed a strong ally if she was to have any chance of restructuring successfully. Most of the government nevertheless favored neutrality but the inner cabal constituted a war party led by Enver Pasha. The cabal favored the Germans because they thought they would win the war and because Anglo-French influence in the Middle East was deeply resented by the Turks. Both the French and the British had longstanding diplomatic influence in Constantinople but German business in trade and banking and German importance in military manufacture and affairs more than counterbalanced the equation. German diplomats made great efforts to tempt the Turks to their cause, in particular offering the inducement of Russian (Turkey's greatest enemy) territory should they win.

In July 1914 Enver Pasha with only a few close confidants signed a defense alliance with Germany; most of the government was not informed and so continued negotiations with Allied diplomats. The Dardanelles were closed to Allied ships in August. Matters resolved in October 1914 when Enver aided a German pre-emptive strike on Russian navy bases along the Black Sea. On October 31 Turkey declared war against the Allies. Britain did not return the declaration until November 5.

The Land War
THE WESTERN FRONT

In August 1914, the major European powers had war strategies, but the key to the opening campaigns was Germany's Schlieffen Plan. Named after a former commander-in-chief, Count Alfred von Schlieffen, it aimed to prevent Germany facing a war on two fronts against France and Russia. Gambling on slow Russian mobilization, the bulk of the German Army was to be launched against France, mostly through Belgium. The aim was to capture Paris in some six weeks, thereby forcing France's surrender, and then use Germany's railways to switch troops to the Eastern Front to crush Russia. The road to victory in France lay with the two German right-wing armies. These had to undertake a great wheeling advance through Belgium and northeast France before arriving to the west of Paris. The plan was an enormous gamble and was recognized as such by the commander-in-chief who had to oversee its implementation in 1914, Field Marshal Helmuth von Moltke.

1914—From movement to stalemate

The Schlieffen Plan began well, with German heavy artillery neutralizing Belgium's fortresses and opening the way for the two right-flank armies to advance into north-east France. A series of encounters, the Battles of the Frontiers, developed all along the Western Front between August 14–25. In Alsace and Lorraine, French attacks into Germany were beaten back, while in the north the British Expeditionary Force under Field Marshal John French and elements of the French Army advancing into Belgium were forced to retreat after the Battles of Mons and the Sambre River. The initiative seemed to lie with the Germans, but weaknesses in their plan were becoming apparent. The troops were advancing at an exhausting rate in order to keep to an inflexible schedule, the northern armies were not strong enough to sweep around Paris to the west without opening gaps between them, and they were rapidly outrunning their supplies. Equally, poor communications were starving the Germans of vital intelligence in a fast-moving campaign.

By late August the French commander-in-chief, Marshal Joseph Joffre, was aware that the Germans were advancing toward the Marne River to the east of Paris and that there was a growing gap between the two armies on the right wing. Joffre acted swiftly. He ordered his forces to hold the line of the Marne, while creating a new army based on Paris. The Germans faced an acute dilemma – if the new threat from Paris was to be dealt with, forces would have to be moved westward, thereby opening a wider gap between their two right-wing armies through which Allied forces could strike. While the Germans delayed, Joffre forced the issue by ordering a wide-ranging counterat-tack from the Marne and from Paris. The First Battle of the Marne, which opened on September 5, forced the Germans to withdraw. Paris was saved and the Schlieffen Plan was in ruins; Moltke was replaced by General Eric von Falkenhayn.

There now followed the 'Race to the Sea', as the Allies and Germans each sought to find an open flank to exploit. The two sides clashed at the First Battle of the Aisne in mid-September, and the fighting northeast of Paris continued into November. Each outflanking attempt involved inconclusive combat that pushed the Allies and Germans ever closer to the North Sea coast. The final attempt to outflank was conducted by the Germans but the First Battle of Ypres in late October ended after some four weeks with the Allies holding their positions around the Belgian town. Both sides dug in to consolidate the ground they held on the Western Front, but the Allies had undeniably defeated the Schlieffen Plan and Germany faced a war on two fronts.

1915—Allied hopes of victory in the west dashed

In early 1915, both the Allies and Germany remained convinced that a great victory could be won. Falkenhayn remained convinced that only battlefield success on the Western Front offered the hope of total German victory. However, he was persuaded by Field Marshal Erich von Hindenburg and General Eric Ludendorff (rising stars in the high command after their successes against Russia in 1914), that Russia could be knocked out of the war quickly. Equally, Falkenhayn was well aware that Austria-Hungary was increasingly weak and needed urgent German support. He agreed to the Russian option. The Western Front was to be stripped of troops and those remaining held on the defensive.

Allied strategy was complicated by Turkey's recent entry into the war, a move which effectively closed the Dardanelles to them and made the flow of much-needed supplies to Russia problematic. In Britain, politicians, many hoping to avoid further slaughter on the Western Front by adopting an 'indirect' approach to the defeat of Germany, decided to force the Dardanelles to reopen the route to Russia and possibly crush Turkey. In contrast, Allied generals supported a knock-out blow against the German Army on the Western Front. The resultant strategy compromised both options by agreeing to both, thereby splitting the Allied forces. Britain's still comparatively small military effort in France was constrained by the decision to earmark troops for the Gallipoli campaign against Turkey. Consequently, France bore the brunt of the Allied offensive effort on the Western Front, although the British did undertake supporting operations.

The French moved first, continuing the First Battle of Champagne, which had be-gun in late December 1914, but little progress was made and German counterattacks at La Bassée Canal and near Soissons in early 1915 brought the offensive to an end. A supporting British attack against Neuve Chapelle made initially good progress, chiefly due to the use of a short but intense preliminary bombardment that caught the Germans unaware, but the British were unable to rush reinforcements forward quickly enough and losses mounted in the face of German counterattacks. Although hamstrung by limited resources in the west, Falkenhayn opted to launch a limited attack against British-held Ypres, chiefly to eradicate the salient in the line around the Belgian town and test the effectiveness of a new weapon – poison gas. The Second Battle of Ypres, the only German offensive in the west during 1915, opened on April 22 and began well as the gas caused considerable panic, but the Allies recovered. Lacking reserves and facing stubborn resistance, Falkenhayn closed the operation down in late May.

The Allies returned to the offensive as the German drive against Ypres subsided, concentrating their efforts in the Artois region. The main assault opened on May 16, with the French attacking toward Vimy Ridge in the Second Battle of Artois with some success, before a lack of reinforcements and German counterattacks regained much of the lost ground, although the fighting spluttered on until late June. Britain's contribution began with the Battle of Aubers Ridge on May 9, but an acute shell shortage (which was to cause outrage in England) and an ill-coordinated infantry assault produced heavy casualties and few gains. A renewal of the British attack, known as the Battle of Festubert, began on the 16th but had only pushed the German line back less than a mile when it ended on the 27th. The French and British attacked again in late September. The French launched the Second Battle of Champagne, while to the north further French forces again attempted to take Vimy Ridge in the Third Battle of Artois, while the British opened the Battle of Loos. None of these battles achieved the decisive breakthrough the Allied generals desired; although the French did reach the crest of Vimy Ridge on the 29th. The main British effort at Loos, despite early successes, was called off in mid-October, while Second Champagne continued until November 6.

By the end of 1915, the Allies had failed to seriously dent the German line in a series of coordinated offensives along much of the Western Front. Their lack of heavy artillery in quantity, acute shortages of shells, poor planning, lack of reserves, and frequent failure to exploit initial advantages had combined with the excellent fighting skills of the often outnumbered German Army, which was holding increasingly sophisticated defensive positions, to preclude any decisive breakthrough, to stymie their efforts. The Allied failures and the huge casualty figures that accompanied them also severely dented the prestige of the British and French commanders-in-chief. Britain's Field Marshal John French was replaced by General Douglas Haig in December, while France's Marshal Joseph Joffre lost the confidence of his superiors due to his reliance on costly and unimaginative massed infantry assaults, a situation that began his fall from grace.

1916—Verdun and the Somme
In 1916 Germany's strategic focus returned to the Western Front. Falkenhayn launched the Battle of Verdun on February 21, after an artillery barrage of unprecedented ferocity against the vastly outnumbered and outgunned French defenders of the fortresses that ringed the town close to France's eastern border with Germany. Although his local commanders thought otherwise, Falkenhayn was not chiefly concerned with gaining territory or even achieving a decisive breakthrough. He wanted to destroy the French Army, an event that would seriously, if not totally undermine the Allied effort and probably force the French to seek peace terms as civilian morale and support for continuing the war plummeted in the face of grievous casualties. Consequently, Verdun was to be a battle of attrition in which the number of French dead was of overriding importance.

Falkenhayn's strategy at Verdun proved ill-judged. In the opening phase, many French troops were undoubtedly killed and the German assaults also gained territory, not least with the capture of Fort Douaumont on February 26. Equally, the French did rush huge numbers of troops into the sector as German pressure intensified and losses mounted as Falkenhayn intended. However, the Germans also persisted in launching attacks to undermine the increasingly effective defense that was being organized by General Henri Philippe Pétain and they too began to suffer mounting casualties on a par with those of the French. Bitter fighting for positions such as Mort Homme Ridge in March and April and at Fort Vaux, which finally fell to the Germans in June, produced roughly equal losses.

By late June, Falkenhayn's Verdun tactics were clearly failing and, equally worrying, it was clear that the British were planning a major offensive on the Somme, with the intention of relieving the pressure on the French and possibly achieving a major rupture in the German trench system. If that were not possible then it was hoped that the German reserves drawn into the battle would be ground down by attritional fighting. Haig had great hopes for his offensive as did the vastly expanded British forces under his command. However, their hopes were largely dashed on the first day of the battle – July 1.

Some 60,000 men were killed, wounded, or posted missing on that day, and British gains were generally limited, although a supporting French attack did well. This catastrophe was partly the result of a lack of heavy artillery to cut the German barbed wire or smash the deep dugouts in which the defenders sheltered. Also many of the shells fired by the British failed to explode. Equally, the prolonged preliminary bombardment forewarned the Germans of the impending attack. Crucially, there was a slight lull in the artillery fire when the British went over the top that gave the Germans the opportunity to man their positions as the assault waves crossed no man's land and cut them down as they advanced.

The Battle of the Somme did not end on July 1, but continued until mid-November, partly to ease the strain on the French at Verdun and partly because the British high command still publicly hoped for a decisive result. A number of smaller-scale attacks were launched and some, such as the capture of Pozières by Australian troops in late July, achieved actual, if limited, successes.

Tanks made their debut on the Western Front at Flers-Courcelette in mid-September, but they had a limited impact on the overall fighting. The capture of Beaumont Hamel – a July 1 objective – in November marked the end of a battle that had cost the British some 420,000 and the French some 200,000 casualties.

While the Somme continued, the fighting at Verdun gradually swung in France's favor, albeit at high cost. The transfer of resources to face the British forced the Germans on to the defensive and the French began their own series of limited counterattacks. Gradually, much of the lost ground was regained – Fort Douaumont was recaptured in late October and Fort Vaux in the first days of November. When the fighting ended, Falkenhayn's strategy was in ruins – the French had suffered some 550,000 casualties but the German Army had recorded some 435,000 losses. It was not the great attritional victory that he had intended. To make matters worse, the fighting on the Somme, where the Germans posted some 500,000 casualties, and at Verdun had destroyed the cadre of junior officers and NCOs that were the backbone of the German Army. Verdun also wrecked the careers of both Falkenhayn and Joffre, who was blamed for the parlous state of the French defenses at the opening of the German attack. Both men were replaced in 1916—Joffre by General Robert Nivelle and Falkenhayn by Hindenburg and Ludendorff.

1917—A year of Allied disappointments
In 1917, the Allies continued their pressure on the Western Front, while the Germans stayed firmly on the defensive, preferring to husband their scarce resources for a decisive push against Italy as well as maintaining their grip on the conquered parts of Russia and Romania and supporting their weaker allies. To reduce the length on their front and free troops for elsewhere, the Germans made a wholly successful withdrawal to the formidable positions of the Hindenburg Line, an operation that ended in March. The Allies were caught off guard by the German move and had to reschedule their joint spring offensive plans. These began with the British-led Battle of Arras, which opened on April 9. The high point of the fighting was the capture of Vimy Ridge by Canadian forces, but hopes of a breakthrough soon evaporated.

As the Arras fighting died down, the French launched what became known as the Nivelle Offensive in the Champagne region and along the Aisne River. Nivelle had promised a swift and total victory, but his optimism was ill-founded. Despite using a heavy preliminary bombardment and protecting the massed infantry with a creeping barrage, the Germans were prepared for the onslaught and Nivelle's plans quickly fell apart. Little progress was made and the French recorded 118,000 casualties between April 16–20. Mounting losses, poor living conditions and the obvious futility of Nivelle's decision to continue the battle combined to provoke a widespread mutiny in the French Army. Nivelle was sacked and replaced by Pétain, who called off the attacks, improved conditions for the troops, and dealt with the ringleaders. The mutiny, which the Germans failed to discover, was quelled by July but the French were unable to undertake any further major operations—the burden on the Western Front for the rest of the year had to be borne by the British.

The British commander, Haig, had laid plans for a major attack from the Ypres salient with the aim of cutting through the German trenches and then advancing along the Flanders coast to capture ports used by Germany's U-boats. As a preliminary he launched the Battle of Messines Ridge on June 7. Preceded by the detonation of some 20 underground mines that obliterated large sections of the German defenses and the men holding them, the attack was generally successful. Haig's main offensive, the Third Battle of Ypres – or Passchendaele, as it became known – began on July 31. Despite a 10-day bombardment from some 3,000 guns, the initial attacks mostly stalled in front of the German fortifications and then heavy rain, a high water table, and the destruction of the area's drainage system by artillery fire combined to turn the battlefield into a morass. Haig, who believed the German army was closed to exhaustion, continued the battle with a series of smaller attacks designed to capture, step-by-step, sections of the German positions until November, but his plan to win a decisive breakthrough was quietly shelved. The fall of the village of Passchendaele on November marked the end of the fighting, which had cost some 320,000 British and 200,000 German casualties.

The Third Battle of Ypres was a public disaster for Haig, who was heavily criticized for continuing the battle even after the opportunity for a breakthrough had evaporated. He needed a face-saving victory and turned to a new weapon, the tank, that was available for the first time in large numbers. Some 500 spearheaded the Battle of Cambrai on November 20 and they quickly pierced the German line. Their attack was heralded as a great victory, one bought at little cost, but the British were hamstrung by a lack of reserves to exploit their advantage and the tanks proved too mechanically unreliable to capitalize on the early gains. German counterattacks recaptured much of the lost ground by December 3. The year ended with the Allies in despondent mood after the Nivelle Offensive, the French mutinies, and the horrors of Passchendaele; the only cheering news was the decision of the United States to enter the war in April. However, America was militarily unprepared to fight war on a large scale and it would be many months before the US Army's presence would be felt on the Western Front.

1918—The year of decision
Hindenburg and Ludendorff were well aware of the potential of the United States to decide the outcome of the war and also recognized Germany's growing weakness. Saddled with collapsing allies and increasingly short of vital war materials due to the Allied naval blockade, their only hope was to launch a decisive blow on the Western Front before the American Expedition Force (AEF) under General John Pershing could make a major contribution to the campaign. Troops were moved from the Eastern

Front, where Russia's collapse into revolution had removed any threat to Germany, special stormtrooper units were trained in infiltration tactics to break the trench deadlock, and new artillery techniques were instituted. What followed was a series of hammer blows against the French and British, opening with Operation 'Michael' on March 21. A huge 40-mile deep salient was created in the British line, but the offensive ground to a halt due to the arrival of French reinforcements and German supply problems. Others offensives followed – Operations 'Georgette,' 'Blücher,' 'Yorck,' and 'Gneisenau'—between April and June. Each followed the course of 'Michael' and the German high command began to receive reports of indiscipline in the ranks. Exhausted and dispirited troops, who had seen thousands of their comrades become casualties, were looting Allied supply depots rather than advancing; getting drunk and frequently disobeying their officers.

On July 15, the final German offensive of the war opened toward the Marne River, but soon stalled. Three days later the French, with some US support, struck in what became known as the Second Battle of the Marne. By the 20th the Germans had been pushed back and the new Allied supreme commander, Marshal Ferdinand Foch, ordered a succession of offensives all along the Western Front. The British in the north launched the Battle of Amiens on August 8, and in many cases were met by demoralized German troops eager to surrender, although many others would continue to fight hard until the end of the war. Nevertheless, Ludendorff spoke of 'the black day of the German army in the war.' In mid-September Pershing's AEF successfully eradicated the St Mihiel salient in the south, while the French continued the pressure along the center of the Western Front.

September put the seal on Germany's defeat. The British undertook a series of attacks that finally cut through the mighty Hindenburg Line, while the AEF began the Meuse-Argonne Offensive. These rolling advances would continue until the armistice on November 11, but the Allied pushes, against crumbling if sometimes effective German opposition, were remorseless. Beset by revolution at home, short of economic resources, and confronted by military indiscipline, Hindenburg and Ludendorff, virtual dictators, abdicated their responsibilities and left the ending of the war to Germany's politicians.

THE EASTERN FRONT

Russia's mobilization in August 1914 was faster than Germany anticipated and was a precursor to fighting in two theaters, one in East Prussia, where Germany had few troops, and the other in the Austro-Hungarian province of Galicia. The ill-coordinated Russian advance into East Prussia did, nevertheless, cause severe concerns in Germany and prompted the appointment of recently retired Field Marshal Paul von Hindenburg to coordinate the province's defense. Greatly assisted by General Eric Ludendorff, he dealt with the two widely spaced Russian armies menacing East Prussia separately. The southern threat was totally smashed during the Battle of Tannenberg in late August. The more northerly Russian force was severely mauled in the First Battle of the Masurian Lakes and forced to retreat. East Prussia was saved and Hindenburg and Ludendorff became national heroes.

In Galicia Russian forces defeated a badly handled and ill-mounted Austro-Hungarian offensive along a 200-mile front, winning a notable victory at the Battle of Lemberg in late August–early September that forced the Austro-Hungarians to retreat to the Carpathian Mountains. Only the fortress of Przemysl remained in Austro-Hungarian hands in Galicia. German forces were rushed south from East Prussia to prevent a total Austro-Hungarian collapse and pre-empt a Russian advance into the key German coal region of Silesia from Poland, a Russian province. The subsequent German spoiling offensive, fought during late September and October, was of limited success but the danger to Silesia was averted. The Russians returned to the attack in November and the Germans fell back before launching their own counterattack. The Battle of Lódz inflicted heavy casualties on the Russians and brought temporary stalemate to the fighting in Poland.

The great Russian retreat

The German high command concentrated on the Eastern Front during 1915. The necessity of this strategy was confirmed when an Austro-Hungarian attempt to relive Przemysl, begun in January, collapsed with heavy losses in March; Przemysl surrendered on the 12th. The Germans began the year with a limited offensive. A thrust toward Warsaw in January and the ensuing Battle of Bolimov acted as a feint, before the main event, a drive to finish off the Russians menacing East Prussia's borders. The subsequent Second or Winter Battle of the Masurian Lakes in February was not the sweeping victory announced by Hindenburg and Ludendorff but it did increase East Prussia's security. After blunting a Russian offensive in the south during March and April, the Germans launched their own attack in the theater. Directed into Galicia, the Gorlice-Tarnow Offensive fought during May and June was a major victory, one that forced a wholescale withdrawal of Russian armies and recaptured Przemysl. The Germans now switched their forces to the north and opened a push into Poland. Warsaw fell on August 5, heralding a further major Russian retreat. By the end of the year, when severe weather, exhaustion and supply difficulties halted the advance, the series of German-led offensives had saved East Prussia, pushed into the Baltic States, occupied Poland, and liberated much of Galicia. Although the Russian Army had been badly mauled, suffering some two million casualties, it remained substantially intact. It would continue to pose a threat to Germany's security in the east and in 1916 would be used to relieve German pressure on the Western Front.

The Brusilov Offensive

In early 1916 the French requested that the Russians conduct a campaign on the Eastern Front to draw German forces away from the fortress of Verdun, where the French garrison was under intense pressure. The Russians obliged with an attack on March 18. Although enjoying a two-to-one superiority over the Germans, the Russians lacked artillery and shells and the Battle of Lake Naroch ended in April with huge Russian losses and no discernible easing of the pressure on Verdun. Although Russia had suffered severe losses, its high command agreed to launch a second major offensive in June, this time in support of Italy, which was under intense pressure following the opening of the Austro-Hungarian Trentino Offensive.

The Russian attack was coordinated by the army's best commander, General Alexei Brusilov, who gave his name to the offensive. Although he had been refused reinforcements to exploit any successes, Brusilov had made meticulous preparations. A high level of secrecy was maintained, artillery registration on targets was excellent, and the assault waves were protected in deep dugouts. Four Russian armies opened the advance on June 4 and rapidly cut through the mainly Austro-Hungarian opposition on a broad front stretching from the Pripet Marshes to the Romanian border. By mid-June, the Russians had captured some 200,000 prisoners and shattered the Austro-Hungarian forces in Galicia. However, exhaustion, supply difficulties, and a lack of reserves forced Brusilov to halt by the end of the month. This pause allowed the Germans and Austro-Hungarians to rush around 16 divisions from other fronts to stabilize the situation. Nevertheless, Brusilov continued to attack during July and August, reaching the Carpathian Mountains before the offensive ran out of steam. The Russian success had three key results. First, Austria-Hungary was fatally weakened, forcing already overstretched Germany to take over the whole of the direction of the war on the Eastern Front. Second, Romania, eager to seize Austro-Hungarian territory, believed that the Brusilov Offensive was a springboard to achieving its regional ambitions and sided with the Allies. Third, the Russian victory was bought at such a high cost, some one million casualties, that morale in the army fell dramatically.

The Russian collapse

In March 1917 Russia was rocked by revolution. Czar Nicholas II, the emperor and supreme commander, abdicated; and the running of the country and its war effort devolved to the Provisional Government. However, its authority was challenged by the radical Bolsheviks, who strove to exploit the war weariness of ordinary soldiers and civilians. The Provisional Government attempted to fulfil its commitments to the Allied cause by launching an offensive in Galicia during July. Named after the government's defense minister, Aleksandr Kerensky, and announced to the Russian public as a 'liberty' offensive to free Russia from foreign occupation, it was organized by Brusilov. However, despite some early successes, the momentum soon died. German-led resistance stiffened as the Russian forces disintegrated. Previous heavy losses, low morale, and Bolshevik agitation combined to undermine their commitment to carrying on the war. By August, the Germans had retaken much of Galicia.

The Germans, who were under intense pressure on the Western Front from the British at the Third Battle of Ypres, did not exploit Russia's instability until September, when they launched a limited attack against Riga in the north to put further pressure on the unstable Provisional Government. The Bolshevik coup in November finished the Russian government and the new leaders immediately began negotiating Russian withdrawal from the war. An armistice was agreed at Brest-Litovsk on December 12, but the Bolsheviks delayed signing any final settlement, forcing the Germans to reopen hostilities on February 17, 1918, with an offensive deep into Russian territory that met little opposition. Two days later, the Bolsheviks signed the Treaty of Brest-Litovsk, which left much of Russia's economic resources under German control. Free of a major entanglement in the east, the Germans stepped up the transfer of forces to the Western Front for their planned spring offensive. However, one million German troops, who might have been better employed elsewhere, were left in Russia to oversee the treaty's draconian provisions.

TURKEY AND THE MIDDLE EAST

Turkey, which sided with Germany in late October 1914, fought the war on four fronts – the Caucasus, where Russia, backed by Armenian insurgents, was the main enemy, and Gallipoli, Mesopotamia, and Palestine, where troops from Britain and its empire were employed. The British also sponsored Arab nationalist uprisings and guerrilla forces in the Turkish province of Arabia from mid-1916, while the Turks and Germans supported similar but unsuccessful uprisings by Senussi tribesmen in North Africa and rebels in Persia, where both Britain and Russia had strategic interests.

The Caucasus campaign

In late 1914, the Turks undertook a disastrous offensive into the Russian Caucasus in the depths of winter that was repelled by the Russians at the Battle of Sarikamish, which ended on January 3, 1915. Following command changes on both sides, the Turks again advanced into the region to deal with an Armenian uprising that had begun in April. The Turks won the Battle of Malazgirt in mid-July and retook Van from the Armenians. In 1916, the Russians counterattacked to considerable effect, winning the Battle of Köprukoy in late January, capturing Trebizond in April, and smashing a Turkish force at Erzinjan on July 25. Due to pressures elsewhere, which led to troop withdrawals, the fighting in the Caucasus died down for the reminder of the war.

Gallipoli and the Dardanelles

The major threat faced by the Turks in 1915 was the Allied effort to open up the Dardanelles sea-way, to force Turkey out of the war and open a key supply route to Russia. Attempts by warships alone to force a passage in February and March failed and the Allies then launched an amphibious assault on the Gallipoli Peninsula with French, British and empire forces. The first landings took place on April 25 and met with considerable resistance. The assault troops failed to advance inland and the Turks rushed in reinforcements, thereby enclosing the invaders in the southern tip of the peninsula. Trench warfare, similar to that on the Western Front, developed under dreadful conditions. The Allies tried to break the stalemate with landings farther along the peninsula's northern coast at Suvla Bay in early August, but failed to capitalize on the initial surprise and advance against the area's few defenders. Turkish reinforcements arrived under Mustafa Kemal and trench fighting commenced. With losses mounting and no hope of a breakthrough evident, the Allies withdrew during December 1915–January 1916. The withdrawal, unlike the rest of the operation, was conducted superbly.

Mesopotamia

Britain moved swiftly after Turkey's war declaration and in November 1914 occupied Basra in Mesopotamia as a base for further operations toward Baghdad. These began in May 1915 with a major advance along the Tigris River. The Turks were brushed aside and the British occupied Kut-el-Amara in late September. However, the British suffered a major reversal at the Battle of Ctesiphon two months later and retreated back to Kut-el-Amara, where they were besieged from early December. Two relief expeditions in January and March 1916 failed to break through the Turkish lines, and the defenders of Kut-el-Amara, who were starving, suffering a variety of illnesses and short of military supplies, surrendered on April 29.

At Basra, the British awaited reinforcements before beginning a second push on Baghdad in early 1917. A victory was won at the Second Battle of Kut in late February and Baghdad fell on March 11. The offensive halted due to high summer temperatures and the need to bring forward supplies, but recommenced in September. The Turks, under intense pressure due to British successes in Palestine, offered only fractured resistance, and the British won the Battle of Ramadi at the end of the month. The Mesopotamian campaign declined in importance in 1918 as Turkey approached the point of collapse, although the British continued to push northward toward Mosul in October, a move running roughly parallel to a similar thrust through Palestine. The Turks agreed an armistice on October 30 and Mosul was occupied a few days later.

Palestine

The Turks recognized that the Suez Canal was a key strategic asset for the British but their efforts to seize the waterway in February 1915 were half-hearted and easily repulsed. Through the remainder of the year and into 1916, little action took place in Palestine due to the Gallipoli campaign and the build-up to the Somme offensive on the Western Front, although the British did push across the canal into the Sinai Peninsula in preparation for an advance into Palestine. Turkish attempts to halt this incursion were rebuffed at the Battle of Rumani on August 3. In early 1917, the British began their major drive into southern Palestine. Advancing along the coast, they attempted to break through the Turkish coastal defenses but were repelled at the First and Second Battles of Gaza during March and April.

The British attacks resumed in late October, when a new commander, General Archibald Murray, outflanked the Turks during Third Gaza, or the Battle of Beersheba, and forced them into retreat. They abandoned Jerusalem, which Allenby occupied on December 9. For much of 1918, Allenby's campaign was hamstrung by the need to transfer units to the Western Front, where the Allies were facing a series of major German offensives, but he returned to the attack in September. The Battle of Megiddo saw the virtual destruction of the Turkish forces in Palestine. Harassed by Allenby's men and Arab guerrillas on their inland flank, the Turks retreated northward. Damascus fell on October 1, and the campaign concluded at the end of the month.

ITALY AND THE BALKANS

The assassination of Austro-Hungarian Archduke Franz Ferdinand by Serbian nationalists on July 28, 1914, led to the outbreak of World War I, and prompted the first offensive of the conflict. Austro-Hungarian forces invaded Serbia in mid-August but were roundly defeated at the Battle of the Jadar River. In September, the Austro-Hungarians advanced again and forced the Serbians to stage an orderly withdrawal. When the invaders resumed their offensive in November, they became dangerously overextended and consequently fell prey to a Serbian counterattack, the Battle of the Kolubra River, and were pushed back over the border.

The Balkan war widens

In 1915, the strategic situation in the theater was transformed by Italy siding with the Allies in May and Bulgaria joining Germany in October. The Italian Army battered away along the line of the Isonzo River in the northeast of the country which bordered Austria-Hungary. The First to Fourth Battles of the Isonzo, fought between July and December, saw the Italians make virtually no progress due to the mountainous terrain, the strong Austro-Hungarian border defenses, and the Italian Army's lack of training and heavy artillery. In early October, the fate of Serbia was sealed. It was attacked on several fronts by Austro-Hungarian, Bulgarian, and German forces and was overrun. The invasion prompted the British and French to send the first of hundreds of thousands of troops to Salonika in early October as the Greek government feared Bulgarian ambitions in the Balkans. In January 1916, the remnants of the Serbian Army were evacuated and made their way to Salonika, where the force was subsequently reformed.

In 1916, the Italians launched the Fifth Battle of the Isonzo, as part of the Allied effort to relieve the pressure on Verdun, but it was halted in late March having achieved little. The Austro-Hungarians, fresh from victory in Serbia, now launched the Trentino Offensive against northern Italy in mid-May. Early progress soon evaporated due to supply difficulties and then the need to transfer troops to the Eastern Front to deal with the Russian Brusilov Offensive. The Italian riposte was to launch four further attacks along the Isonzo but only the Ninth Battle in August gained any ground and the attacks were called off in mid-November. In what was to prove a disastrous move to grab Austro-Hungarian territory, Romania sided with the Allies in August. The response was swift and devastating. German-led forces swiftly overran the country, capturing Bucharest in early December, confining the remains of the Romanian Army to the northeast of the country.

Italy comes close to collapse

In March and May 1917, the Allied forces in Salonika launched two limited but ineffective offensives. Neither altered the strategic stalemate in the theater, but subsequent political changes in Greece saw the country finally side with the Allies. The Italians launched the 10th and 11th Battles of the Isonzo between May and September 1917; in the latter, fighting gained some important ground against weakening Austro-Hungarian resistance. Austro-Hungary's plight led to the transfer of German forces to the battlefront; they spearheaded the 12th Battle of the Isonzo (also known as the Battle of Caporetto), in late October. The attack was overwhelmingly successful. The Italians were forced back in confusion to the line of the Piave River, although the arrival of 11 British and French divisions and the enemy's supply problems prevented a total collapse.

The Allies triumph

In June 1918, the Austro-Hungarians made one last attempt to knock Italy out of the war. However, the Battle of the Piave River only confirmed the poor state of the empire's armed forces. Riven by nationalist sentiments, short of supplies, and lacking German assistance, they were unable to fulfil the mission and the attacks were called off by the end of the month. Italy's response was not immediate, but in late October the Battle of Vittorio Veneto confirmed Austria-Hungary's impoverished state. Aided by British and French units, the Italians broke out from the line of the Piave and forced the Austro-Hungarians into headlong retreat. An armistice was agreed on November 3, signaling Austria-Hungary's total defeat. A similar collapse was occurring in the Balkans, following the launch of the Battle of the Vardar River by the Allied forces in Salonika during September. By the end of the month the Bulgarians were granted an armistice: the Allies reached the Danube by the end of the war on November 11.

THE WIDER WAR

All of the leading combatant nations were colonial powers, although Britain was by far the most important. Germany's colonies were few, but concentrated in Africa, China and the Pacific. Germany had few resources to spare to protect its possessions and most were lost in the first months of the war. For example, the Samoan Expeditionary Force from New Zealand captured the German colony of German Western Samoa in the Pacific at the outbreak of war. Japan, which had wide-ranging ambitions in both China and the Pacific and sided with the Allies on August 23, 1914, quickly seized the greater part of Germany's other Pacific colonies, the Caroline, Marshall, and Mariana Islands, during October, and captured the concession port of Tsingtao on the Chinese mainland with some British support on November 7.

In similar fashion, the bulk of Germany's colonies in Africa were taken by the Allies in the first half of the war as they were isolated, short of troops and usually bordered by Allied possessions. Togoland, Cameroon, and German Southwest Africa were all overrun by Allied forces between 1914 and 1916. However, the war in East Africa proved much more protracted and a drain on Allied resources. This was chiefly due to the skilful guerrilla campaign conducted by the local German commander, General Paul von Lettow-Vorbeck. He ranged far and wide across the region, evading far larger Allied forces and only agreed to lay down his arms after the armistice of November 11, 1918. Because of communications difficulties, this did not take place until the 25th, making it the last act of the German Army in World War I.

THE ARMISTICE

Following the Treaty of Brest-Litovsk, on March 3, 1918, which settled World War 1 on the Eastern Front, Germany was no longer faced by the necessity of fighting a war on two fronts. Relieved of the need to keep sizeable forces in the east to defend East Prussia, the German army on the Western Front was significantly reinforced. The strengthened German army was able to launch a number of major spring offensives: in March and April 1918 the Kaiserschlacht saw the Germans advance south of Arras toward Amiens; this was followed later in April by the Lys Offensive and in May by a third phase on the River Aisne. Heavy fighting in May and June, however, stopped the German advance and, by the time of the Second Battle of the Marne (in July/August), the initiative was once more with the Allies. In August, the Amiens Offensive saw the Allies rout the German Second Army and, from this point, German defeat became inevitable.

The first attempts to negotiate an armistice occurred in early October, but it was not until November, with the German forces in retreat, that an armistice was agreed. On November 9, Kaiser Wilhelm II abdicated and fled; he was replaced by a provisional socialist government in Berlin following a revolution. The armistice was agreed and came into effect at the 11th hour of the 11th day of the 11 month—a time that is still marked to this day.

The nature of the armistice, the collapse of the wartime leadership, and the fact that war barely impinged on much of Germany helped to foster the myth that the army had been 'stabbed in the back'—a myth that was to be much promoted as Fascism took hold. The reality was, however, that Germany – like all other combatant nations – had suffered immense losses, both in terms of manpower and economic power, from which it would struggle to recover.

Casualties and Remembrance

The number of human casualties, both military and civilian, is almost impos-sible to calculate. (This was the first war to have a real impact on the civilian population away from the battle fronts through aerial bombing.) Estimates for the number of military casualties range from nine to 12 million, with many millions more injured. Many of those injured were also to die from the long-term effects of war, in particular gas and tropical diseases, while for many of the survivors there was a feeling of great guilt, with many refusing ever to talk about their experiences. The civilian casualties also numbered many millions, particularly in the east, where some two million Russians died and there were massacres of Armenians and other ethnic populations. In addition the impact of economic warfare, blockades, and famine was dramatic; it is estimated that at least half a million Germans died from starvation.

Apart from the human cost, there was also an immense economic cost. The primary effect of the war was to shift the global economic balance toward the New World, as European indebtedness led to the United States becoming the major creditor nation. For many of the returning troops in Europe, there was little prospect of employment as many of the traditional industries suffered an almost inexorable decline.

The scale of the human cost can best be seen through the vast wartime cemeteries that can be found throughout much of the area fought over during the war. The British and Empire graveyards are managed by the Commonwealth War Graves Commission, while numerous other cemeteries house the combatants from other nations. Many of the structures in the British and Empire cemeteries were designed by the noted architect Sir Edwin Lutyens, who also designed the Cenotaph in London where Britain marks Armistice Day annually on the Sunday closest to November 11. Remembrance Day sees services at war memorials throughout the world. The human cost led to the creation of a charity, the Royal British Legion, that provides help and assistance to veterans and their families. One of the founders of the Legion was Field Marshal Haig, a leading British commander during the war.

Undoubtedly, one of the most important consequences of the war was its impact on the various national feelings. Mention has already been made of the German resentment, which was to be further fostered by the Treaty of Versailles, but for most nations there was a desire that the war would be the war to end all wars. For France, the consequence of war was a defensive strategy based around the Maginot Line that was to prove fatally flawed when the Germans launched their attack on the west in May 1940. For Britain, the loss of a generation was to result in a desire to avoid similar loss in the future and was an undoubted factor in the policy of appeasement in the late 1930s. For the United States there was a feeling that, having assisted the Old World once, the country should not get involved in European squabbles again; a policy of isolationism was the result, a policy that was ultimately doomed to failure in the dark days of December 1941.

The Legacy
VERSAILLES

Following the Armistice on the Western Front, there were demands that the conquered powers, in particular Germany and the Habsburg Empire, should be made to pay for their defeat. Although there were politicians who warned that the imposition of too harsh a settlement would lead only to resentment and the likelihood of further conflict, these siren calls were ignored in the general rush for retribution. The result was the Treaty of Versailles, signed on June 28, 1919 (although only reluctantly by Germany).

Perceived in Germany as unfair, particularly as it labeled the country guilty of causing the war, the treaty was a major factor in the ultimate rise of Adolf Hitler. The treaty saw certain parts of the former German state transferred. Denmark received (after a plebiscite), the area of North Schleswig; France regained Alsace-Lorraine; Upper Silesia and part of East Prussia passed to Poland; the port of Danzig was administered by the League of Nations; and both Belgium and the newly created Czechoslovakia also received territory. In addition, France was allowed to occupy the Saarland for 15 years and the Rhineland was to be demilitarized. The end result was that Germany was split in two, with the remains of East Prussia separated from the rest of the country by a Polish corridor. It also resulted in sizeable German minorities in many surrounding countries. Finally, Germany was stripped of its overseas colonies, forced to pay significant financial reparations, and was restricted in the scope of military equipment that the postwar armed forces could operate.

The other major casualty of the war was the Austrian Empire. The Treaties of St Germain and Trianon in 1919 and 1920 effectively brought the end of the empire and the creation of new independent states, such as Hungary and Czechoslovakia. To the south, the various Slav states (Serbia, Montenegro, Croatia, Slovenia, and Bosnia) were united to form the new Kingdom of Yugoslavia. Romania was also to gain a considerable amount of land (despite having been virtually defeated and only reentering the war on November 9, 1918). Romania gained Transylvania and Bessarabia along with much of the Hungarian Plain. This resulted in the country acquiring a sizeable Hungarian minority.

THE NEW WORLD ORDER

One further consequence of World War 1 was the creation of the League of Nations. Established in 1920, the League was designed to encourage peace by the settlement of disputes through arbitration. It was based in Geneva and had the backing of a number of highly influential politicians, among whom was President Wilson of the United States. However, as a result of the country's refusal to ratify the Treaty of Versailles and the resultant move toward isolationism, the US never became of member of the league. This fatally weakened the League of Nations, particularly when after 1930, fascist states such as Italy and Germany increasingly ignored it. Germany resigned its membership in 1933 (having joined only in 1926) and Italy did likewise in 1937. In the build up to World War II, the league was powerless to intervene as the world's great powers acted without reference to it, in particular over Japanese aggression against China and the Italian invasion of Abyssinia (Ethiopia). The league, however, was not to be formally dissolved until 1946 when the new United Nations was established.

In terms of the world order, however, the major shift had occurred with the rise of the United States. From the mid-19th century onward, the United States' economic power had increased immeasurably and, in a low-key way, the country had also ex-panded its territorial possessions, particularly after the 1898 war with Spain, which had brought it control of the Philippines, Puerto Rico, Cuba (temporarily), and Hawaii. Despite this, in terms of world politics, the US remained rigidly isolated from affairs in Europe. It was President Woodrow Wilson who reflected the US position well when he said in 1915, 'We have stood apart, studiously neutral.' In entering the war in 1917, to bring the new world to the assistance of the old, Wilson had subtly altered the balance; however, in proclaiming, as he did in April 1917, that, 'The world must be made safe for democracy,' he implied that the US would assume a much greater role after victory was assured. In reality, after the Versailles settlement, the US reverted to its traditional political isolationism although its economic power was to dominate increasingly the world economy.

RUSSIAN CIVIL WAR

Following the Bolshevik Revolution of October 1917 in the east, there was a period of civil war in Russia. Britain and others supplied support – albeit in a fairly half-hearted form – to the opponents of Lenin while World War I was still progressing. However, with peace in the west, the imperative to keep the Eastern Front alive disappeared, and between 1918 and 1921 resistance to the new regime was eliminated.

Resistance to the Bolshevik revolution came from a number of sources and in different parts of the country. At the start of the civil war, the new regime lacked an army; this was hastily organized by Leon Trotsky. Becoming known as the Red Army, the force was able ultimately to achieve victory over the counter-revolutionary forces – the so-called White forces – as a result of a lack of close cooperation between the various anti-communist forces. There were five main theaters of operation in the civil war. In the Crimea, from December 1917 until General Wrangel was defeated in November 1920, the Cossacks had initial success. In the Ukraine, the Germans installed General Skoropadsky as head of a puppet regime, which survived until the Germans withdrew in November 1918, after which Cossack forces under General Deniken occupied the region from August until December 1919; resistance in the Ukraine ceased in the summer of 1920 after a brief occupation of Kiev by Polish forces in May of that year. The third theater was in the Baltic states where, in October 1919, an army under General Yudenich had advanced to Petrograd, but failed to take the city. This theater also saw campaigns against the armies of Finland, Latvia, Estonia, and Lithuania, although all these campaigns were concluded by late 1920. In Northern Russia, British and French forces landed at Murmansk in June 1918 and captured Archangel in July that year. Establishing a puppet government, Anglo-French occupation of the region continued until October 1919. Finally, in Siberia, a counter-revolutionary government, backed by Czech ex-prisoners of war and a small

Japanese force that had landed in December 1917 at Vladivostock, was set up by Admiral Kolchak. However, he was captured and executed in early 1920; the Japanese, meanwhile, continued to hold Vladivostock until late 1922. Apart from the threat of civil war, the new Bolshevik regime also had to face peasant uprisings, many caused by famine, and mutiny among naval forces at Kronstadt in early 1921.

The leader of the October Revolution, Lenin (Vladimir Ilyich Ulyanov) was to remain in power only until his death on January 21, 1924. Lenin was ultimately replaced as Soviet leader by Stalin, but not until internal conflict within the Communist Party was concluded. Leon Trotsky, Stalin's great rival, was forced into exile (and later murdered). During the 1930s Stalin's power was further increased by systematic 'purges' of the party and the military. It is claimed that one factor in the German army's initial successes in 1941 was Stalin's elimination of most of the higher echelons of the Soviet military.

THE REBUILDING OF EMPIRE

Although the war led to the defeat and dismemberment of four empires in Europe and the Middle East – Germany, Austria-Hungary, Russia, and Turkey – the two nations with the greatest global empires, Britain and France, were to emerge from the war and from Versailles with their imperial prestige enhanced, although the victory was in many ways shallow. Both Britain and France had been economically weakened by the war and the strains of maintaining their respective empires would undermine their military power within Europe.

Of the defeated and dismembered empires, only two had territories that could have been regarded as colonial possessions. Germany had, albeit relatively late, joined Britain and France in the acquisition of territories in Africa and the Far East, while Turkey had had control over much of the Middle East and Arabia.

One of the consequences of the Treaty of Versailles was that Germany was stripped of its overseas possessions – another cause of German resentment – and these were then held under a mandate of the League of Nations. Of German territory in Africa, German East Africa (Deutsche Ost Afrika; German since 1884) was became a British mandated territory and renamed Tanganyika; Southwest Africa (German since 1884) was captured by South Africa in 1914–15 and became a mandated territory under South Africa; Togo (German since 1884) was under joint French and British mandated control; Cameroon (Kamerun; a German protectorate since 1884) saw mandated control pass to Britain and France. In the Far East, the northern part of the Solomon Islands, controlled by the German New Guinea Company, and New Guinea (Kaiser-Wilhelmsland) were mandated to Australia. Other German possessions in the Pacific, such as the Caroline Islands and the Marshall Islands were mandated to Japan, while Samoa passed to New Zealand.

Many of the territories of the former Ottoman Empire were given their independence; it was during this period that countries such as Iraq (under British mandated control until 1932) and Saudi Arabia emerged, although other territories again passed under League of Nations' mandate to Britain and France. In the Middle East, France gained control of Lebanon and Syria through these means, while Britain gained a mandate over Palestine.

These post-Versailles mandates subsisted until, in many cases, after World War II and into the period of decolonization. However, while the post-World War I settlement helped to create the illusion that all was well with both the British and French empires, the reality, certainly for the former, was the economic powerhouse of the 19th century – the 'Workshop of the World' – was being overtaken both economically and militarily by the United States. Although events, such as the Silver Jubilee of King George V in 1935, helped to foster the illusion of one great Imperial family, there were signs that the process of evolution from Empire to Commonwealth was already underway.

Following the Easter Rising in Ireland, the country was partitioned as a result of the Anglo-Irish Treaty of 1921. Although the Irish Free State retained the monarch as its head of state until 1937, the period between 1922 and 1937 was marked initially by civil war in the Free State and by a gradual severing of ties between Britain and the Free State from the early 1930s onward, particularly under the leadership of Eamonn de Valera. As, at that time, there was no concept that a nation could remain part of the Empire (or Commonwealth) without accepting the monarch as head of state, constitutional ties between Britain and Ireland ended when it became a republic.

Elsewhere in the empire, greater autonomy was granted to the great dominions – Australia, Canada, New Zealand, and South Africa – when, following the Imperial Conference of 1926 and the Statute of Westminster, they were recognized as independent save for the continued allegiance to the crown. In other parts of the empire, most notably in India where Mahatma Gandhi and the Congress party were becoming increasingly influential, there were greater moves for increased independence. How the empire would have evolved if World War II had not occurred is difficult to say; certainly, World War II was to accelerate a process of decolonization as the concept of self-determination became more prevalent.

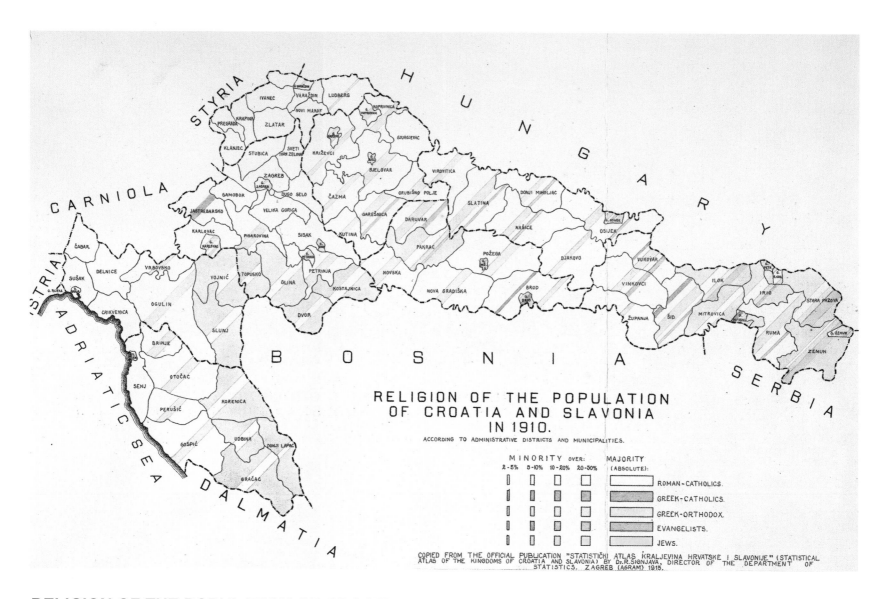

RELIGION OF THE POPULATION
OF CROATIA AND SLAVONIA
IN 1910.

ACCORDING TO ADMINISTRATIVE DISTRICTS AND MUNICIPALITIES.

MINORITY over:				MAJORITY (ABSOLUTE):	
2-5%	5-10%	10-20%	20-50%		
					ROMAN-CATHOLICS.
					GREEK-CATHOLICS.
					GREEK-ORTHODOX.
					EVANGELISTS.
					JEWS.

COPIED FROM THE OFFICIAL PUBLICATION "STATISTIČKI ATLAS KRALJEVINA HRVATSKE I SLAVONIJE" (STATISTICAL ATLAS OF THE KINGDOMS OF CROATIA AND SLAVONIA) BY Dr.R.SIGNJAVA, DIRECTOR OF THE DEPARTMENT OF STATISTICS, ZAGREB (AGRAM) 1915.

RELIGION OF THE POPULATION OF CROATIA AND SLAVONIA, 1910

ABOVE: The map clearly shows the complicated religious affiliations in the Balkans in the early years of the 19th century. As the Austro-Hungarian Empire weakened so did its hold over the diverse peoples of the area. Nationalism and religion would cause the spark that would lead Europe to war. Events in the last years of the 20th century show that the unrest exists to this day. MPK 291 (2)

TURKEY IN EUROPE, 1914

RIGHT: The Ottomans had lost their hold over the Balkans and their African provinces during the 19th and early 20th centuries. This map shows the positions of the Turkish-Bulgarian border following the First Balkan War of 1912, the Bulgarian border following the Treaty of Neuilly of November 27, 1919, and the peace settlement between the Allies and Bulgaria that gave Western Thrace to Greece, the Dobrudja region to Romania and required Bulgaria to pay reparations. MPK 509 (3)

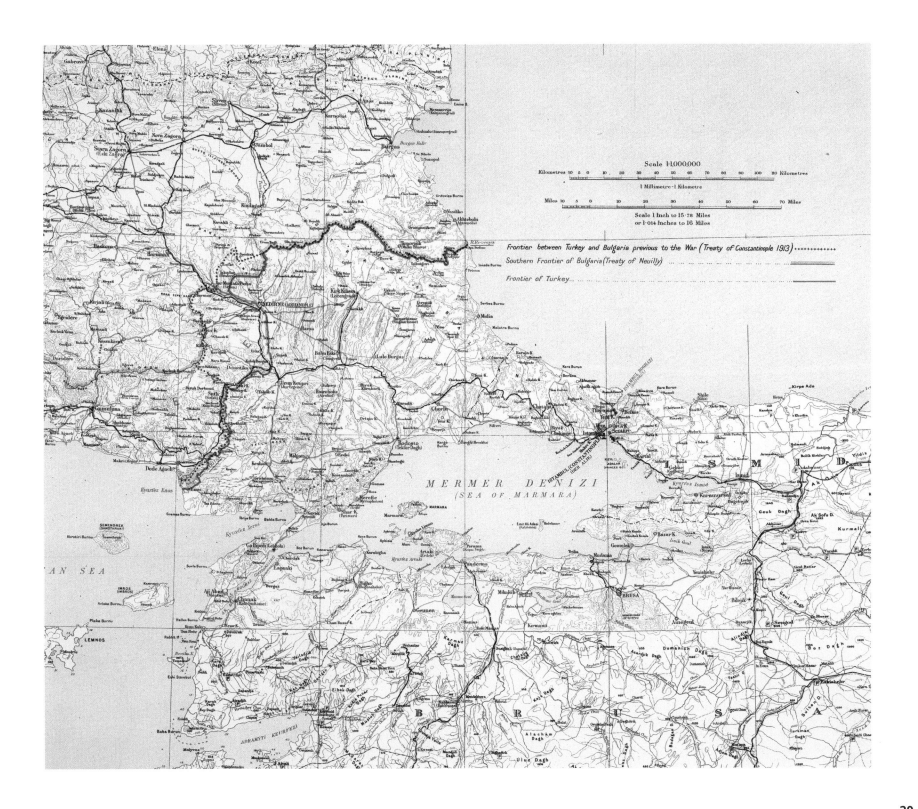

Scale 1:1,000,000

Kilometres 10 5 0   10   20   30   40   50   60   70   80   90   100   110 Kilometres

1 Millimetre=1 Kilometre

Miles 10   5   0   10   20   30   40   50   60   70 Miles

Scale 1 Inch to 15·78 Miles
or 1·014 Inches to 16 Miles

Frontier between Turkey and Bulgaria previous to the War (Treaty of Constantinople 1913) ++++++++++

Southern Frontier of Bulgaria (Treaty of Neuilly) ....

Frontier of Turkey ....

MERMER DENIZI
(SEA OF MARMARA)

GERMAN WAR AIMS, 1914

LEFT: Stanford's map of Europe, Africa, and West Asia shows the areas embraced by *Mittel Europa* and *Mittel Afrika*, the German ideals in the Great War. *Mittel Europa* sees a corridor of territory with Germany at one end, through Austria, the Balkans (but not Greece), and Turkey. *Mittel Afrika* stretches across the continent providing Germany with the empire its leaders had dreamed about, and a position on the world stage that befitted its ideals. The policy was predicated on keeping internal unrest unfocused and fighting a short war if necessary: it was a policy of confrontation that would lead to war. WO 300/14

U-BOAT POSITIONS AROUND THE NORTH SEA COAST AND ENGLISH CHANNEL, AUGUST 19, 1914

LEFT: This map, corrected up to 1924, shows the 'approximate positions of German submarines on the occasion of the High Sea [sic] Fleet sortie,' some two weeks after Great Britain declared war on Germany. The text says: 'This is considered to have been the greatest concentration directed against war ships.' The German Navy had the largest and best contemporary fleet of submarines. Relatively few Allied and neutral ships were lost to German submarines in 1914, but in 1917 almost 2,500 were sunk as the German U-boat Service nearly won the war for the Central Powers. Around the date of this map, on August 9, *U15* had been sunk by British cruiser *Birmingham* off Fair Isle; around August 12, *U13* was lost in the Heligoland Bight; and on November 23, *U18* was rammed and surrendered. The losses on the British side were the cruiser *Pathfinder* off the Firth of Forth on September 5, the cruisers *Aboukir*, *Hogue* ,and *Cressy* sunk by *U9* on September 22; and the cruiser *Hawke* on October 15, again to *U9*. MPI 671 pt 1 (5)

DEFENSES OF MAUBERGE, 1914

LEFT: A French map of the defenses of Mauberge, where the main fortifications were built by Louis XIV's military architect, Vauban. Many of the cities of the Low Countries and Northern France had been fortified over the centuries and in 1914 these sophisticated latterday castles included Liège, Antwerp, and Namur. The Germans bypassed the fortifications when they attacked, bringing up artillery to pound them into submission once they had taken the surrounding area. The only French fort attacked at this time, Mauberge benefited from a more active defense and faired better than the others, surviving an epic 11-day siege before surrendering on September 8. Mauberge had been identified as the BEF's concentration area since 1911. From August 16–24, 1914, Mauberge aerodrome was the HQ of the Royal Flying Corps, with its 63 machines and 860 personnel. Following the retreat after the Battle of Mons on August 23, the British, rather than getting trapped in the fort, retreated southward, leaving the city to its fate. WO 153/116

BATTLE OF TANNENBERG, AUGUST 1914

RIGHT: This map is actually taken from a 1944 document about the topography and defenses of East Prussia – information the War Office passed to the invading Russians. It shows the attack by the Russian First (Rennenkampf) and Second (Samsonov) Armies during the battle fought between August 26 and 30, 1914. The Russian attacks took place during their early war incursion toward Königsberg, on the back of what appeared to the Russians as a victory at Gumbinnen on August 20. Personal emnity between the two Russian generals, the folly of sending uncoded radio messages, and the discovery by the Germans of a dead Russian staff officer with their military plans in his pocket, all contributed to a resounding tactical victory for German generals Hindenburg and Ludendorff. The Russian loss was a great shock to the Allies, who were hard pressed in northern France. WO 208/686

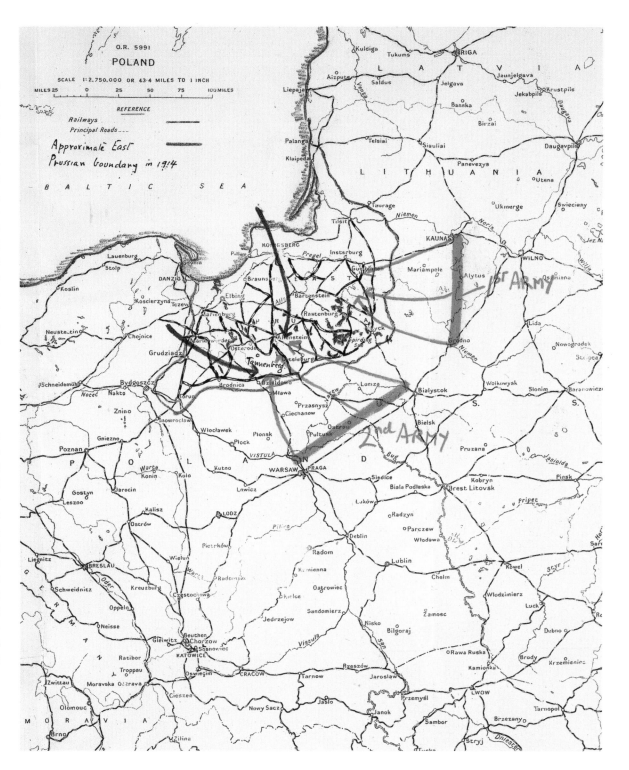

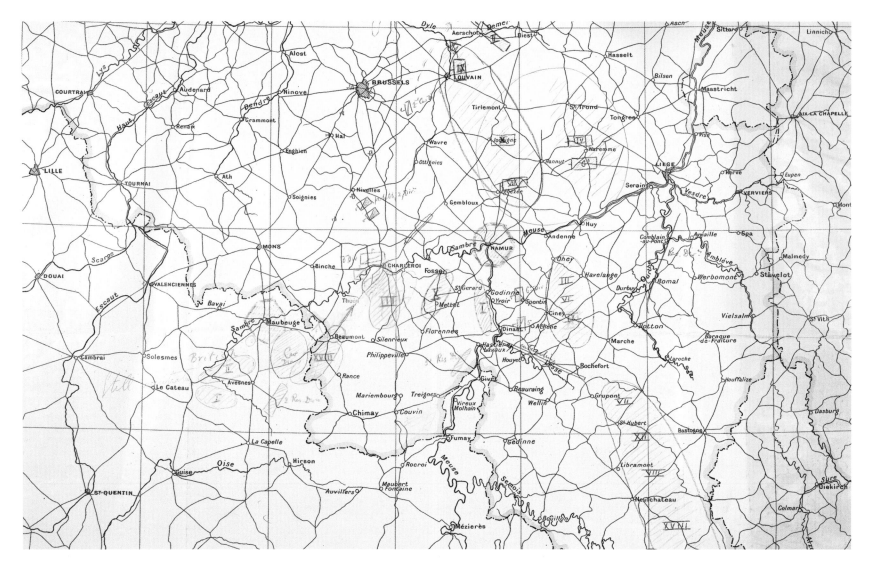

THE BEF AT MONS, AUGUST 20–23, 1914

ABOVE: This map shows the BEF moving up to take its position alongside the French Fifth Army on August 20. Within hours the German First Army reached its lines: the Battle of Mons saw the opening salvos of World War I for British ground forces. Five divisions of the BEF – about 70,000 British troops with 300 guns – under the command of Sir John French had disembarked on the Belgian coast heading for the Sambre. They were late, their commander didn't realize the size of the enemy force in front of him, and they were in a defensive formation on a 20-mile front along the Mons-Condé Canal when the German First Army attacked at 06:00hrs on August 23. Von Kluck's 14 divisions – about 160,000 men and 600 guns – was the vanguard of a German invasion force of 38 divisions.

The BEF, experienced troops who had learned their trade all over the globe, was well dug in with II Corps (under General Smith-Dorrien) to the west, I Corps (under General Douglas Haig) to the east, and the Cavalry Division in reserve. The Germans initially made no progress against lethal British rifle fire from Smith-Dorrien's marksmen but, recognizing the size of the force against them, during the day the BEF started a slow withdrawal to the second line of defense while von Kluck called up his reserves. Rather than head for the coast – as the commander wanted – it was crucial that the BEF should stay in touch with the French on their flanks. So began the Great Retreat that lasted until September 6, and was punctuated by serious engagements such as that of the BEF at Le Cateau or the French success at Guise. In total the British lost some 1,600 men at the Battle of Mons. WO 153/50

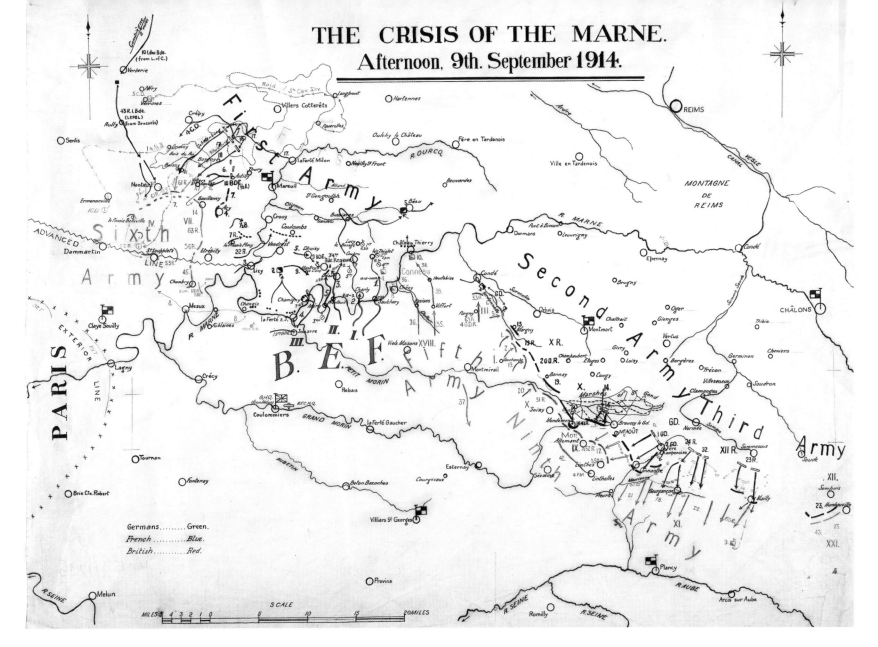

THE CRISIS OF THE MARNE.
Afternoon, 9th. September 1914.

Germans........Green.
French..........Blue.
British..........Red.

SCALE

MILES 5 4 3 2 1 0   5   10   15   20 MILES

THE CRISIS OF THE MARNE, SEPTEMBER 9, 1914

ABOVE: This map shows the critical moment in the 'Miracle of the Marne,' as the BEF, attacking between the German First and Second Armies, advanced across the Marne. Joffre's counterattack – at one stage only held together by 6,000 reservists brought up to the frontline by Paris taxis – had broken the German attackers. With von Kluck's and von Bülow's forces in retreat the Allied armies advanced cautiously to the Aisne. With hindsight it is argued that a more vigorous push would have broken the Germans completely: that doesn't take into account the condition of the troops, exhausted and with some 25 percent casualties. WO 153/1259

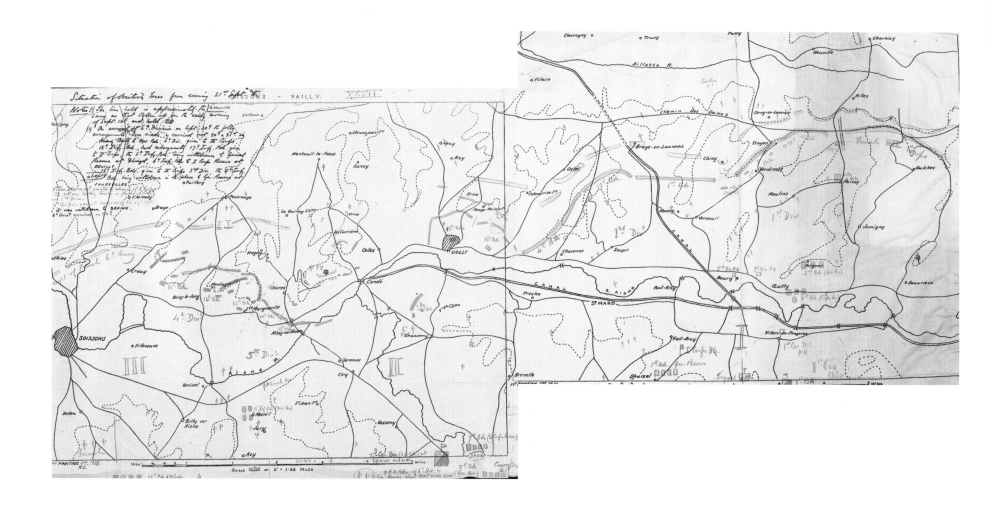

THE BEF AT THE AISNE, SEPTEMBER 21, 1914

ABOVE: The Allied counterattack reached the Aisne on September 12. The crossings began under heavy fire from the Germans who had taken position on the Chemin des Dames Ridge above the river. The slow followup to success on the Marne had given the Germans time to dig in and – more importantly – plug the gap between the First and Second Armies, that the BEF had been trying to exploit, with the Seventh Army under General von Heeringen. Operations on the north bank of the Aisne lasted until September 28, but in the face of severe casualties sustained by frontal attacks on the heights, the line stabilized into trench warfare. This was the start of the 'Race to the Sea' as both sides tried to outflank each other on the seaward flank, the last mobile warfare the Western Front would see until 1918. This map shows the position of the BEF on the evening of September 21. The annotation on the map identifies this line as being 'the same as that taken up in the early morning of the 14th.' It goes on to talk about the disposition of 6th Division on its arrival on September 20 – the Heavy Battery and Howitzer Brigade to III Corps, 17th and 18th Infantry Brigades to I Corps, the 5th Infantry Brigade to General Reserve, the 6th Infantry Brigade to I Corps Reserve. The BEF would move to Flanders as the 'Race to the Sea' took place, and as its numbers swelled its two original corps became armies. WO 153/50

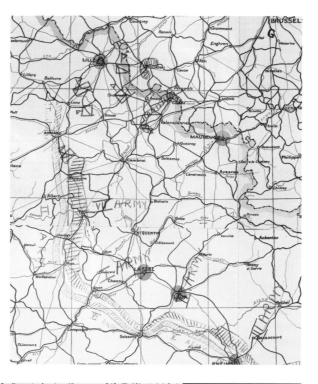

THE 'RACE TO THE SEA,' OCTOBER–NOVEMBER, 1914

LEFT: The 'Race to the Sea' describes mutual out-flanking attempts by both the Allies and the German forces to gain the advantage of the Channel coast. It became the last mobile phase of the war on the Western Front. German forces commanded by the newly appointed General Erich von Falkenhayn had withdrawn to the Aisne after the Battle of the Marne. There the Germans were well dug in and the Allies, under Marshal Joseph Joffre, failed to make any headway against them in the First Battle of the Aisne.

With stalemate on the Aisne, both sides rushed their forces north toward the coast in late September 1914 in an attempt to control the strategically important Channel ports. On the way the Allies unsuccessfully attempted to take Arras and Albert from the Germans before both sides converged on Flanders in early October. Much of the region was unoccupied as the Belgian Army retreated west after the fall of Antwerp leaving the coast undefended. The Germans were determined to win control of the area and launched a massive offensive from the coast to Armentières. Bitter fighting lasted for six weeks and was at its heaviest around the Yser Canal (Battle of the Yser, October 18–November 30) and the town of Ypres (First Battle of Ypres, October 30–November 24). Despite enemy determination the Allies were just able to prevent the German breakthrough. The fighting tailed off in late November with neither side having won the 'race.'

The three maps show the position on September 30/ October 1 (**above left**); on October 4/5 (**above right**); and on October 6/7 (**left**). WO 153/426 (1/4/6)

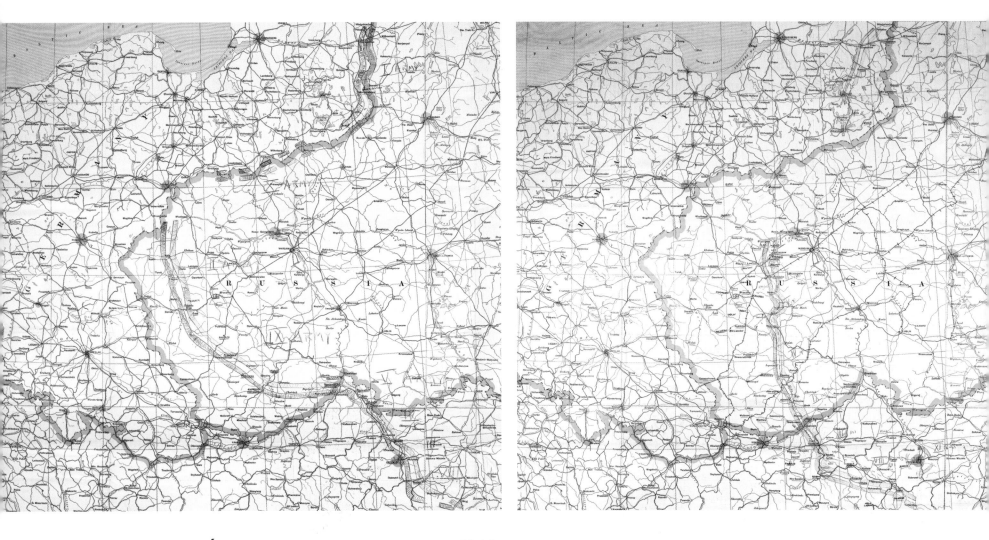

BATTLE OF LÓDZ, NOVEMBER–DECEMBER 1914

The three maps show the main area of combat on the Eastern Front in fall 1914: Poland, at that time under Russian control. In October the Russian First, Second, Third, Fourth, Fifth, and Ninth Armies pushed towards Germany; the First aimed towards Thorn, the others southwest towards Silesia. On November 1, Paul Hindenburg was promoted Field Marshal and became C-in-C of German forces on the Eastern Front. Command of the Ninth Army was taken over by General August von Mackensen, whose forces were in the path of the Russian drive. The first map (**above left**) shows the lines on November 4, as the Russians were pushing west. The second (**opposite page**) shows the lineup for the battle itself. Lódz was a major supply center and when threatened by German attack the Russian Second and Fifth Armies force-marched over 60 miles in two days in time to block the German forces that arrived on November 18. The battle raged for seven days, with von Mackensen's forces

making little headway at first for the town was well supplied with men, mun-itions, and supplies. The Russians held off the German attacks for a week until the attackers began to run short of supplies. By November 25, the Germans had run out of ammunition and the assault on Lódz was halted. Hindenburg was convinced he had gained an important strategic victory and to consolidate his advantage carried on the attacks when reinforcements – four German corps – arrived in early December. Weakened by the heavy fighting (some 100,000 casualties since November 18) and lack of supplies, the Russians withdrew eastward on December 6. The German forces continued to attack hoping to rout the Russians, but by December 13 the Germans had losses approaching 100,000, and the counterattack lost momentum. The third map (**above**) shows the position on December 26 as the two sides ended 1914 in trenches and stalemate. WO 153/789 (9/30), MPI 647 pt 2 (28)

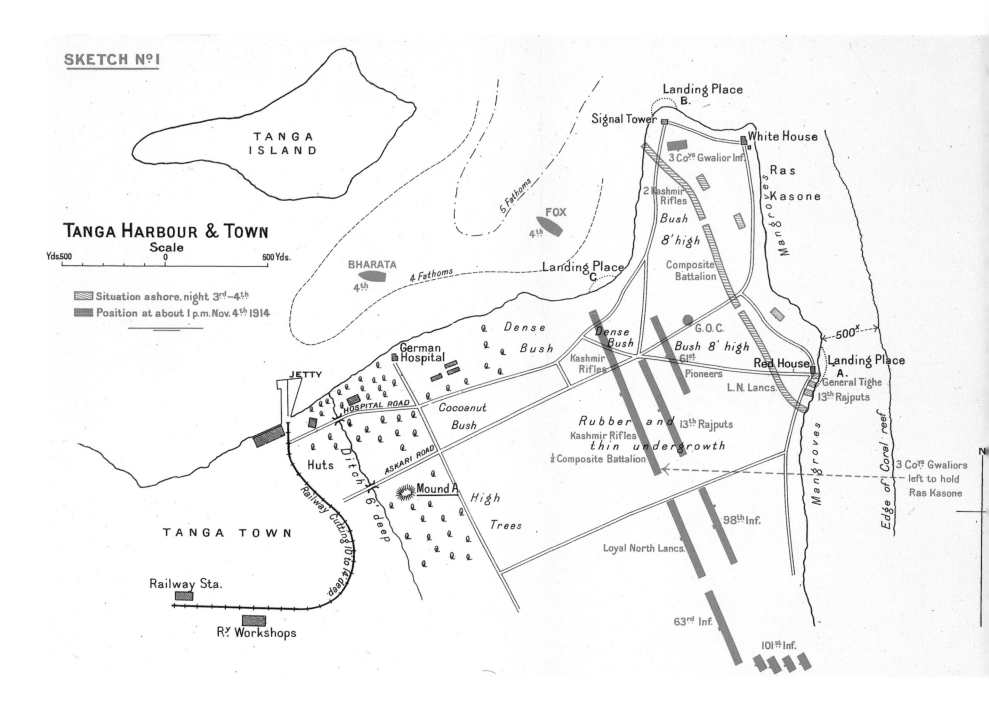

SKETCH Nº1

TANGA ISLAND

Tanga Harbour & Town

Scale

Yds 500   0   500 Yds.

▨ Situation ashore, night 3rd–4th
▬ Position at about 1 p.m. Nov. 4th 1914

5 Fathoms

FOX
4th

BHARATA
4th

4 Fathoms

Landing Place
C

Landing Place
B.

Signal Tower

White House

3 Coys Gwalior Inf

2 Kashmir Rifles

Bush 8' high

Composite Battalion

Ras Kasone

Mangroves

Dense Bush

German Hospital

Dense Bush

G.O.C.

Bush 8' high

61st

Red House

Landing Place A.
General Tighe
13th Rajputs

500

Kashmir Rifles

Pioneers

L.N. Lancs.

JETTY

Huts

HOSPITAL ROAD

Cocoanut Bush

Rubber and 13th Rajputs
Kashmir Rifles thin undergrowth
½ Composite Battalion

3 Coys Gwaliors left to hold Ras Kasone

Ditch 6' deep

ASKARI ROAD

Mound A

High Trees

98th Inf.

Edge of Coral reef

Mangroves

TANGA TOWN

Loyal North Lancs.

Railway Cutting 10 to 14 deep

Railway Sta.

63rd Inf.

Ry. Workshops

101st Inf.

N

TANGA, GERMAN EAST AFRICA, DECEMBER 1914

LEFT: This map, from a dispatch by Major General A E Aitken of the Indian Expeditionary Force, shows the position in Tanga on the night of November 3/4, 1914 and at about 13:00hrs on November 4. Tanga was the terminus of the Usambara Railroad from Uganda, and the most important port in German East Africa. Sitting on a high plateau above a safe harbor it had been visited by a British warship in mid-August but was left unharmed after giving a promise of local non-aggression. On November 3, 1914, an amphibious attack by Indian Army Forces started the first major engagement of the war in German East Africa. The German forces, including 'Askaris' (as native troops were called) were led by Colonel Paul von Lettow-Vorbeck, an excellent commander who inspired great trust in all his troops. His colonial army (the *Schutztruppe*) would only surrender on November 25, 1918 after a brilliant campaign. Aitken's 'Force B' was an 8,000-strong force comprising 27th Bangalore Brigade and an Imperial Service Brigade, few of them well-trained troops. Ordered to take German East Africa, Aitken arrived in Mombasa on October 31, making no secret of his orders. Forewarned, Lettow-Vorbeck quickly reinforced his position with troops from the interior using the railroad to muster around 10,000 men. On November 2, the British cruiser Fox visited Tanga to renounce the non-aggression agreement. Led to believe that the harbor was mined, Force B landed after dark on November 3, two miles along the coast from Tanga. Advancing next morning they met German troops and by the evening Force B began a haphazard withdrawal that took all of November 5. Aitken's forces left behind a large quantity of munitions on the beach – 16 machineguns, 200 or so rifles, 600,000 rounds of ammunition – and lost 360 men killed 487 injured; the Germans lost 67 killed, and 81 injured. WO 158/439

FIRTH OF FORTH: INCHKEITH DEFENSES, 1915

RIGHT: The island of Inchkeith in the Firth of Forth, midway between Edinburgh and Kingholm, became a fortification in 1881. Three batteries were built there to give clear fields of fire on any surface vessels that attempted to pass upriver toward the naval base of Rosyth, during World War I the home base for the British Grand Fleet's battlecruisers, under the command of Vice Admiral David Beatty. It was from Rosyth that Beatty's battlecruisers would sortie to Heligoland Bight (1914), Dogger Bank (1915), and Jutland (1916). Beatty succeeded Jellicoe as the Grand Fleet's C-in-C in 1916, and it was at Rosyth that he took the surrender of the German High Seas Fleet at the end of the war. WO 78/5162 (2)

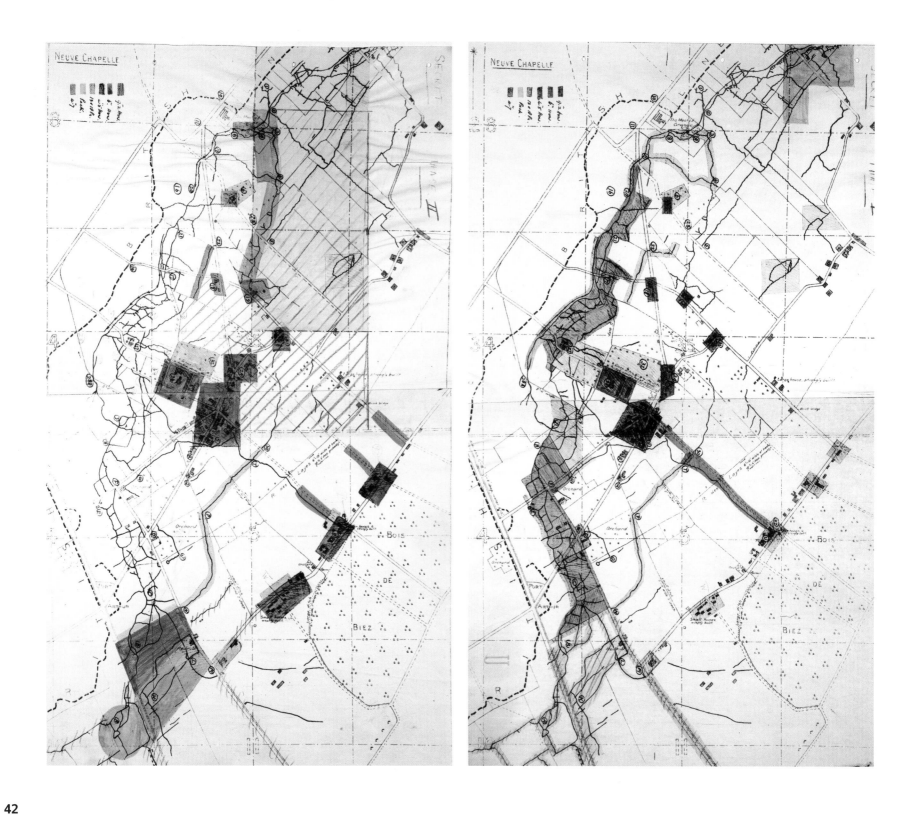

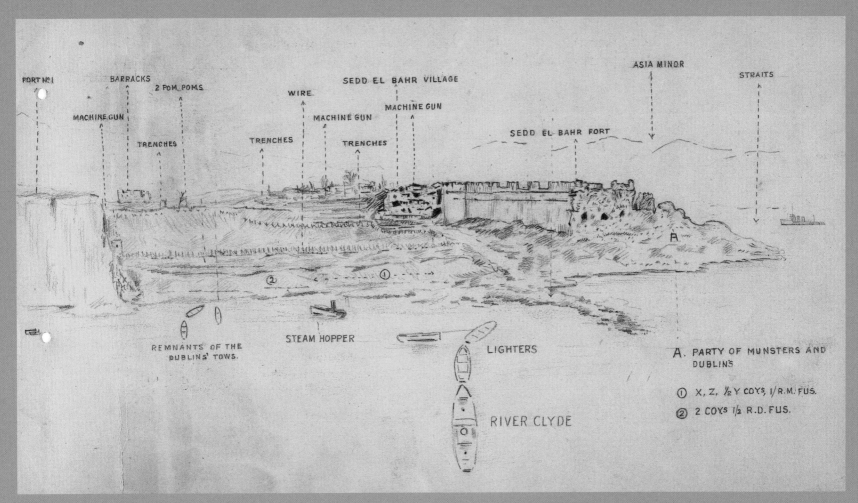

The illustration contains the following labels:

FORT N°1 · BARRACKS · 2 POM POMS · SEDD EL BAHR VILLAGE · ASIA MINOR · STRAITS

MACHINE GUN · WIRE · MACHINE GUN · MACHINE GUN

TRENCHES · TRENCHES · MACHINE GUN · TRENCHES · SEDD EL BAHR FORT

REMNANTS OF THE DUBLINS' TOWS. · STEAM HOPPER · LIGHTERS · RIVER CLYDE

A. PARTY OF MUNSTERS AND DUBLINS

① X, Z, ½ Y COYS, I/R.M. FUS.

② 2 COYS ½ R.D. FUS.

BATTLE OF NEUVE CHAPELLE, MARCH 10–12, 1915

LEFT: Part of the Allied offensives of spring 1915, the battle also served the purpose of pinching out a salient left in the British lines at the end of 1914. Following an artillery bombardment the attack was prosecuted by 7th and 8th Divisions of British IV Corps and the Meerut Division of the Indian Corps. By March 12, Neuve Chapelle had been taken but the attack got bogged down after a German counterattack had been held and nearly 13,000 casualties had been sustained. These maps show two phases of the artillery bombardment. Neuve Chapelle is at the crossroads under the large purple block of first phase (**left**). Gun types are identified by different colors (below). WO 153/124 (2/3)

purple	9.2-in howitzers		green	13- and 18- pounders
blue	6-in howitzers		yellow	pack howitzers
brown	4.5-in howitzers		magenta	4.7-in guns.

GALLIPOLI, 1915

ABOVE (**and pages 44–45**): Sketches from the sea of the positions on the Gallipoli peninsula. First (**above**), V Beach showing the *River Clyde* and Sedd El Bahr Fort. The British suffered 1,200 casualties during the April 25 landings. On page 44 (from **top** to **bottom**): the Gallipoli peninsula from one mile west of X Beach, showing Gully Beach and Y Beach on which the landings were effected without casualties; panorama of Anzac Cove from about a mile northeast of Ari Burnu; Suvla Bay from a mile south of Suvla Point. The landings at Anzac and Suvla both suffered from deviations; nevertheless they would fight to link up and achieve this on August 10. The panoramas on page 45 show (from **top** to **bottom**): Cape Helles, from a mile south of W Beach that saw 533 British casualties during the landings; Chunuk Bair, from three miles south of Nibrunesi point; and Suvla Bay, from a mile east of Suvla Point. A main objective, Chunuk Bair was occupied for a few hours on August 7. WO 153/1337 (1/5/7/8)

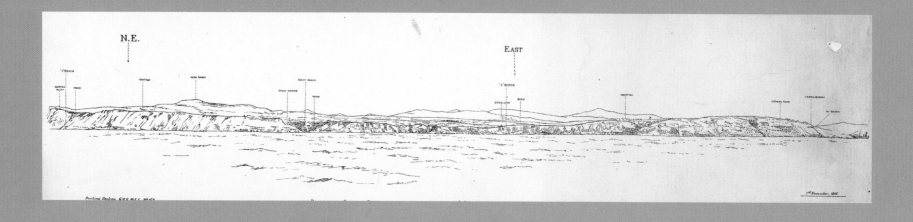

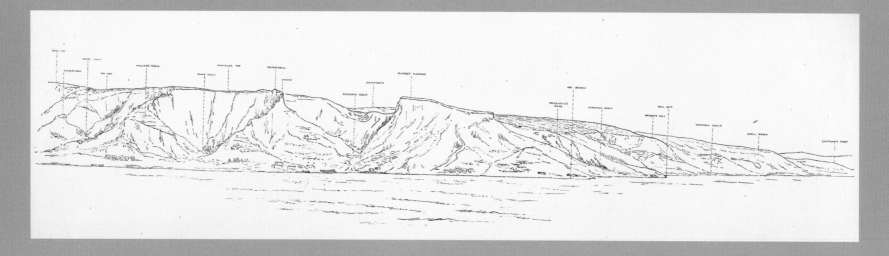

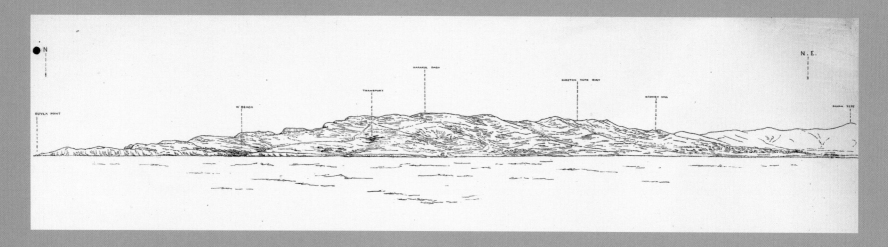

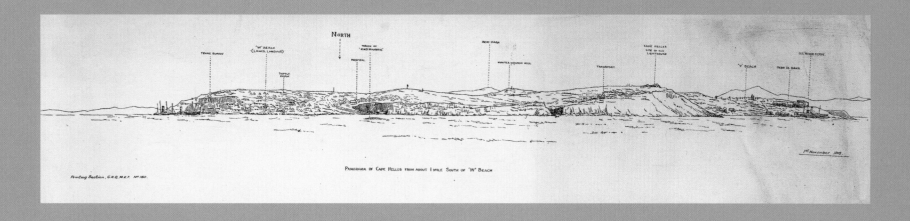

Panorama of Cape Helles from about 1 mile South of 'W' Beach

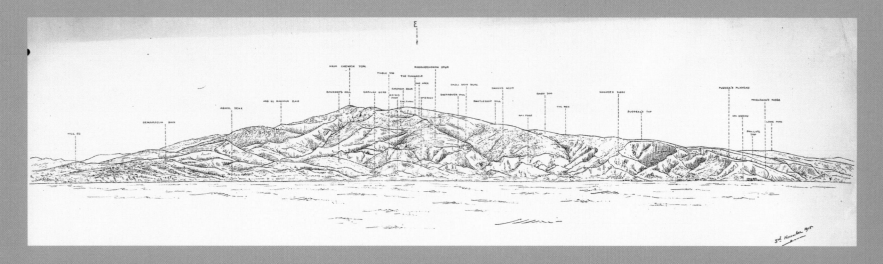

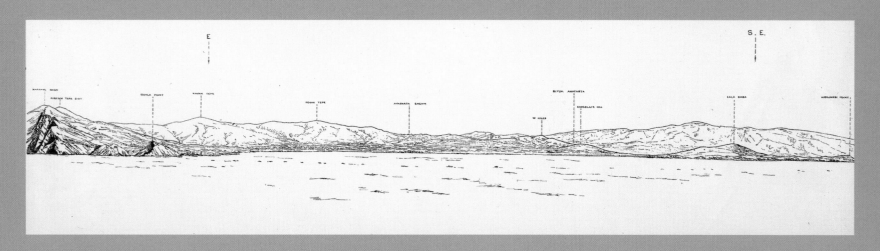

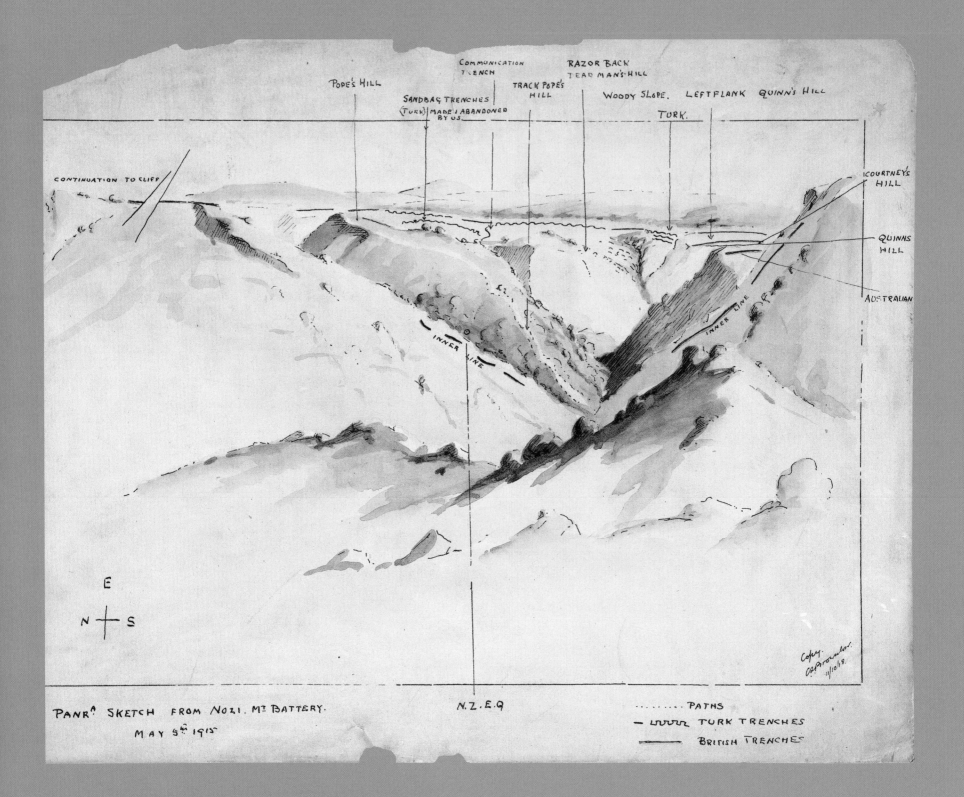

POPE'S HILL

SANDBAG TRENCHES
(TURK) MADE & ABANDONED
BY US

COMMUNICATION
TRENCH

TRACK POPE'S
HILL

RAZOR BACK
DEAD MAN'S HILL

WOODY SLOPE.   LEFT FLANK   QUINN'S HILL

TURK.

CONTINUATION TO CLIFF

COURTNEY'S
HILL

QUINNS
HILL

AUSTRALIAN

INNER LINE

INNER LINE

E

N ⟶ S

Copy
CAPBrownlow
11/10/18.

PANRA. SKETCH   FROM No 21. Mᵗ BATTERY.
        MAY 5ᵗʰ 1915

N.Z.E.G

.... PATHS
─ ⟿⟿⟿ TURK TRENCHES
───── BRITISH TRENCHES

46

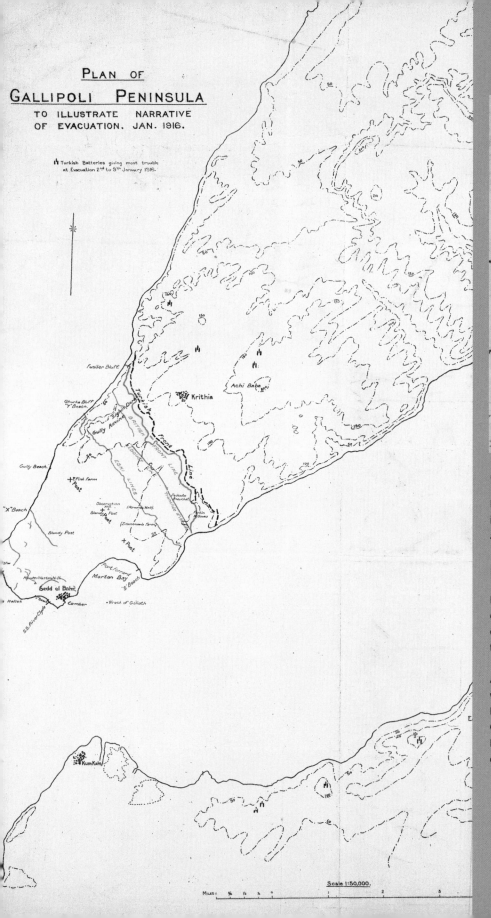

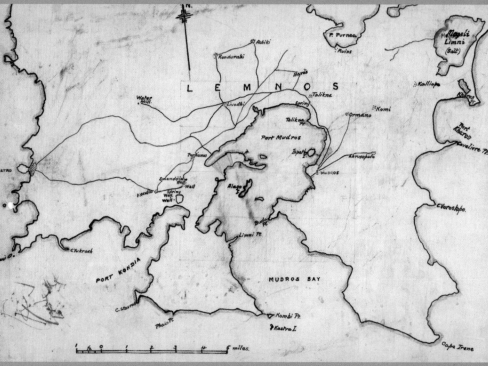

GALLIPOLI, 1915

FAR LEFT: Panoramic sketch from the position of No 21 MT Battery on May 5, 1915. Just inland from Anzac Cove and southeast of Chunuk Bair, the evacuation of the New Zealand and Australian forces took place here between December 10 and 19 without loss. WO 317/6

EVACUATION OF GALLIPOLI, 1915

LEFT: Plan of the Helles positions on the peninsula. The troops were evacuated on the night of January 8/9, 1916. In the week leading up to the final evacuation, vehicles, equipment, over 35,000 troops, and over 3,500 horses and mules were evacuated. On the final night, the rearguard was stealthily evacuated without loss. WO 153/1050 (2)

ABOVE: Map of Lemnos showing Mudros Bay, critical to the whole Gallipoli operation. It was from here that the main force left for the original landings. Commandeered by the Royal Navy in 1915, the armistice between the Allies and Turkey was signed in the harbor on October 30, 1918. The hospital ship *Britannic*, sister ship to the *Titanic*, was often seen in Mudros Harbor before it sank after hitting a mine laid by *U73* in the Kea Channel, off Athens, on November 21, 1916. WO 153/1050 (4)

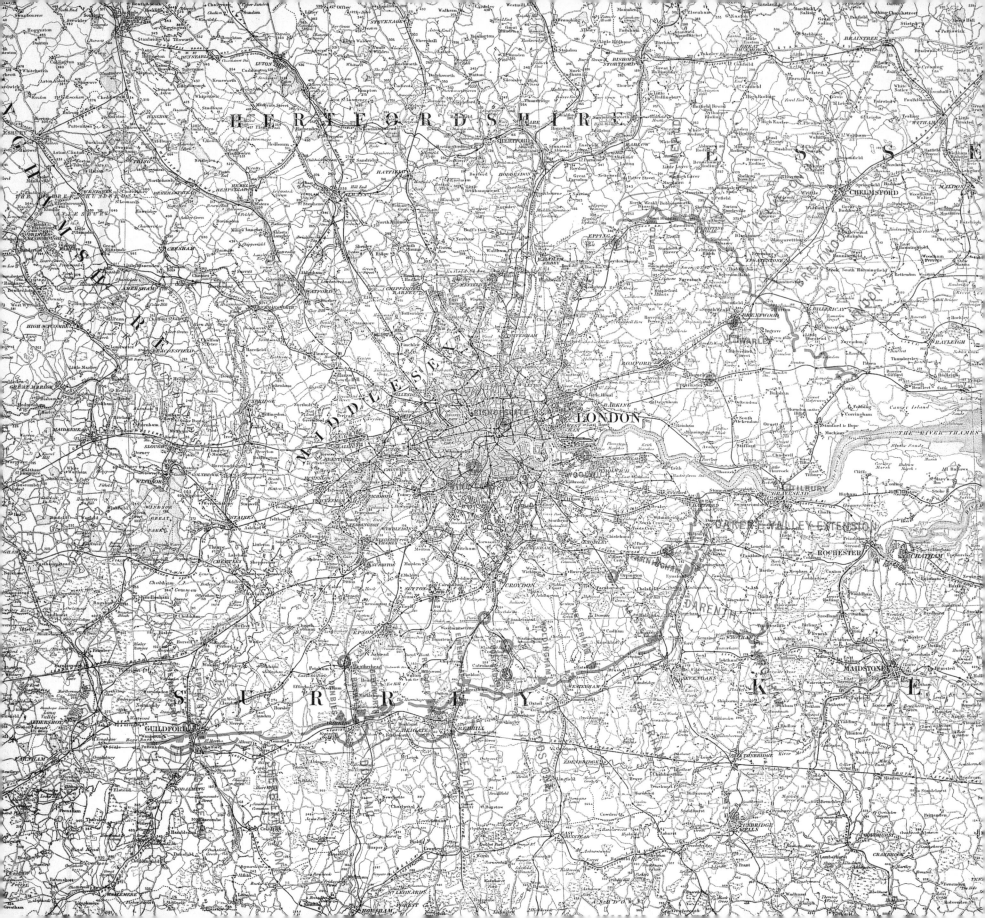

DEFENSES AROUND LONDON, 1915

LEFT: Plan of the London defense positions in 1915, showing a line along the North Downs to the south of London in Surrey, and to the northeast of the city in Essex. The key identifies entrenched lines, forts and depots. WO 78/4420

BATTLE OF LOOS: RFC OPERATIONS, SEPTEMBER 25, 1915

RIGHT: Disposition of No 1 Wing HQ, Nos 2, 3, 10, and 16 Squadrons, and kite balloon sections with graphic representations of the operations they carried out – trench bombardment, artillery counter-battery, tactical reconnaissance, and patrolling. See also page 50. MPI 647 pt 1 (1)

BATTLE OF LOOS: HOHENZOLLERN REDOUBT

BELOW RIGHT: Large scale plan of the Hohenzollern redoubt and Fosse 8 (The Dump), part of the German defensive lines, taken by 9th Division of General Sir Hubert Gough's I (BR) Corps on September 25, 1915, during the Battle of Loos. The plans were prepared by Royal Engineers of First Army after the battle in October 1915. There's no doubt that German defensive positions were better than those of the British, as was shown by the way they withstood the heavy bombardment leading up to the Somme offensive. WO 153/1096

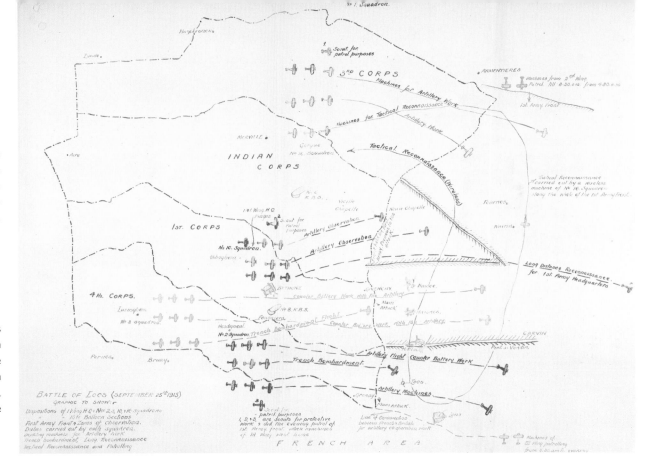

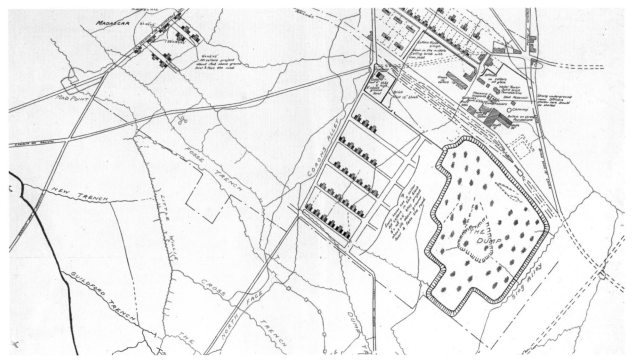

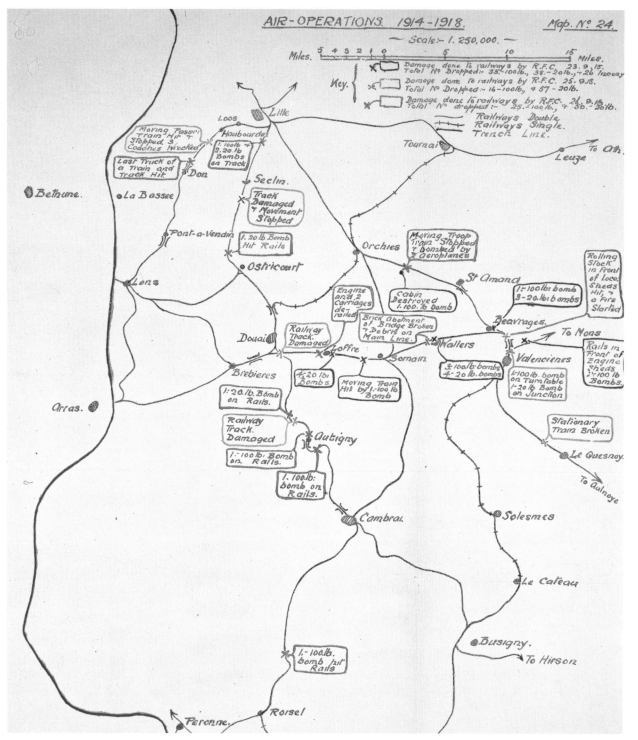

Map No. 24 — Air-Operations 1914–1918. Scale 1:250,000

BATTLE OF LOOS: RFC OPERATIONS, SEPTEMBER 25, 1915

LEFT: This map shows the damage done by RFC aircraft September 23–26, 1915, on railroads just south of the Loos battlefield. Note the details of the numbers of bombs dropped and their effects. Railroads – as the most obvious method for the German Sixth Army to bring troops and supplies to the front – were immediate targets for bombers – as they would be again in World War II. MPI 647 pt 1 (3)

THIRD BATTLE OF ISONZO, OCTOBER 23, 1915

RIGHT: Between June 23, 1915, and September 12, 1917, the Italians attacked Austrian positions along the Isonzo River no fewer than 14 times – six times in 1915, six times in 1916, and twice in 1917. After the final battle, when they had taken Gorizia, the Austrians were drained to such a degree that they had to appeal to Germany for help. The 12th Isonzo River battle on October 24, 1917, is better known as the Battle of Caporetto and saw the Germans rout the Italians and push them west to the Piave River. This map shows the position five days after the start of the third battle, which would set minor Italian gains against 67,000 casualties. Italian forces are shown in green, with their HQ in Udine; Austrian units are in red. See also page 89. WO 153/772

Note: Italian Troops, Green
Austrian, Red

AIRSHIP RAIDS, MARCH 5/6 AND MARCH 31/APRIL 1 1916

RIGHT AND FAR RIGHT: The first German Army Zeppelin was commissioned in 1908. Strictly speaking, only airships designed by Count Graf Zeppelin were officially Zeppelins: the Schütte-Lanz airships and Parseval craft were not. Airships were used for reconnaissance and strategic bombing, their main drawback was their vulnerability to strong winds and weather conditions. Navigation was also problematic as raids had to be conducted at night because of their vulnerability to enemy fire – even moonlight was too dangerous. Target identification was another problem, as was hitting the target from above 10,000ft. Airship bombing raids were not very effective even though they were able to operate largely unhindered until aircraft and ordnance was developed that was able to reach above 11,000ft. As AAA fire improved, airships were forced to fly above the cloud level, decreasing their chances of hitting their designated targets. In 1917 the Military Airship Service was discontinued and all remaining craft were transferred to the German Navy which used them for reconnaissance. Some 135 German airships were built, of which 37 were destroyed by enemy action. About 270 crew members were lost in operations against Britain, against 501 civilians killed. No British pilots were killed as a direct result of Zeppelin actions. These two maps show the tracks of airship sorties over eastern England in spring 1916, including bombs dropped and AAA guns in action. Opposite is an example of the sort of ordnance carried. MPI 512 pt 3 (41, 43)

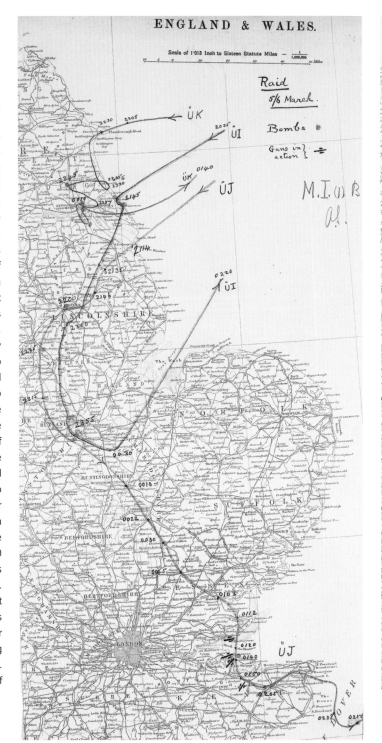

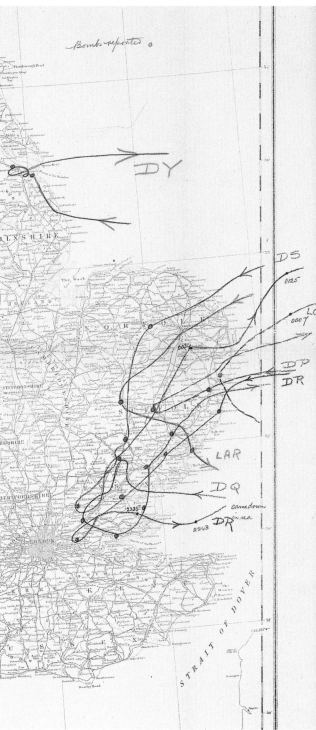

AIR RAID BOMB, SEPTEMBER 25, 1916

ABOVE AND RIGHT: Photograph and drawing of a German bomb dropped from an airship on Clough Fold, Rawtenstall, Lancashire. Germany sanctioned strategic bombing of English military targets by Zeppelins on January 7, 1915, but this was soon extended to include English cities. London was first attacked by Zeppelin on May 31, 1915, when seven people on the ground were killed and a further 35 wounded. The largest Zeppelin raid was on September 2/3, 1916, and involved 14 Zeppelins heading for London, but none of them got there. In total there were just over 100 airship raids over Britain during the course of the war. MPI 512 pt 1 (36)

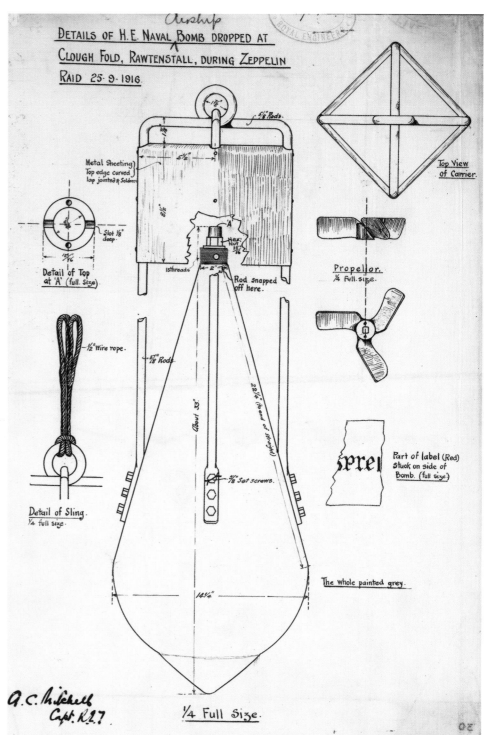

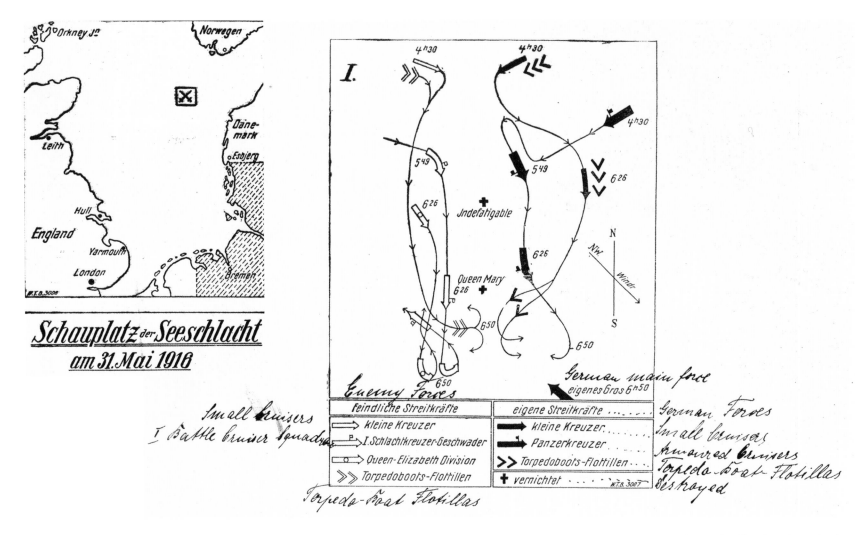

Schauplatz der Seeschlacht am 31. Mai 1916

BATTLE OF JUTLAND, MAY 31, 1916

ABOVE (AND PAGES 55–6): This massive encounter was the biggest naval battle of the war and saw some 250 warships and some 100,000 sailors take part. Known as the Battle of Jutland to the British (Skagerrak to the Germans) it was fought between the British Grand Fleet led by Admiral Sir John Jellicoe on board the *Iron Duke*, and the German High Seas Fleet, led by the newly appointed C-in-C Vice-Admiral Reinhard Scheer, on board the *Friedrich der Grosse*.

The Royal Navy had been trying to lure the German fleet into battle in the North Sea, but the smaller German fleet avoided large-scale confrontation. Scheer was criticized in Germany for the lack of results, so he embarked on a plan to trap British ships – especially battlecruisers – by luring them to the Danish coast. He knew from aerial reconnaissance that the main British fleet was still in harbor, so he sent Admiral Hipper to Danish waters to raid

the coast with 40 ships. The main High Seas Fleet followed, sailing from the Jade River on May 31 at 01:00hrs. Scheer was mistaken in thinking the British were completely unaware of his plans. German radio traffic, monitored by the Room 40 codebreaking unit, gave away the High Seas Fleet muster point, although not what they were going to do. The British Grand Fleet set sail in response. At the same time, Admiral Beatty's fleet of battlecruisers sailed out from Rosyth to rendezvous with the main fleet. First contact between the adversaries was made in midafternoon, the battlecruisers clashing at around 1430hrs. There ensued a brief exchange of gunfire, with each side congratulating themselves on springing their trap. What followed is described in the accompanying maps – the first five being German with English annotations. Military historians view the encounter as indecisive, although the German gunnery was certainly more effective than the British, but one thing is clear: strategically itwas a triumph for the Royal Navy. The High Seas Fleet returned home and only came out again to surrender. The maps show: Unnumbered **(page 54, left)** the lo-

continued on page 56

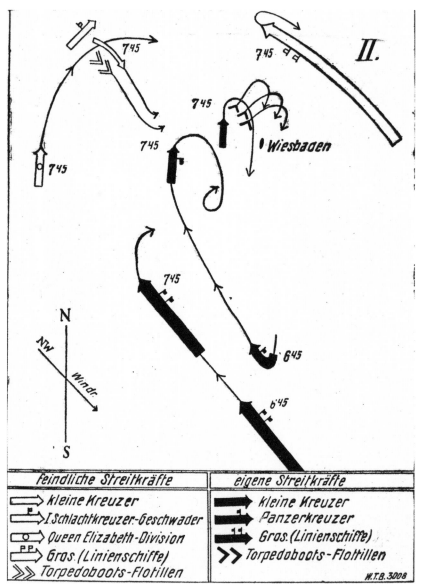

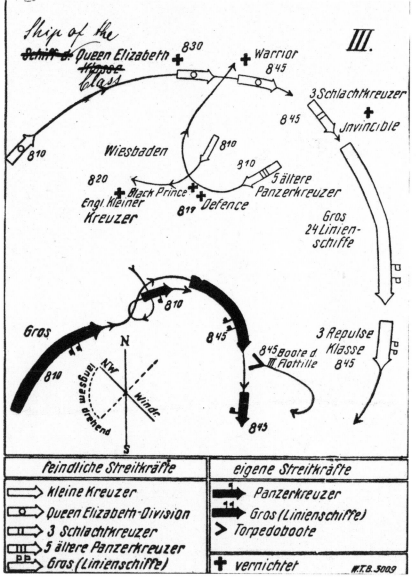

THE FLEETS

British Grand Fleet included 72 capital ships, plus Beatty's battlecruiser fleet of 42 ships. The force included eight less-useful armored cruisers, six vulnerable pre-dreadnoughts, 26 light cruisers, and one seaplane carrier, *Engadine*. Total 151 ships.

Losses: *Invincible, Defence, Black Prince, Tipperary, Ardent, Fortune, Sparrowhawk, Shark, Queen Mary, Indefatigable, Turbulent, Nestor, Nomad; Warrior* sank the next day. In total three battlecruisers, three armored cruisers, eight destroyers/torpedo boats. Out of 60,000 officers and men serving in the Grand Fleet, 6,748 died.

German High Seas Fleet included 37 capital ships, plus Hipper's battlecruiser fleet of 35. Total 99 ships.

Losses: *Elbing, Lützow, Frauenlob, Pommern, Rostock, Wiesbaden, S35, V4, V27, V29, V48*. In total one battleship, one battlecruiser, four light cruisers, five destroyers/torpedo boats. Out of 36,000 men 3,058 died.

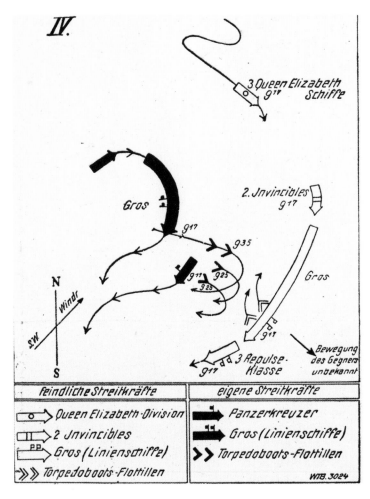

cation of the battle; I (**page 54, right**), II (**page 55 left**) the first action between the two battlecruiser fleets 14:30hrs to 18:50hrs; III (**page 55 right**), IV (**above**) the main action between the two fleets, 18:45hrs to 21:45hrs.

In the maps: *Feindliche Streitkräfte* – enemy [English] forces, *eigene Streitkräfte* – own [German] forces, *kleine Kreuzer* – small [light] cruisers, *Schlachtkreuzer Geschwader* – battlecruiser squadron, *Panzerkreuzer* – armored cruisers, *Gros (Linienschiffe)* – main force (ships of the line), *ältere Panzerkreuze* – old armored cruisers, *vernichtet* – destroyed/sunk, *langsam drehend* – slowly changing direction [of the wind], *Bewegung des Gegners unbekannt* – movement of the opposition unknown; the rest are self-explanatory. ADM 137/4825 (1–5)

RIGHT: Another German plan showing the engagements between 18:45hrs and 21:50hrs. MPI 671 pt 2 (28)

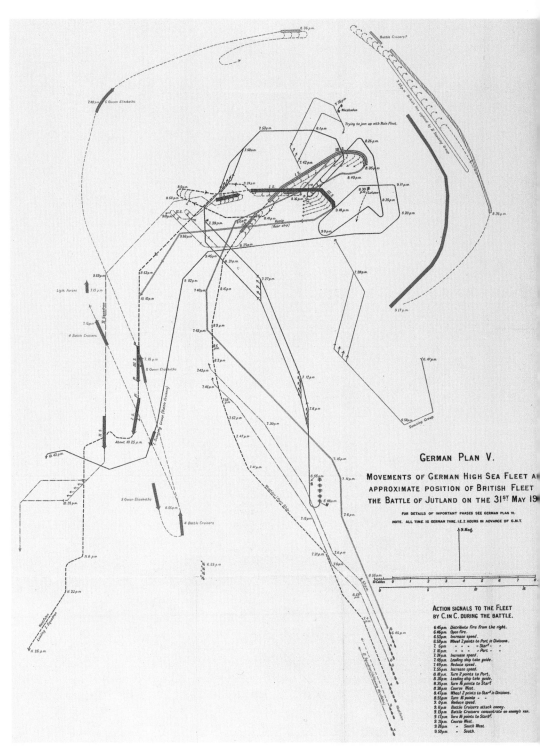

BATTLE OF JUTLAND: TRACK OF THE *MARLBOROUGH*, MAY 31, 1916

RIGHT: *Marlborough* commanded by Captain G P Ross was part of the British High Seas Fleet, and the flagship of the 1st Battle Squadron commanded by Vice-Admiral Sir Cecil Burney. Jellicoe had been trying to lure the German High Seas Fleet into battle for almost two years, but the Germans had managed to avoid fighting a pitched battle. The engagement was carried out in poor visibility and confusion, exacerbated by only sporadic and often inaccurate reported positions on both sides. Jellicoe deployed his ships while still out of range of enemy fire into six columns each of four ships in line ahead with the *Marlborough* leading the starboard column. After a stiff engagement the German fleet performed a *Gefechtskehrtwendung* (battle turn) and reversed course. During this period, at 18:55hrs, a torpedo from the crippled Wiesbaden struck the *Marlborough*. Burney transferred his flag to the *Revenge*. *Marlborough* was attacked again as she was escorted slowly back to port, by U46, but sustained no further injury. Although damaged she was quickly repaired and returned to join the High Seas Fleet at Scapa Flow in early August 1916. MPI 671 Pt 3 (38)

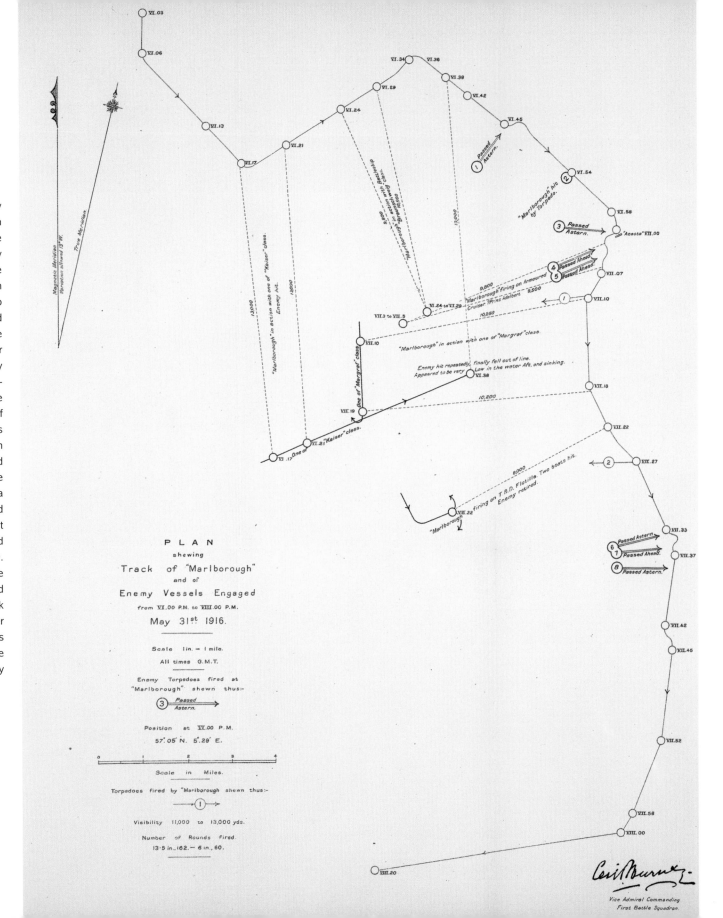

PLAN
shewing
Track of "Marlborough"
and of
Enemy Vessels Engaged
from VI.00 P.M. to VIII.00 P.M.
May 31st 1916.

Scale 1in. = 1 mile.

All times G.M.T.

Enemy Torpedoes fired at "Marlborough" shewn thus:—

Position at VI.00 P.M.
57° 05′ N. 5° 29′ E.

Scale in Miles.

Torpedoes fired by "Marlborough" shewn thus:—

Visibility 11,000 to 13,000 yds.

Number of Rounds fired.
13.5 in., 162. — 6 in., 60.

Vice Admiral Commanding
First Battle Squadron.

MINING DAILY BLOW CHART, JUNE 30– JULY 1 1916

RIGHT: These two blow charts show the mine explosions in late June and early July in First and Second Armies' areas; the blue dots representing British mine explosions, the red German ones. The sectors covered are given on the left of the charts. Note: those for Armagh Wood and Lille Road in the Second Army chart and see page 59. Mining in World War I hadn't changed much since the Middle Ages when it was an important part of siege warfare and used to bring down many a besieged castle. The underground battlefield, populated not just by people digging but by listening parties and armed soldiers, is graphically described in *Birdsong* by Sebastian Faulks (Hutchinson, 1993). The start of the Battle of the Somme was heralded by enormous mines and the Battle of Messines in June 1917 saw 19 mines detonated, one of whose explosions, it was said, could be heard in England. WO 153/1249 (11, 13)

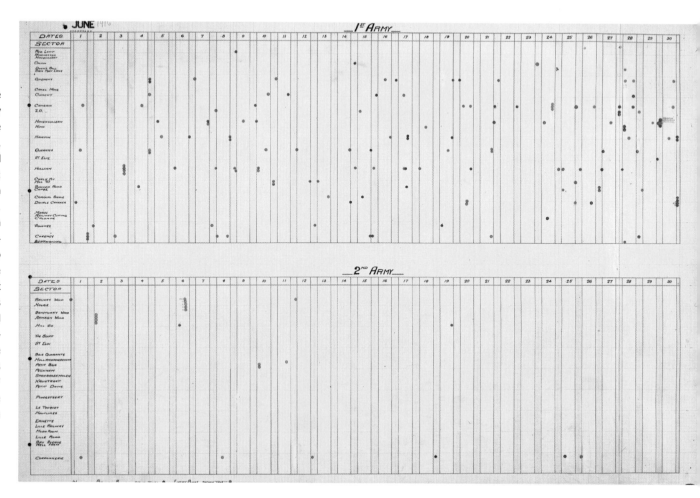

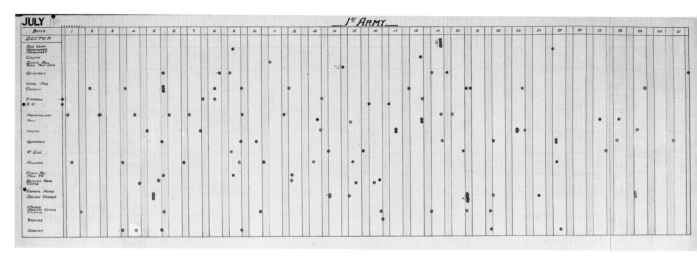

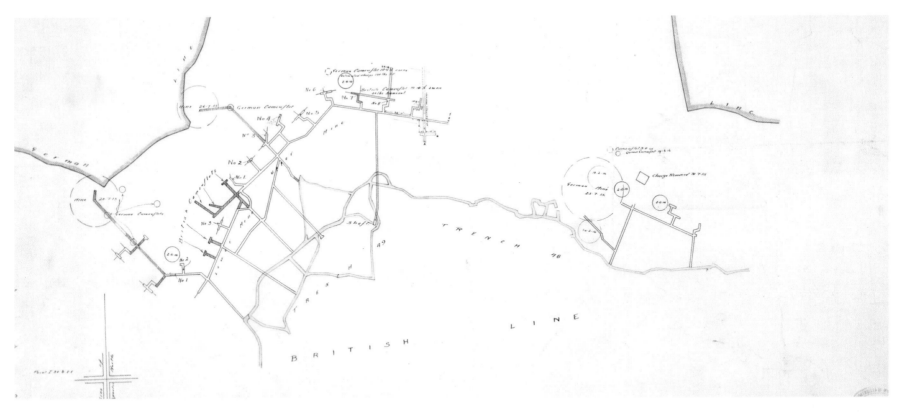

ARMAGH WOOD MINING 1916

ABOVE: Second Army Mining Plans by No 2 Canadian Tunneling Company. Note the position of the trench lines and the German *camouflets* (chambers containing explosives that were used to countermine the mining operations of the other side). WO 153/908

LILLE ROAD MINING, 1916

RIGHT: Mining plans for Carency-Ecurie (Lille Road). The RE mining operations. WO 153/913 (41)

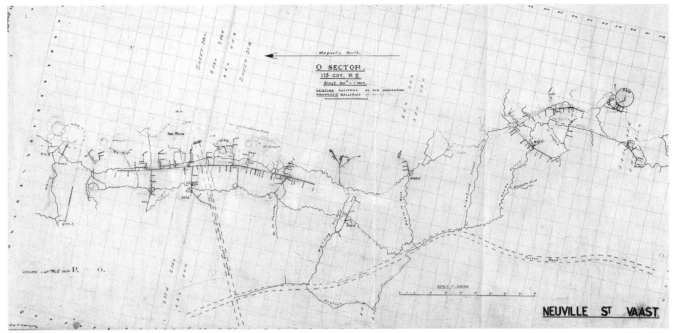

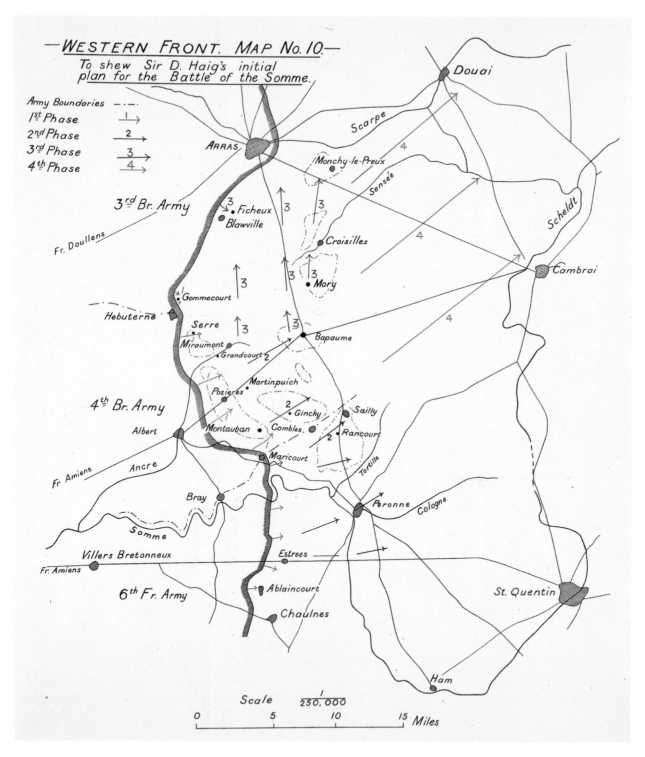

-WESTERN FRONT. MAP No. 10.-
To shew Sir D. Haig's initial
plan for the Battle of the Somme.

Army Boundaries -.-.-
1st Phase →1→
2nd Phase →2→
3rd Phase →3→
4th Phase →4→

3rd Br. Army

Fr. Doullens

Fr. Amiens

4th Br. Army

Albert

6th Fr. Army

Fr. Amiens

Villers Bretonneux

Somme

Ancre

Bray

Hebuterne

Gommecourt

Serre

Miraumont

Pozières

Montauban

Maricourt

Estrees

Ablaincourt

Chaulnes

Ficheux

Blawville

Grandcourt

Martinpuich

Combles

Ginchy

Sailly

Rancourt

Croisilles

Mory

Bapaume

Tortille

Peronne

Cologne

Ham

ARRAS

Monchy-le-Preux

Scarpe

Sensée

Scheldt

Cambrai

Douai

St. Quentin

Scale 1/250,000
0   5   10   15 Miles

BATTLE OF THE SOMME, JULY–NOVEMBER 1916

LEFT: The Somme offensive was meticulously planned by Haig, with much thought given to the assault lines after the breakthrough. Note the phases of battle that see the British Fourth Army punch through the German defenses in Phases 1 and 2, move north in Phase 3, and then east in Phase 4. What actually happened is illustrated on the next page (**right**). The battle started with a preliminary bombardment of the German lines that lasted for eight days. This sustained barrage was intended to eliminate the German forward defenses. However, much of the ammunition issued to the BEF was of such poor quality that it did not penetrate as far as the concrete bunkers beneath the German trenches and, furthermore, even failed to destroy the fences of barbed wire protecting the German lines. Thus the German troops were well able to withstand the British Infantry assaults when they started their advance at 0730hrs on July 1. About 58,000 BEF troops were put out of action that day with around 20,000 of them killed outright. MPI 647 pt 1 (8)

BATTLE OF THE SOMME, JULY–NOVEMBER 1916

LEFT: The phases of advance between the opening on July 1, and October 18. In fact the campaign continued into November when a final thrust saw Beaumont Hamel fall into British hands. The southern part of this map shows the successes of the French Sixth Army whose area of operations stretched from around Combles southward. Note the apparent break in the middle of the map: this is the River Somme itself. Initial French gains, and the long grinding British battles saw immense casualties—around 420,000 British and 200,000 French. Ironically, the actual territory captured over the period of four months would fall in a matter of days to the Germans during their 1918 offensive. However, when assessing the Somme it must not be forgotten that half a million Germans died during the battle and the loss of so many experienced troops had a dramatic attritional effect on their army. The figures and colors on the map are explained in the key below. WO 153/189

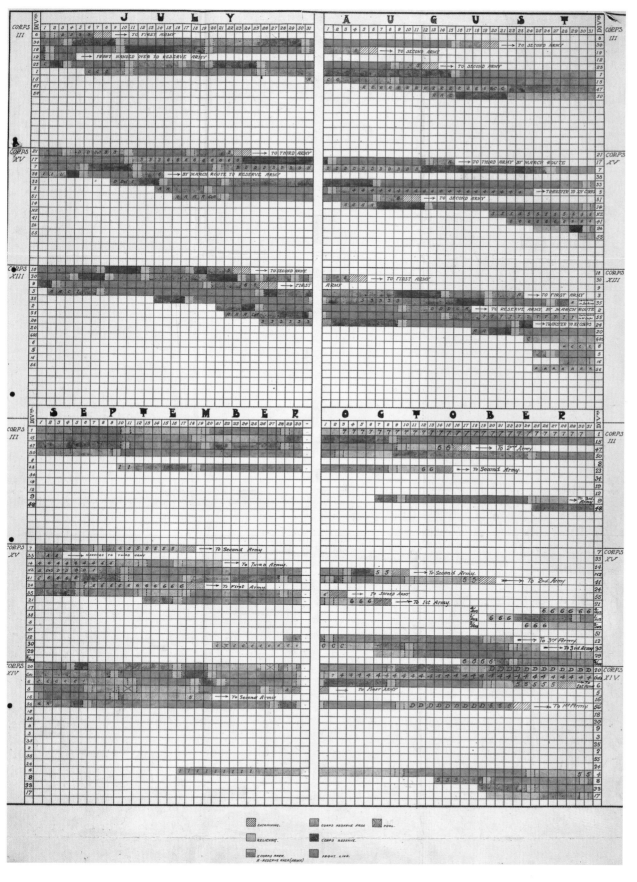

BATTLE OF THE SOMME, JULY–NOVEMBER 1916

LEFT: This chart – nicknamed a 'Tartan' for its similarity to the Scottish cloth – shows the length of time divisions from III, XIII, XIV, and XV Corps spent at the front in the period July–October 1916. The colors represent: black hatching – entraining; yellow – relieving; green (with number) – X corps area (A, reserve; R, St Ricquier); green (with cross) – pool; brown – corps reserve area; blue – corps reserve; red – front line. So, for example the 1st Division, and the 8th, spent half of July 1 in the front line, half of the 1st and the 2nd being relieved, the next four and a half days on reserve, and the next two days entraining to go to First Army. This hides the other statistics. The 8th, a regular division led by Major General H Hudson, suffered 5,121 casualties on July 1. WO 153/1265 (2)

RIGHT: The trenches (blue – British, red – German) between Beaumont Hamel and Thiepval correct to June 14, 1916. Beaumont Hamel was not taken until November. Thiepval, taken in September, is the location of the memorial to 73,077 British soldiers missing on the Somme in 1916 and 1917, although some bodies or graves have been found since it was built. The memorial stands on what was one of the strongest parts of the German line, the grounds of the chateau (see square 25 on map). Nearby, the Schwaben Redoubt was taken by the 36th (Ulster) Division whose memorial – the Ulster Tower – stands just outside Thiepval village. WO 297/1489

1:10,000   BEAUMONT   EDITION 2. B   57d S.E. 1 & 2. (parts of)

TRENCHES CORRECTED TO 28-4-16.
TRENCHES CORRECTED TO 14-6-16.

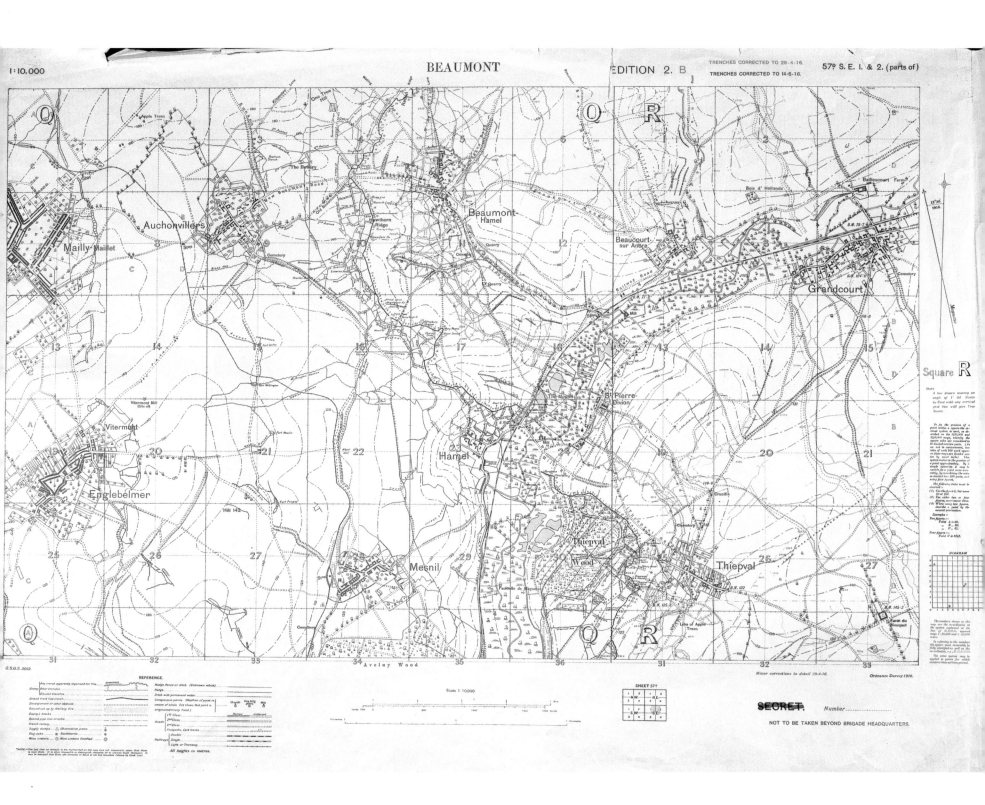

G.S.G.S. 3002.

REFERENCE.

Scale 1:10,000

SHEET 57d.

SECRET. Number..............

NOT TO BE TAKEN BEYOND BRIGADE HEADQUARTERS.

Minor corrections to detail 28-4-16.   Ordnance Survey 1916.

All heights in metres.

Square R

DIAGRAM

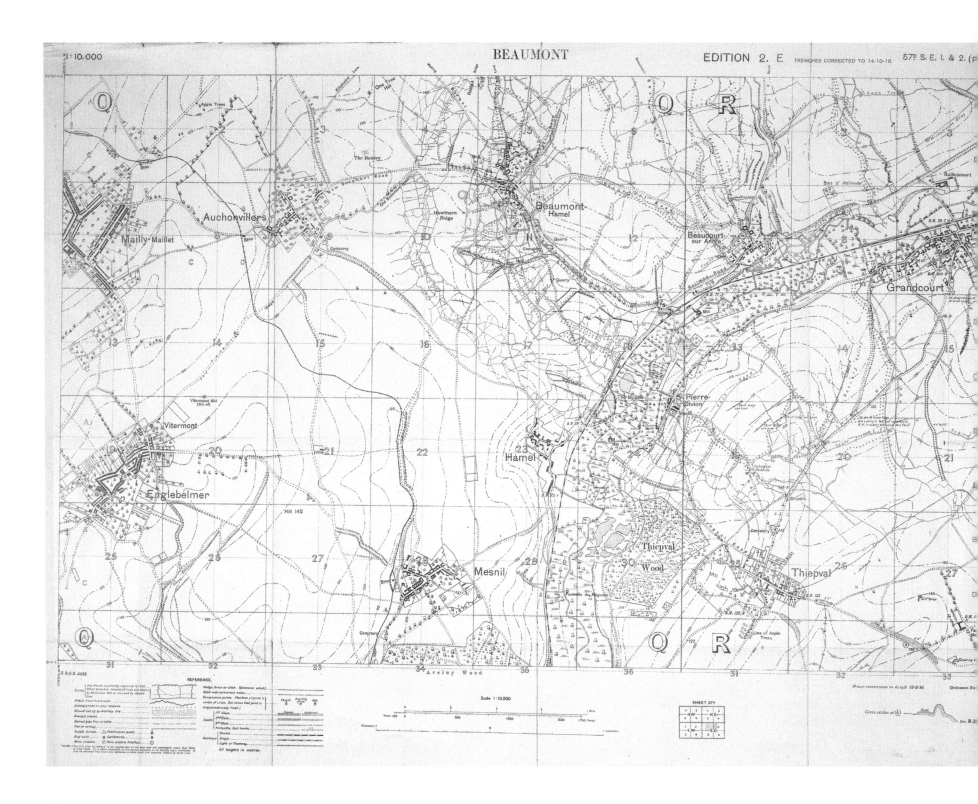

BATTLE OF THE SOMME, JULY–NOVEMBER 1916

FAR LEFT: The same area as that covered in the map on page 63, this shows the position four months later. The trenches around Beaumont Hamel are correct to October 14, 1916, just a month before the weather brought an end to the Somme off-ensive in late November, and just before the last action along the Somme – the Battle of Beaumont Hamel. Also known as the Battle of Ancre, this last effort by the BEF to capture territory started on November 13, 1916. It was hampered by the encroaching winter weather but the BEF managed to capture Beaumont Hamel, just before heavy snowfall stopped operations along the Somme altogether. It is said that only one pane of stained glass, removed by a German officer and returned many years later, survived the destruction of the church of Beaumont Hamel. WO 297/1495

LEFT: Detailed map showing the disposition of the BEF and German divisions and their movements over the period of the Battle of the Somme (from July 1 to November 23, 1916). The red units are British forces and the blue units are German troops in situ on the battlefield as at November 23. The orange units are those (British and German) withdrawn from other fronts or the reserve, and sent to the Somme together with the date of their first appearance. The green units are those (British and German) withdrawn exhausted from the battle and the date of posting elsewhere. The red lines around units whose numbers are circled in green indicate units taken out of and then returned to battle. Note the 8th Division (in green) removed from the battlefield on July 6 as per the 'Tartan' on page 62.
WO 153/158

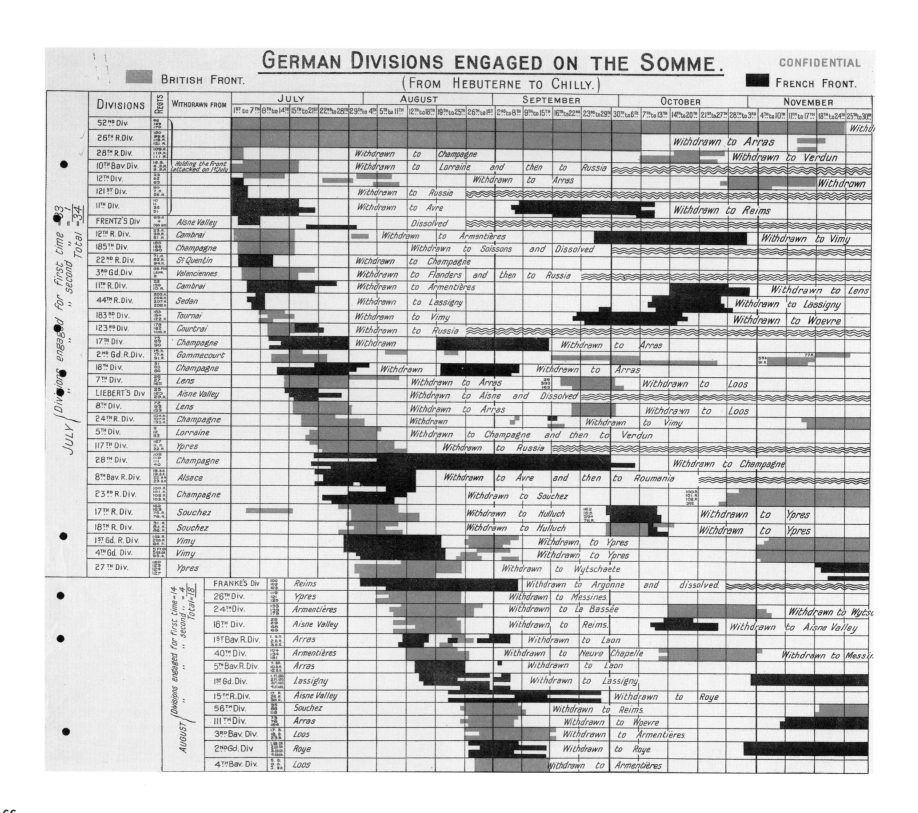

GERMAN DIVISIONS ENGAGED ON THE SOMME.
(FROM HEBUTERNE TO CHILLY.)

BRITISH FRONT.
FRENCH FRONT.
CONFIDENTIAL

Division	(regiments)	Withdrawn From	Note
53RD R.DIV.	241 R. 242 R. 243 R. 244 R.	La Bassée	Withdrawn to Loos and then to Champagne
35TH DIV.	61 141 176	Chaulnes	Withdrawn
23RD DIV.	108 101 177	Reims	Withdrawn to Roye
54TH R.DIV.	245 R. 246 R. 247 R. 248 R.	Neuve Chapelle	Withdrawn to Loos and then to Lorraine
10TH ERS.DIV.	369 370 371	Woevre	Withdrawn to Champagne
New 185TH DIV.	65 161 186	Aisne Valley	Withdrawn to Aisne Valley
45TH R.DIV.	209 R. 210 R. 211 R. 212 R. 213 R.	Messines	Withdrawn to Oise Valley
5TH BAV. DIV.	7 B. 14 B. 19 B. 21 B.	Lens	Withdrawn to Fromelles
46TH R.DIV.	214 R. 215 R. 216 R.	Wytschaete	Withdrawn to Reims
13TH DIV.	13 55 158	Verdun	Withdrawn to Verdun
58TH DIV.	106 107 120 R.	Reims	Withdrawn to Ypres — Withdrawn
6TH BAV. DIV.	6 10 B. 11 B. 13 B.	Argonne	Withdrawn to Neuve Chapelle
21ST DIV.	80 81 87	Aisne Valley	Withdrawn to St. Mihiel
25TH DIV.	115 116 117	Aisne Valley	Withdrawn to St. Mihiel
50TH R.DIV.	229 R. 230 R. 231 R.	Bois Grenier	Withdrawn to La Bassée
52ND R.DIV.	238 R. 239 R. 240 R.	Ypres	Withdrawn to Champagne
51ST R.DIV.	234 R. 235 R. 236 R.	Ypres	Withdrawn to Champagne
213TH DIV.	149 368 R. 74 R.	New	Withdrawn to Soissons
214TH DIV.	50 358 363	New	Withdrawn to Woevre
212TH DIV.	20 114 38 R.	New	Withdrawn — Withdrawn
36TH DIV.	5 128 175	Roye	
10TH R.DIV.	37 37 R. 155	Champagne	Withdrawn to Verdun
7TH R.DIV.	36 R. 66 R. 72 R.	Argonne	Withdrawn to Argonne
6TH BAV.R.DIV.	16 B.R. 17 B.R. 20 B.R. 21 B.R.	Fromelles	Withdrawn to Souchez
15TH DIV.	160 186 389	Aisne Valley	Withdrawn to Aisne Valley
9TH R.DIV.	6 R. 19 R. 395	Champagne	Withdrawn to Argonne
4TH ERS.DIV.	360 361 362	Ypres	Withdrawn to Ypres
2ND NAVAL DIV.	1 Mar. 2 Mar. 3 Mar.	Flanders	Withdrawn to Flanders
113TH DIV.	36 48 32 R.	Oise Valley	Withdrawn to Verdun
29TH DIV.	112 113 142	Champagne	
6TH DIV.	24 64 396	Champagne	Withdrawn to Argonne
19TH R.DIV.	78 R. 78 R. 92 R.	Argonne	Withdrawn to Woevre
1ST BAV.DIV.	1 B. 2 B. 24 B.	St. Mihiel	Withdrawn to St. Mihiel
2ND BAV.DIV.	12 B. 15 B. 20 B.	St. Mihiel	Withdrawn to St. Mihiel
103RD DIV.	32 71 116 R.	Champagne	Withdrawn to Champagne
211TH DIV.	27 75 R. 103 R.	New	Withdrawn to Aisne Valley
5TH ERS.DIV.	3 R.E. 73 L.W. 74 L.W.	Ypres	Withdrawn to Flanders
8TH ERS.DIV.	365 51 E. 92 E.	Woevre	Withdrawn to Woevre
38TH DIV.	94 95 96	Verdun	Withdrawn to Flanders
221ST DIV.	41 60 R. 1 R.E.	New	
BAV. ERS. DIV.	15 B.R. 28 E. 30 E.	Verdun	Withdrawn
30TH DIV.	99 105 143	Verdun	Withdrawn
39TH DIV.	126 132 172	Verdun	Withdrawn
206TH DIV.	359 4 R.E.R. 394	Flanders (New)	Withdrawn
222ND DIV.	193 397 B.R.	Alsace (New)	
16TH R.DIV.	190 390 29 R.	Aisne Valley	
223RD DIV.	144 173 29 E.	Alsace (New)	Withdrawn
208TH DIV.	25 185 65 R.	Russia (New)	
32ND DIV.	102 103 177	Argonne	
14TH BAV. DIV.	4 B. 8 B. 25 B.	Verdun (New)	

Left margin, Sept. group: Divisions engaged for first time = 26, second = 8, Total = 34

Oct. group: Divisions engaged for first time = 18, second = 10, third = 1, Total = 29

Nov. group: Divisions engaged for first time = 6, second = 9, third = 3, Total = 18

BATTLE OF THE SOMME, JULY–NOVEMBER 1916

LEFT AND FAR LEFT: Another chart showing troop movements involved in the Battle of the Somme, this shows in detail the movement of German units on the British and French fronts between the locations of Hebuterne and Chilly between July 1 and November 30. Over the period a total of 97 German divisions were involved in the battle: 33 in July; another 14 in August; 26 in September; 18 in October; and 6 in November. Many — 32 — of the divisions that took part in the battle were relieved, left the area, and then returned; four divisions had the misfortune to do so twice. WO 153/1261 (20, 21)

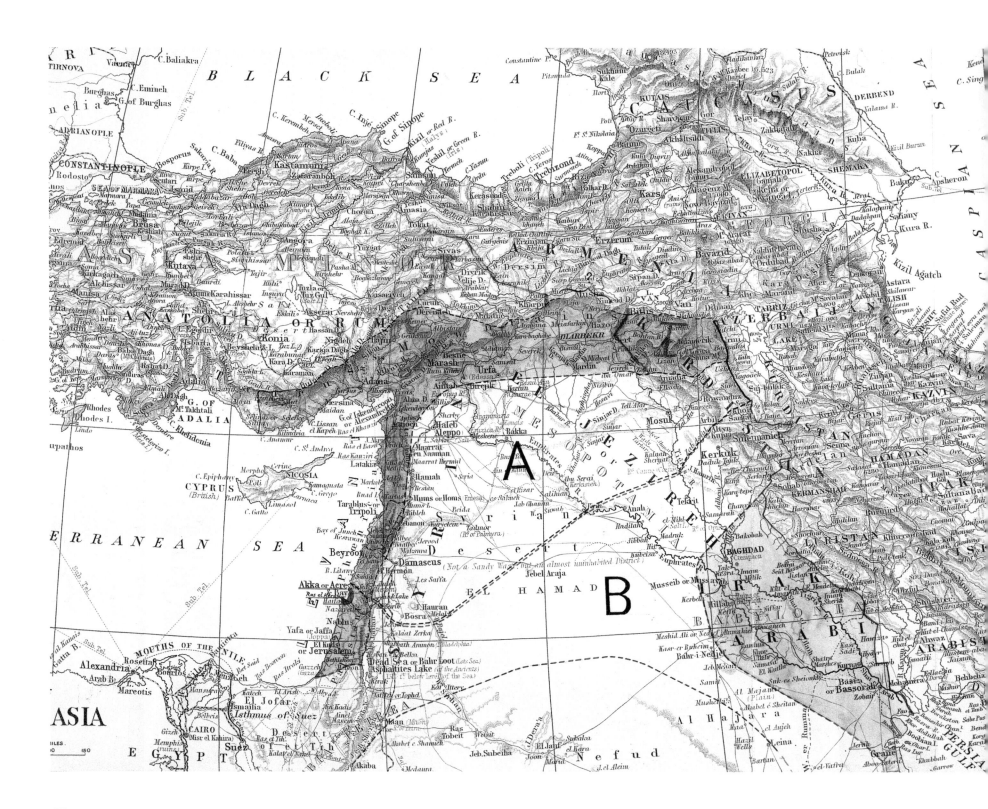

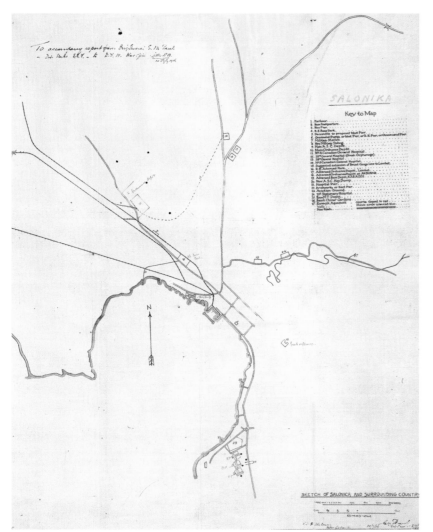

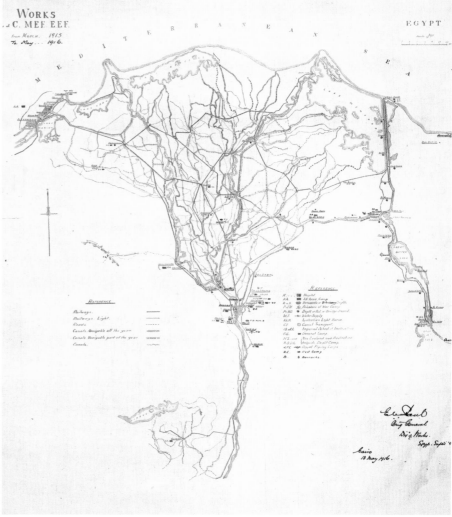

MIDDLE EAST, 1916

LEFT: From the Foreign Office archives (with spheres of French and British influence marked out) this map shows well the Palestinian and Middle Eastern theater of operations. Events in the Middle East hinged around Britain's lifeline, the Suez Canal. Fearful of Turkish threats (an attempt to take it was made by crossing Sinai in early February 1915), Britain pushed towards Palestine with its Egyptian Expeditionary Force. With assistance from the Arabs (see pages 106–107) the Turks were beaten by General Sir Edmund Allenby, who transferred to the front in June 1917. The war in the Middle East did much to assist the operations in Mesopotamia (see pages 90–91) as it forced the Turks to switch forces from that front to Palestine. A byproduct of the Arab Revolt against Turkey, who had ruled the area since the 16th century, would be the increase in Arab nationalism that has echoes in the area to this day. FO 371/2767

SALONIKA, 1916

ABOVE LEFT: From the Director of Fortifications and Works, Egypt and Palestine, this sketch map shows works around Salonika, the Greek port on the Aegean that was seen as the main artery of Allied assistance to Serbia. In fact little was achieved on the front except the invaliding out of theater of nearly half a million men with malaria. MFQ 1/516 (1)

NILE DELTA, 1916

ABOVE: Another sketch map from the Director of Fortifications and Works, Egypt and Palestine, this shows rail road and canals around the Nile delta and Suez Canal in 1916. MFQ 1/516 (2)

MAMETZ AND MONTAUBAN, 1916

RIGHT: Blueprint of plans of German Fifth Army trenches bearing the admonition: 'Taking into the front line forbidden.' While dated November 1916, it shows the lines as they were at the start of the battle of the Somme with Mametz still in German hands. WO 153/593

VIMY RIDGE, 1916

FAR RIGHT: Three illustrations: an aerial composite photograph associated with a map showing its coverage and a Canadian Corps barrage map of Vimy Ridge. Lying above the town of Arras, this strategically important 7.5-mile long chalk outcrop saw near constant fighting from September 1914, when it was occupied by German forces, until the Allies finally took the ridge in late 1917. German engineers had dug in deep and reworked the network of medieval caves and passages to make a formidable defensive position from where the Germans shelled Arras with heavy artillery. The British Third Army was assigned the sector in March 1916, taking over from the French who had tried to take the position to their heavy cost. During April 9–14, 1917 four divisions of the Canadian Corps under the command of the Hon. Sir Julian Byng successfully assaulted and captured the Ridge in the action known as the Battle of Arras. Today it is the site of one of the most memorable of all the war memorials erected postwar, with twin towers on which the Spirit of Canada weeps for her fallen countrymen. The undated barrage map shows the same terrain, from Givenchy in the north. WO 316/21, WO 153/1160

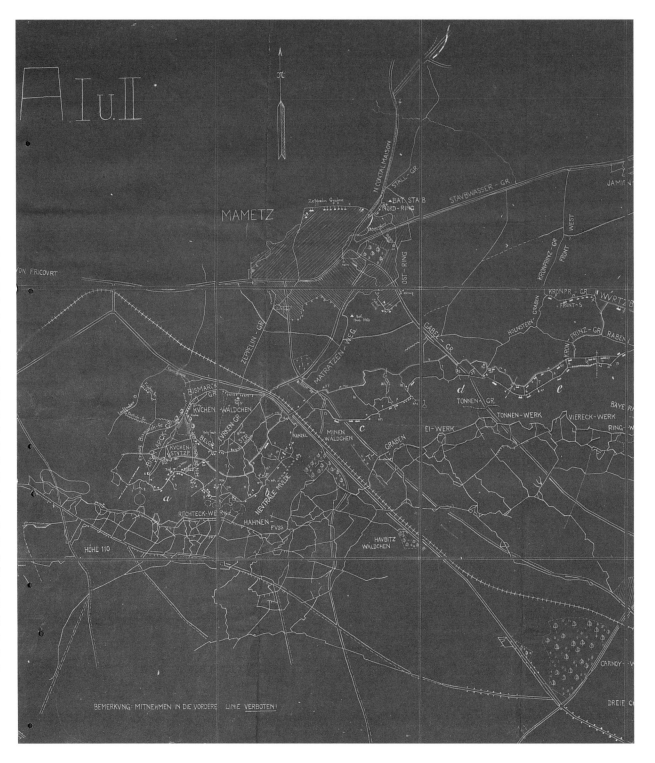

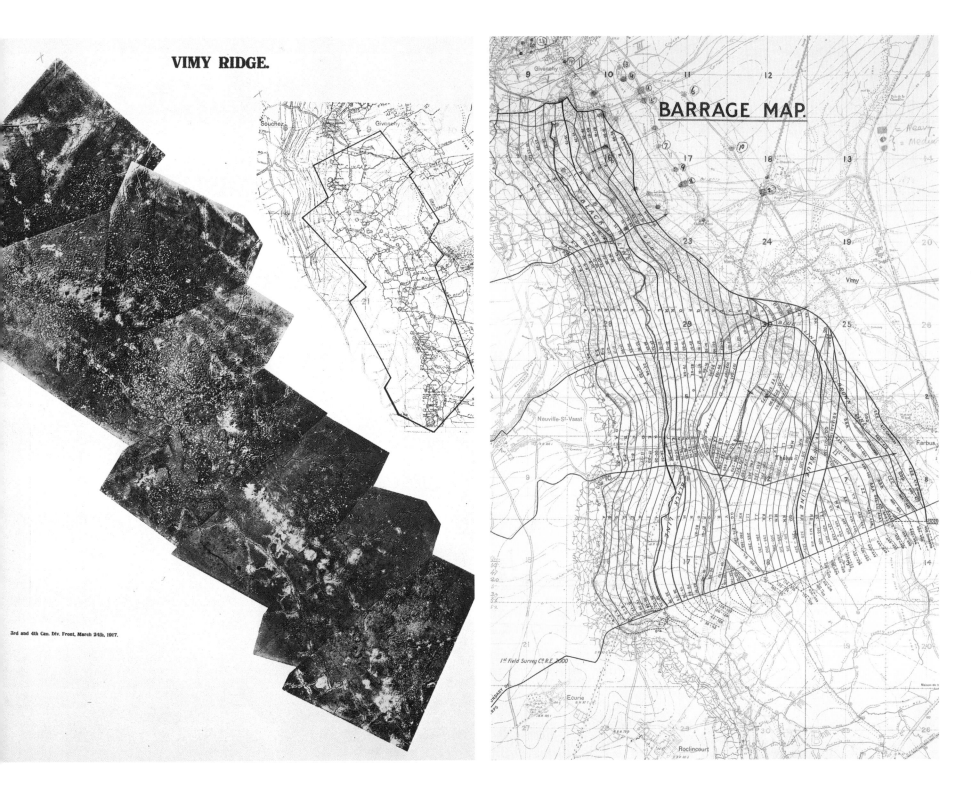

VIMY RIDGE.

BARRAGE MAP.

3rd and 4th Can. Div. Front, March 24th, 1917.

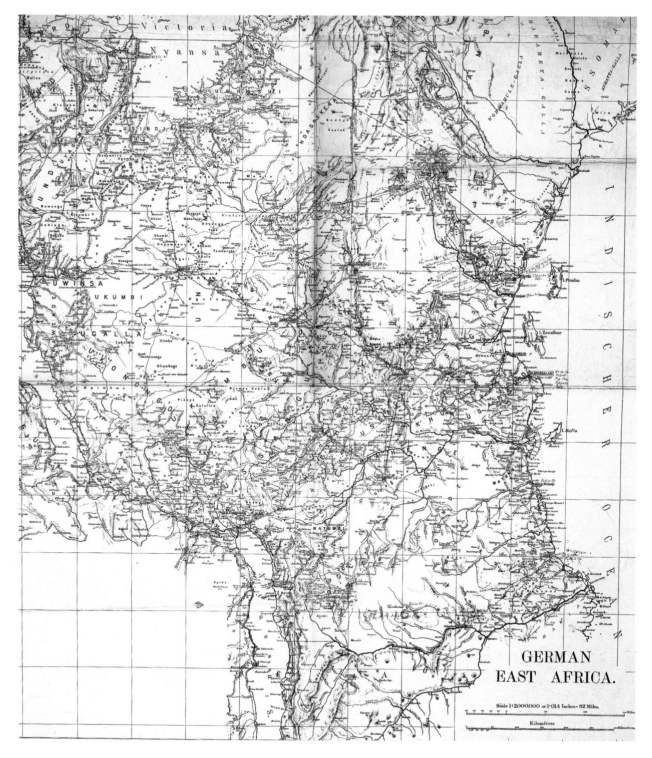

EAST AFRICA, 1916

LEFT: British operations in East Africa after the landings in Tanga by Aitken's Force B (see page 40) were defensive, while Lettow-Vorbeck waged a guerilla war. In early 1916 Lieutenant General Jan Smuts took command of the British forces which were reinforced considerably. In spite of these advantages, Lettow-Verbeck and his forces continued to run rings round the British. WO 153/804

YUGOSLAVIA, 1916

RIGHT: During the war there were many plans and discussions, often premature, about the fate of the belligerents and the areas involved. This map shows thoughts on the creation of a single state to unite the Balkan Slavs – Yugoslavia – that was promoted by the Treaty of London in 1915 between the Allies and Italy. By 1916 this was the view of what Yugoslavia would be, and the red line shows (as the key to this French map says) 'the limits of the Italian pretensions after the Convention of London.' While a Balkan superstate may have seemed the solution, in reality it did little but bottle up problems and when the top came off after the fall of communism at the end of the century, all the troubles that existed in 1914 became apparent once more. MPK 291 (5)

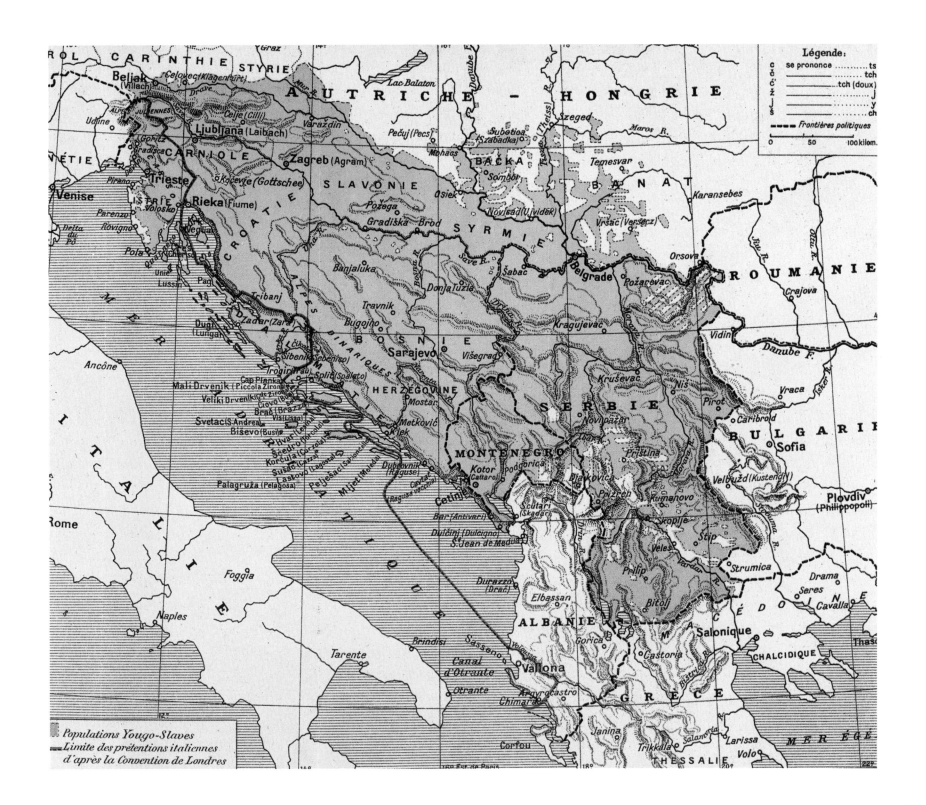

Légende:

c	se prononce	ts
c č		tch
č		tch (doux)
ž		j
j		y
š		ch

- - - *Frontières politiques*

0   50   100 kilom.

▨ *Populations Yougo-Slaves*
── *Limite des prétentions italiennes
d'après la Convention de Londres*

73

ARMOURED CAR FORCE, ROMANIA, 1916–17

RIGHT: The maps on this spread are all drawn by Petty Officer John D Sinclair of the British RN Armoured Car Division that was crewed by Royal Marines and served with the Russians. The maps explain a little-covered campaign, waged around the Danube as British units moved from Odessa toward the Romanian capital of Bucharest, to assist Russian forces attempting to aid the Romanians who had declared for the Allies on August 27, 1916. Buoyed by the initial success of the Russian Brusilov Offensive, the Romanian declaration of war on the Central Powers proved to be a horrible mistake. The Romanian Army was just not capable of withstanding the German Ninth Army, commanded by General Erich von Falkenhayn, when it came as reinforcements to the Austrians. The Germans pushed the Romanians out of three quarters of their country, took Bucharest on December 6, and took control of the Ploesti oilfields. The Allies had promised an offensive from Salonika, but this did not materialize. The first map (**right**) shows the route the RN Armoured Car Division took. The second (**far right, above**) shows the defense of Vizirul by the armored cars and Russians, at the end of December 1916/early January 1917; the final map (**far right, below**) shows the defense of Harsova on the Danube. MPI 1/10 (1/3/3B)

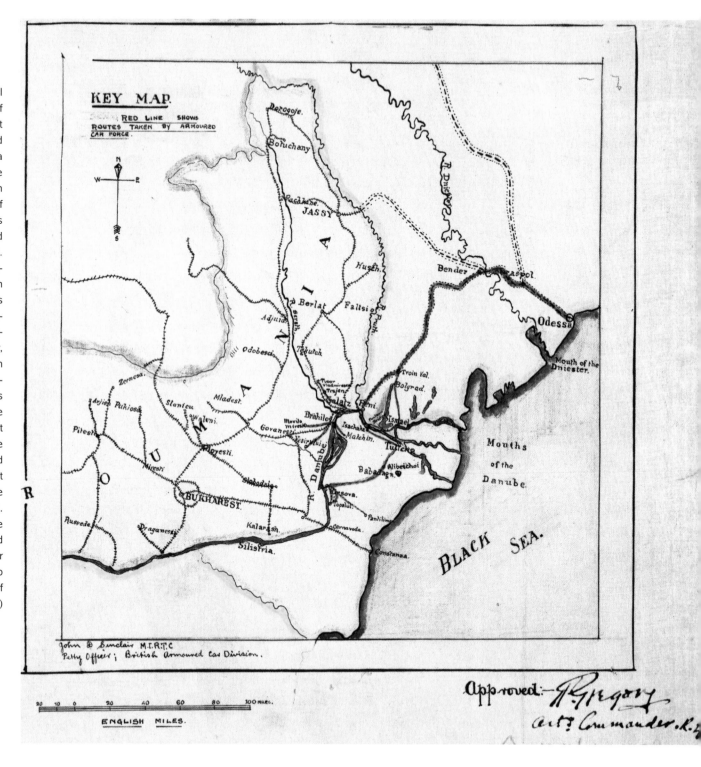

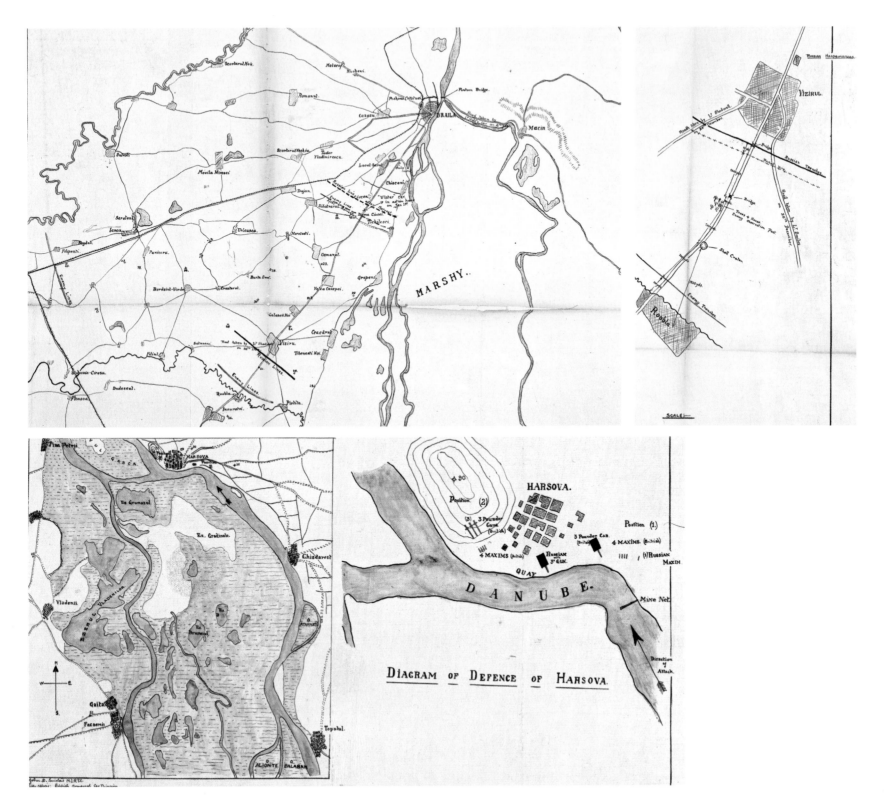

DIAGRAM OF DEFENCE OF HARSOVA.

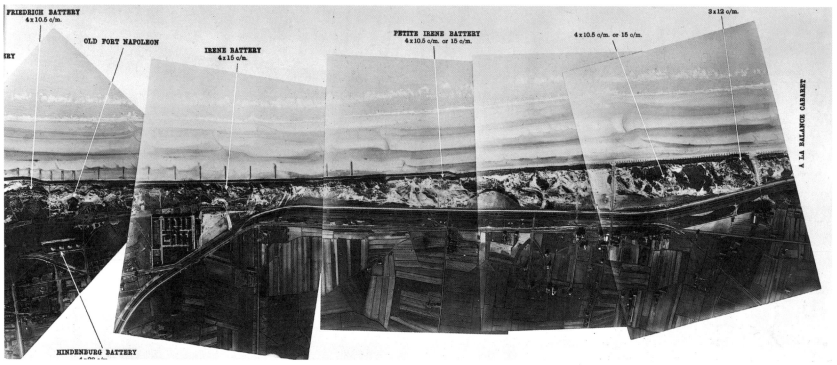

TRENCH LINES, 1917

TOP: This photograph is of enemy positions west of Bucquoy, and makes an interesting comparison with the aerial shots shown on this spread. It is one of a pair of strereographic photographs taken from British trenches, looking out toward the enemy. These images could supply information that maps could not; particularly in the undulating terrain of Flanders. WO 316/3

DUTCH COAST, 1917

ABOVE AND RIGHT: One of the big changes to the way people saw the battlefield was the birth of aerial reconnaissance. The state of the art in 1917 is shown by these composite photographs of the coast from the Dutch frontier to Ostend, showing gun batteries and coastal features. Maps were, of course, still important and continue to be to this day: but for a snapshot of a moment, as an intelligence tool, and as a view of behind enemy lines, the photographs supplied by reconnaissance aircraft were able to provide something that military commanders had not seen before. WO 153/883

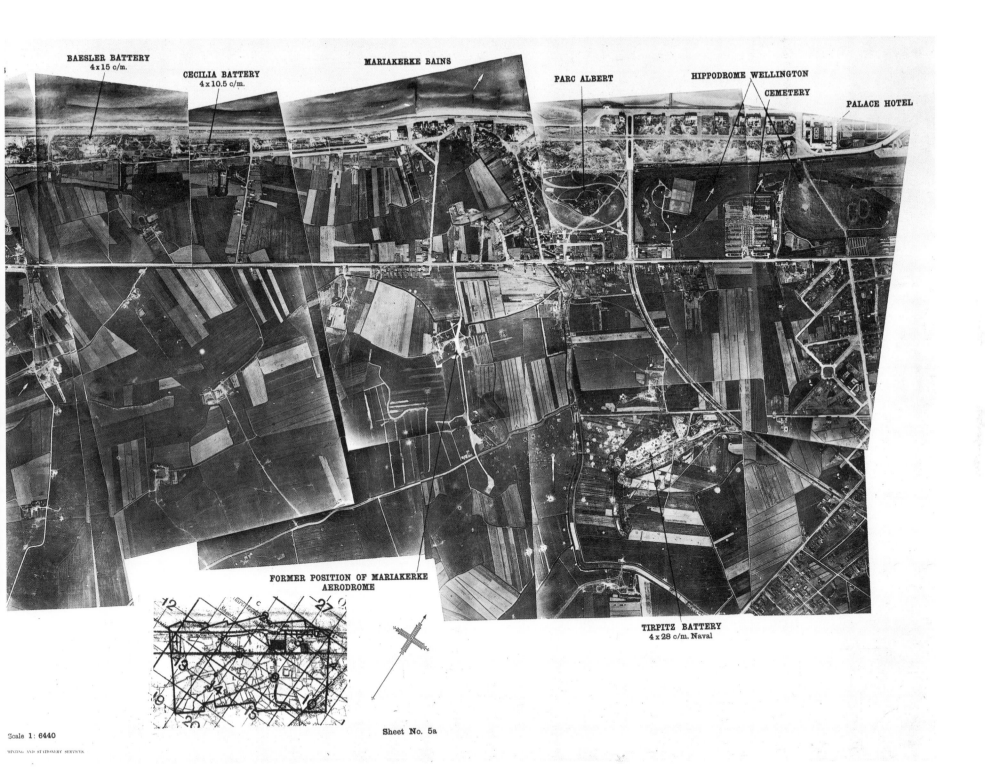

BAESLER BATTERY
4 x 15 c/m.

CECILIA BATTERY
4 x 10.5 c/m.

MARIAKERKE BAINS

PARC ALBERT

HIPPODROME WELLINGTON
CEMETERY

PALACE HOTEL

FORMER POSITION OF MARIAKERKE
AERODROME

TIRPITZ BATTERY
4 x 28 c/m. Naval

Scale 1 : 6440

Sheet No. 5a

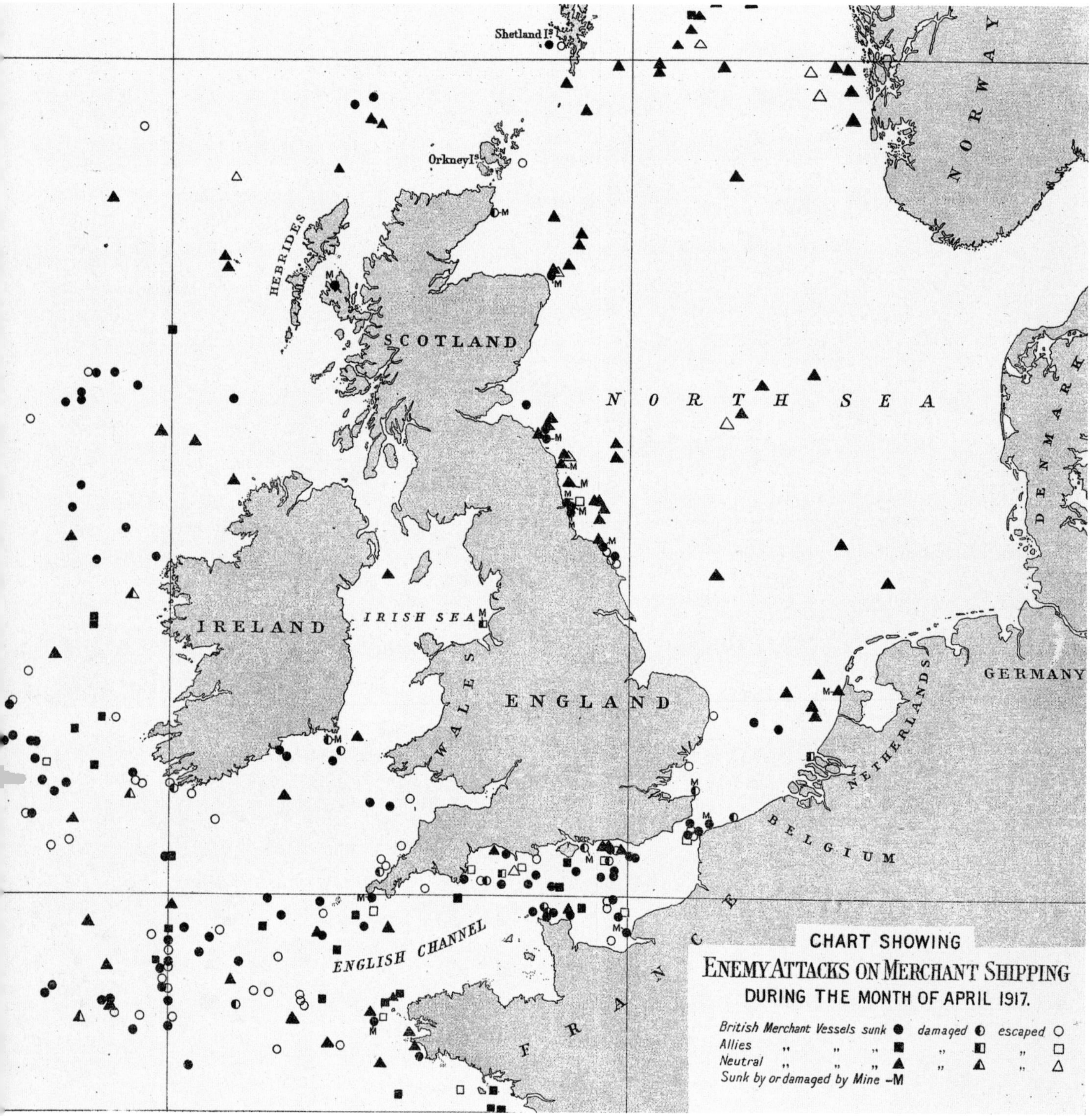

Map labels: Shetland Is, Orkney Is, HEBRIDES, SCOTLAND, NORTH SEA, NORWAY, DENMARK, GERMANY, NETHERLANDS, BELGIUM, IRELAND, IRISH SEA, ENGLAND, WALES, FRANCE, ENGLISH CHANNEL

CHART SHOWING
ENEMY ATTACKS ON MERCHANT SHIPPING
DURING THE MONTH OF APRIL 1917.

British Merchant Vessels sunk ● damaged ◑ escaped ○
Allies   "   "   " ■   " ◪   " □
Neutral   "   "   " ▲   " ◬   " △
Sunk by or damaged by Mine —M

GERMAN ATTACKS ON MERCHANT SHIPPING, APRIL 1917

LEFT: As the title suggests, this map shows the enemy attacks on British and Allied shipping in April 1917, also identifying mine damage and loss. The U-boat war was a significant feature of World War I and one that impinged directly on the land war. German unrestricted U-boat warfare, while certainly affecting Britain, did not damage her suffi-ciently to weaken her resolve for the land battle. It also had a large part in bringing the United States into the war on the side of the Allies following passenger ship losses such as the *Lusitania* and *Sussex*. What the story would have been had the Germans had more U-boats is difficult to surmise. MPI 671 pt1 (1)

ABOVE RIGHT: The enemy attacks on shipping in the Mediterranean.
MPI 671 pt 1 (2)

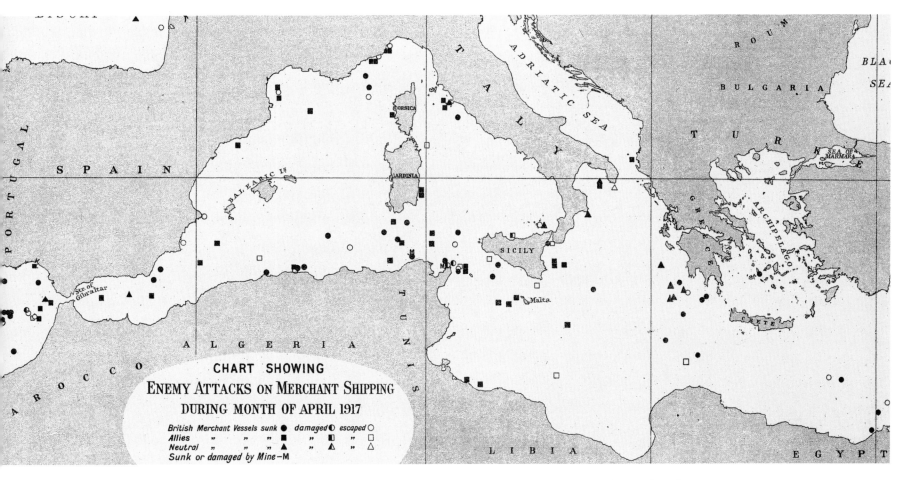

CHART SHOWING

ENEMY ATTACKS ON MERCHANT SHIPPING

DURING MONTH OF APRIL 1917

British Merchant Vessels sunk ● damaged ◑ escaped ○
Allies   "   "   ■   "   ◨   "   □
Neutral   "   "   ▲   "   ◮   "   △
Sunk or damaged by Mine—M

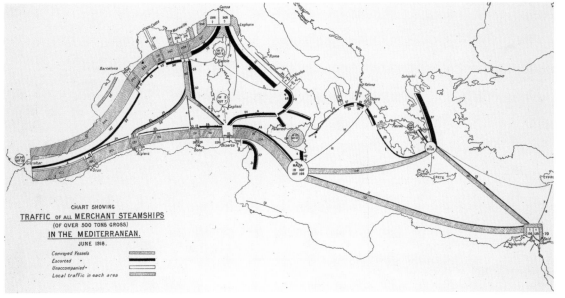

CHART SHOWING
TRAFFIC of all **MERCHANT STEAMSHIPS**
(OF OVER 500 TONS GROSS)
IN THE MEDITERRANEAN.
JUNE 1918.

Convoyed Vessels
Escorted   "
Unaccompanied "
Local traffic in each area

MERCHANT STEAMSHIP TRAFFIC, JUNE 1918

LEFT: This diagram, although slightly out of date sequence, shows the volume of merchant steamship traffic over 500 tons gross in the Mediterranean during the month of June 1918. It combines well with the map above to show how important the Mediterranean was to the Allies, both as a natural conduit for reinforcements, and also as the shortcut for British Empire traffic through the Suez Canal.

MPI 671 pt 1 (4)

THIRD BATTLE OF ARRAS, APRIL 1917

LEFT: The opening phase of the Nivelle offensive, the Battle of Arras, is seen as one of the successes of 1917, particu-larly because it was during this battle that the Canadian Corps took Vimy Ridge. The attrition rate was also seen to be in better proportion between attacker and defender than hitherto: British First, Third, and Fifth Armies suffered 158,660 casualties during the Battle of Arras (46,826, 87,226, and 24,608 respectively), as against German Sixth Army's 100,000. WO 153/519

MEDICAL POSTS ON THE WESTERN FRONT, 1917

ABOVE RIGHT: Overlaid on a base map of trench positions as at November 27, 1916, this map shows the distribution of medical posts – so essential with the attrition levels of World War I. In a world that is used to seeing casualties casevaced from the battle area by helicopter, where modern western armies have extremely high survivability levels (so long as the wounded are taken off the battlefield), it is hard to comprehend the problems associated with the estimated 20 million wounded. It was during this war that the basis for modern battlefield medicine – including triage – were developed. WO 153/1169

SCARPE RIVER, 1917

BELOW RIGHT: Another of Flanders' rivers, the Scarpe, runs from just south of Arras through to Antwerp and the sea. It was the scene of many battles during the period. WO 297/142

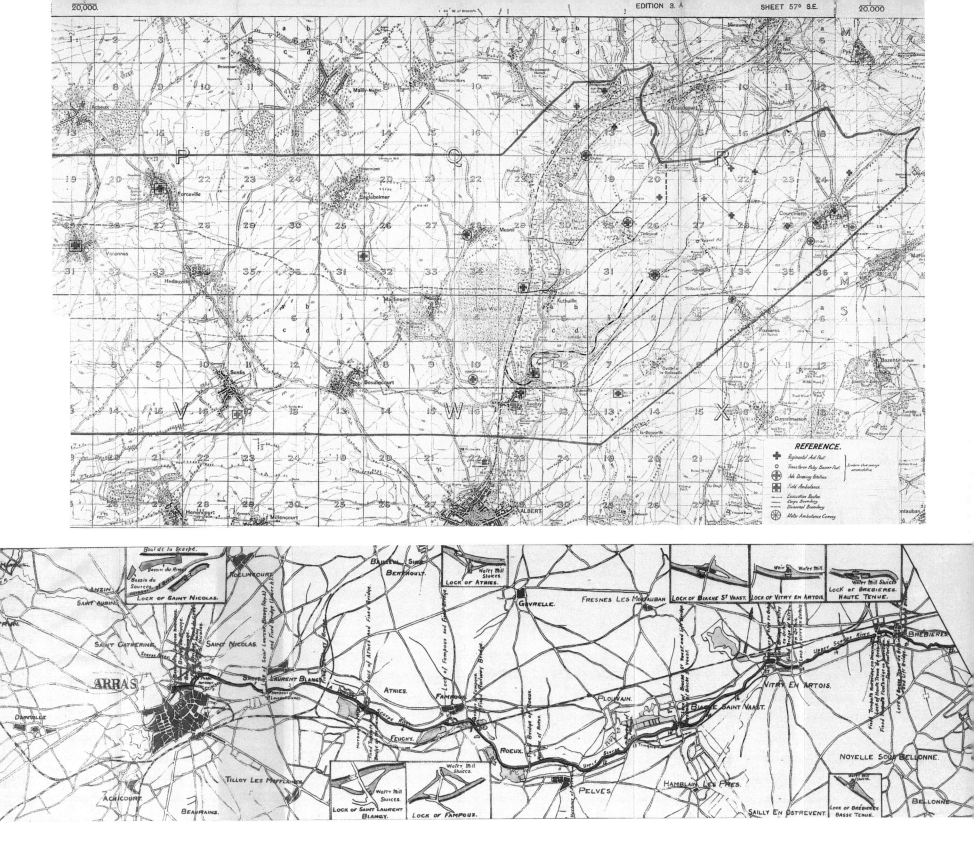

REFERENCE.

Regimental Aid Post
Transfer or Relay Bearer Post
Adv. Dressing Station
Field Ambulance.
Evacuation Routes
Corps Boundary.
Divisional Boundary
Motor Ambulance Convoy

BATTLE OF MESSINES, JUNE–JULY 1917

RIGHT: The Battle of Messines was fought by British Second Army from late May and ended with the German salient under British control. Preceded by 19 massive mine explosions, that were heard in London and are estimated to have killed 10,000 men, and a creeping barrage all objectives were taken quickly. This map shows the area of the battle with progressive gain lines up to July 31, 1917. WO 297/623

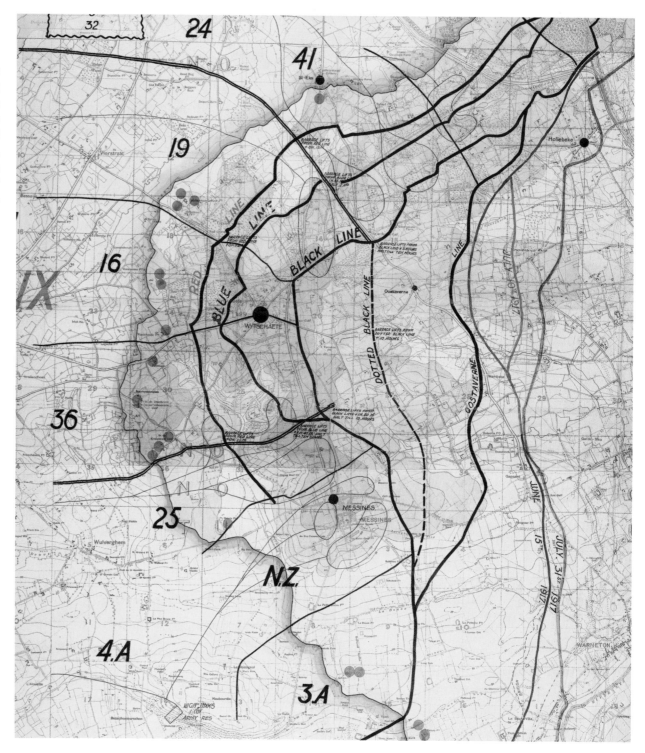

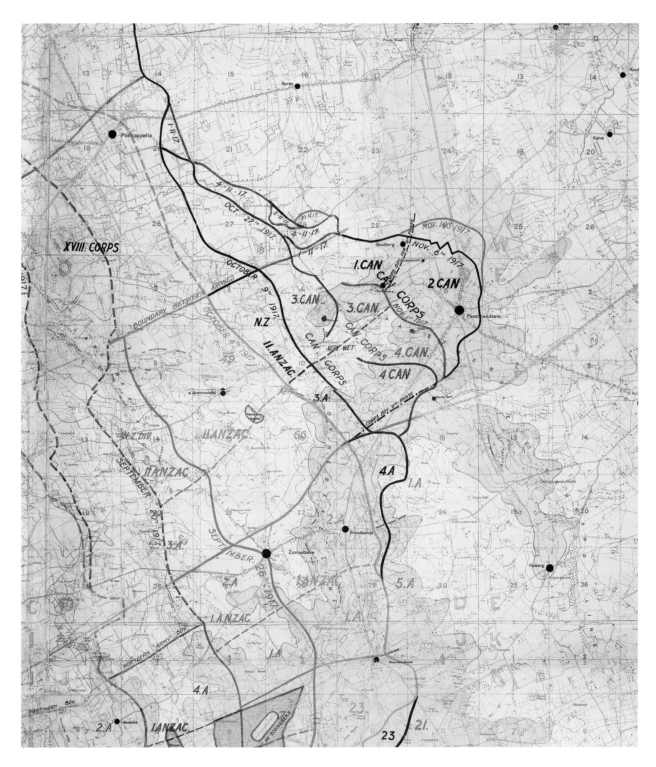

THIRD BATTLE OF YPRES, SEPTEMBER–NOVEMBER 1917

LEFT: This map shows the Allied gains from September to November 10, 1917, at the third Battle of Ypres. Following the success at Messines, the attack at the Ypres salient started on July 31. The French First, British Fifth, and British Second Armies attacked the German Fourth Army in heavy going: deep mud after heavy rains and constant artillery barrages. Overall control moved from Gough (commander Fifth Army) to Plumer on August 25, and the operation continued into November. After the Somme, 'Passchendaele' – as the Third Battle of Ypres was known – has become the most obvious symbol of the pointlessness of the tactics of attrition and frontal attack practiced by the Allied generals. In total 320,000 Allies and 200,000 Germans died for a paltry gain of some five miles. WO 297/623

84

THIRD BATTLE OF YPRES, SEPTEMBER–NOVEMBER 1917

Three aerial photographs giving a panorama of Passchendaele and showing the blasted terrain. The village of Passchendaele (**left**) gave the battle its alternative name. WO 316/22

BATTLE OF YPRES: HOSTILE TACTICAL MAPS, SEPTEMBER 18–OCTOBER 21, 1917

The three maps on this spread were produced by British Second Army and look at hostile threats during the Third Battle of Ypres – Passchendaele – which took place between June 6, and November 10, 1917, and lost the BEF around 310,000 men. The maps identify 'Enemy Reserves, Concentrations and counterattack Methods East of Ypres.' The first (**Right**), dated September 18, 1917, looks at attacks north of the Menin Road in August and is overprinted on a map whose trench lines are correct to September 9.

WO 153/496 (1)

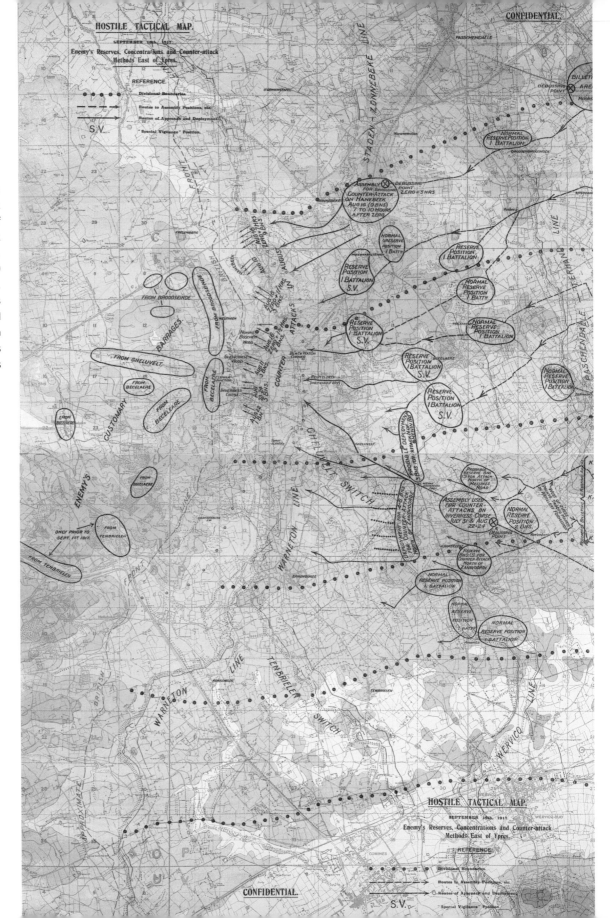

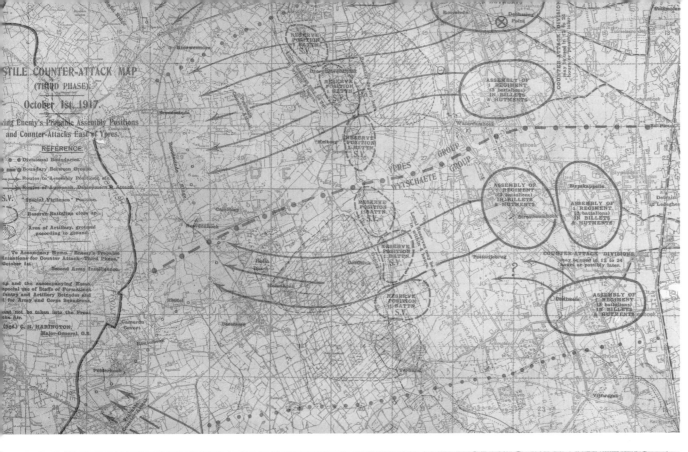

LEFT: Section of Hostile counterattack Map dated October 1, 1917, with trenches correct to September 29. The circulation is identified at left with the restriction, 'They must not be taken into the Front Line or the Air' signed by Major General G S Harrington. It looks at the units and location of a probable German counterattack south of the village of Passchendaele. The village would fall in the final, costly attack of the battle in early November. WO 153/496 (5)

BELOW LEFT: Section of Hostile counterattack Map dated October 24, 1917, with trenches correct to October 10. It looks at the units and location of a probable German counterattack east of Ypres. WO 153/496 (9)

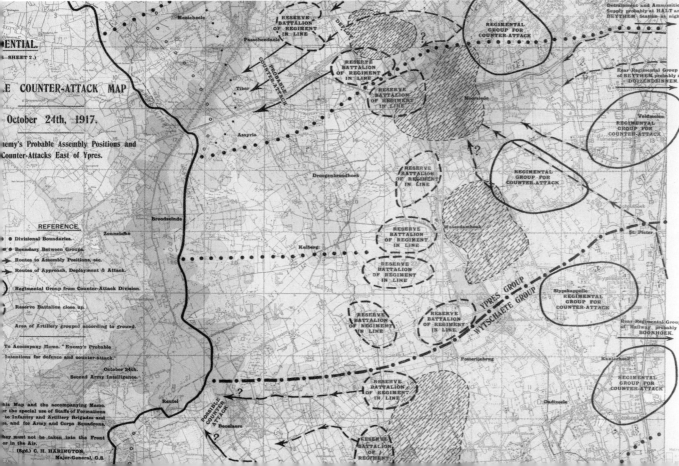

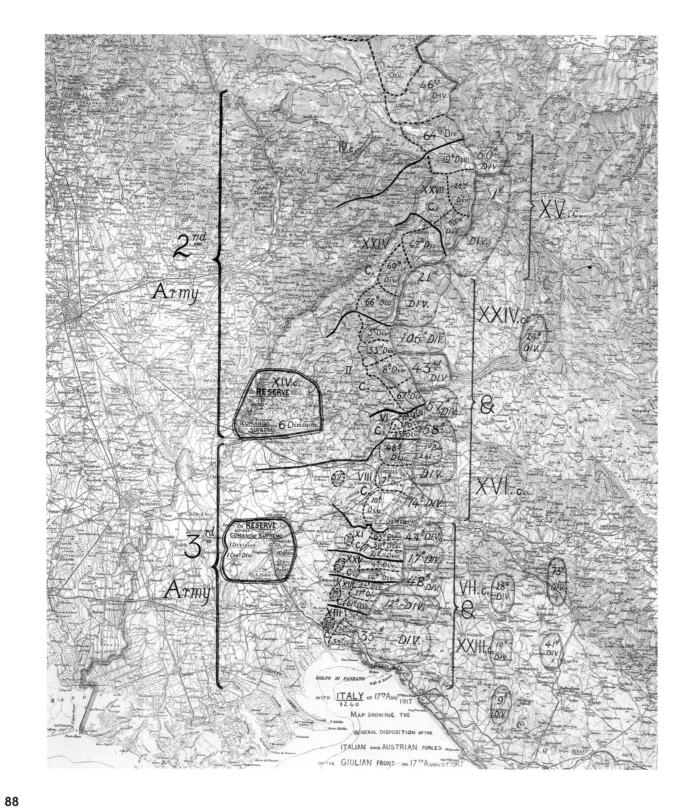

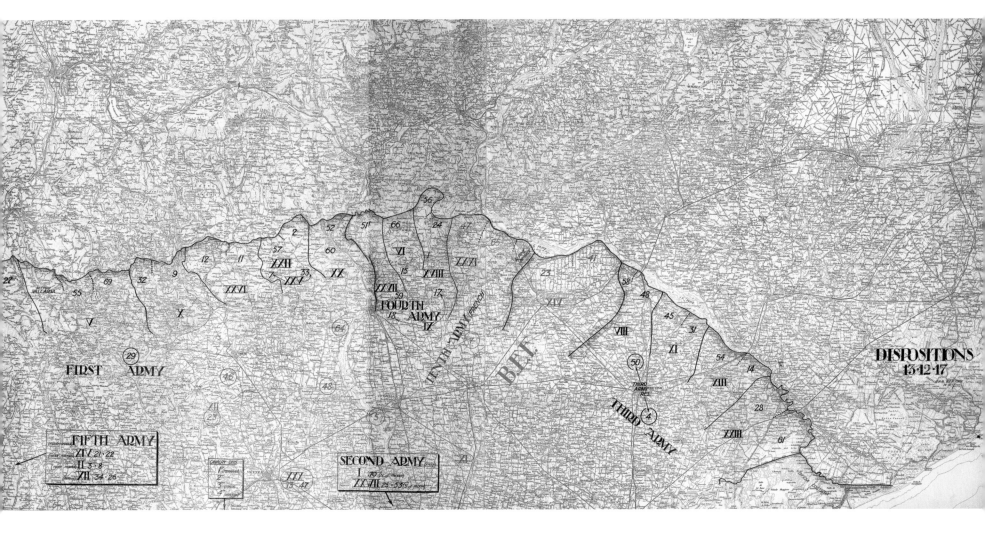

SIXTH BATTLE OF ISONZO, AUGUST 17, 1917

LEFT: At the start of the war the Isonzo River was held by Austrian forces. The Italians and Austrians fought between 10 and 12 battles (depending what is counted as part of the Isonzo contest) in the area (see also page 51). This map shows the movements during the Sixth Battle which took place between August 6 and 17. General Luigi Cadorna commanded 22 Italian divisions against nine Austrian divisions. The initial Italian assault was successful and the main attack got across the River Isonzo and went on to take Gorizia (Görz) by August 9. Once their positions were reinforced Cadorna further advanced his troops until August 12, by which time the Italians had taken 45 square miles of land—making this the biggest Italian land victory so far of the war. Five days later the fighting died down. At the end of the Sixth Battle the Italians had taken 51,250 casualties as against 41,850 Austrian casualties. WO 153/772

ITALIAN CAMPAIGN, DECEMBER 13, 1917

ABOVE: The position on December 13, 1917 showing Italian, French, and British dispositions on the Piave River following the general Italian retreat after the Battle of Caporetto on October 23. The Germans and Austro-Hungarians had opened their attack on the Italian front line at Isonzo on October 24, with a massive bombardment as a precursor to the infantry advance. Shocked and demoralized, the Italian troops fell back to avoid getting trapped by the sea at their backs, to a position beside the Tagliamento River by October 31. In the face of overwhelming German-Austrian superiority they were unable to hold this position and were forced even further back to the Piave River by November 7, where they were able to join up with arriving French and British troops. WO 153/772 Parts 1 and 2

OPERATIONS OF THE 'DUNSTERFORCE' IN NORTH PERSIA, 1917

RIGHT AND FAR RIGHT: Before the outbreak of World War I Persia was the object of intense rivalry between Russia and Britain for possession of the valuable oil fields. The 1907 Anglo-Russian accord split Persia into northern (Russian) and southern (British) zones of influence. Germany had long wanted to muscle in on Persia, too, and was successful in destabilizing British influence. Indeed, by outbreak of war the British only had influence in the gulf ports where they had garrisons. In late 1917 with the agreement of the Persian government, a multinational force of nearly 1,000 men was gathered together at Hamadan to guard the oilfields and restore order: malign Turkish and German agitators were making the country ungovernable. Titled 'Dunsterforce' the men were elite troops from Britain, Australia, New Zealand, and Canada, called in from the Western and Mesopotamian Fronts to work under the command of Major-General L C Dunsterville. In January 1918 Dunsterforce was ordered to march north to prevent a joint Turkish-German force invading India through Persia. Just over 200 miles into their journey Dunsterforce encountered 3,000 Bolshevik Russian troops at Enzeli, on the Caspian coast, who forced them to turn back to Hamadan. Meanwhile a German division had occupied Tiblisi in Georgia and their allies the Turks were close to occupying the important oil port of Baku. Ordered north again Dunsterforce set out with armored cars accompanied this time by 3,000 Russians. In June 1918 they easily beat resistance and took Enzeli. In July the Russians departed to support the new nationalist regime there, which was threatened with overthrow by the approaching Turkish forces. The Russians requested Dunsterforce's assistance and they set off across the Caspian Sea for Baku. Arriving at Baku on August 16, about 1,000 British troops (39 Brigade) joined the town garrison of 10,000 local volunteers. Heavy fighting against the Turks came to a head on the night of September 14, when Turkish pressure and heavy fighting made Dunsterforce's position untenable. As Dunsterfore withdrew, 14,000 Turkish troops prepared to attack the port: Baku fell that day. Accompanied by a large number of Armenian refugees Dunsterforce returned to Enzeli. On the declaration of Armistice a Russo-Armenian force, and Dunsterville's 39 Brigade operating on the Caspian Sea, reoccupied Baku on November 7. General Dunsterville was ordered back to Britain where he received criticism for the expedition. WO 153/1032 (1/2)

КАРТА
АПШЕРОНСКАГО ПОЛУОСТРОВА
БАКИНСКОЙ ГУБЕРНІИ и УѢЗДА

Scale 1/84,000; 1 inch = 1.32 miles.

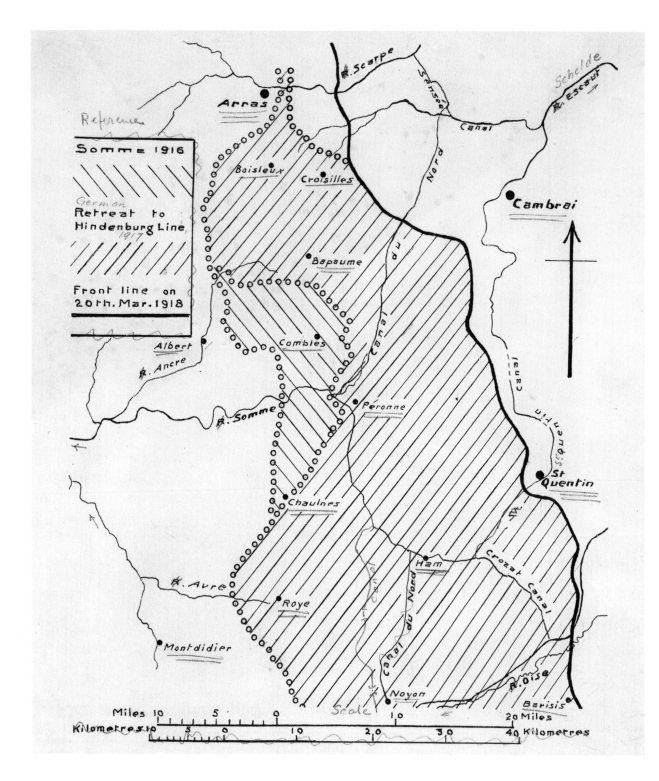

Reference

Somme 1916

German
Retreat to
Hindenburg Line,
1917

Front line on
20th. Mar. 1918

Miles 10 5 0 Scale 10 20 Miles
Kilometres 10 5 0 10 20 30 40 Kilometres

GERMAN RETREAT, MARCH 1918

LEFT: This map shows two sorts of war devastation – the devastation of battle as caused by the Battle of the Somme in 1916, and the devastation caused when the Germans retreated to the Hindeburg Line in 1917 leaving an enormous swathe of scorched earth behind them. It is said that they destroyed every church spire, entire villages, crops, livestock and every possible source of cover and food that the pursuing Allies could make use of. More importantly the devastated land disrupted Allied offensive plans in 1917 and allowed the Germans to concentrate behind very strong fortifications. This map shows the front line on March 20, 1918. WO 153/1298

MILITARY HQS IN FRANCE, BELGIUM, AND GERMANY AS FROM NOVEMBER 28, 1917

RIGHT: This is one of a set of maps produced for the Cambrai Enquiry in 1918. WO 158/56

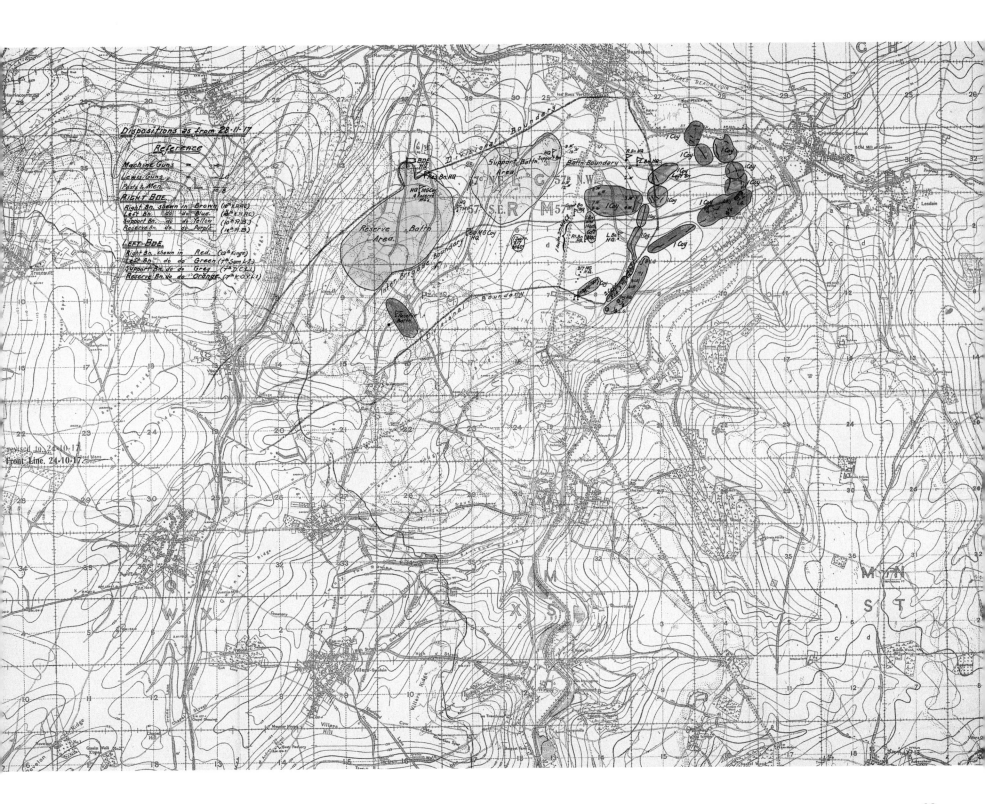

Dispositions as from 28·11·17

Reference

Machine Guns =
Lewis Guns
Posts & Men

RIGHT BDE.
Right Bn. shewn in Brown (10ᵗʰ K.R.R.C.)
Left Bn. do do Blue. (8ᵗʰ K.R.R.C.)
Support Bn. do do Yellow (10ᵗʰ R.B.)
Reserve Bn. do do Purple (11ᵗʰ R.B.)

LEFT BDE.
Right Bn. shewn in Red. (12ᵗʰ Kings)
Left Bn. do do Green (7ᵗʰ Som.L.I.)
Support Bn. do do Grey (7ᵗʰ D.C.L.I.)
Reserve Bn. do do Orange (7ᵗʰ K.O.Y.L.I.)

Revised to 24·10·17
Front Line. 24·10·17

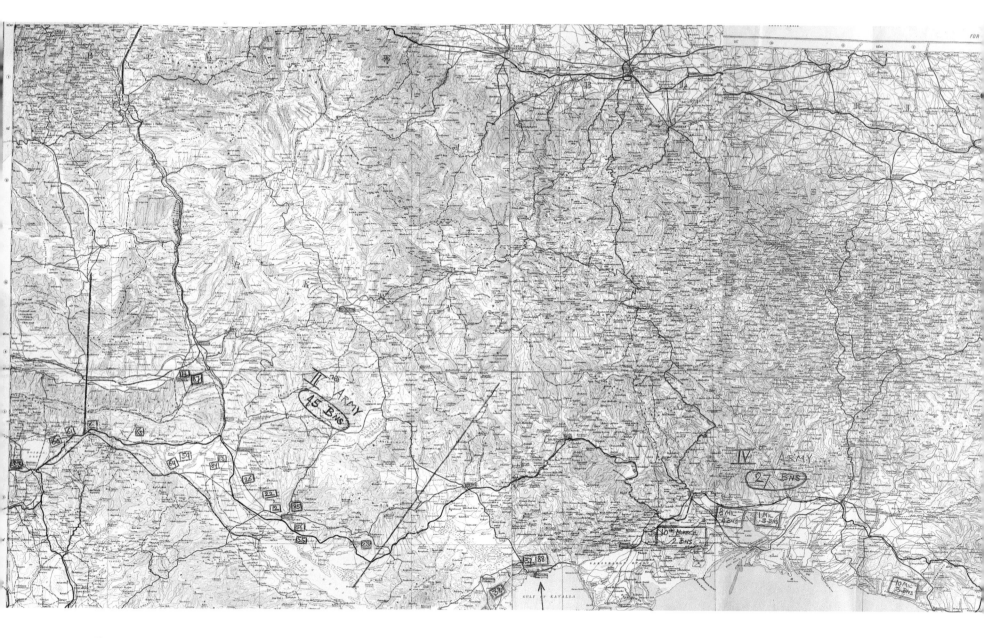

SALONIKA, 1917

ABOVE: The Salonika campaign, like the attack on Gallipoli, was strategically sound but didn't have the effect that the Allies had hoped for. Easily contained, the front line remained static and more troops were affected by malaria than fought the Central Powers. The direct railway link to Belgrade meant that it was an excellent location for the Allies to channel assistance to Serbia. In the end, five Allied divisions were sent to Salonika – four

French and one British – under the French commander General Maurice Sarrail. This map shows proposals for an offensive near Thasos by Serbian, Greek, and Romanian ministers. Salonika is at the bottom left of the map. It was called 'Germany's biggest internment camp' because the troops did little to help the Allied cause. WO 153/1011 (1) (2)

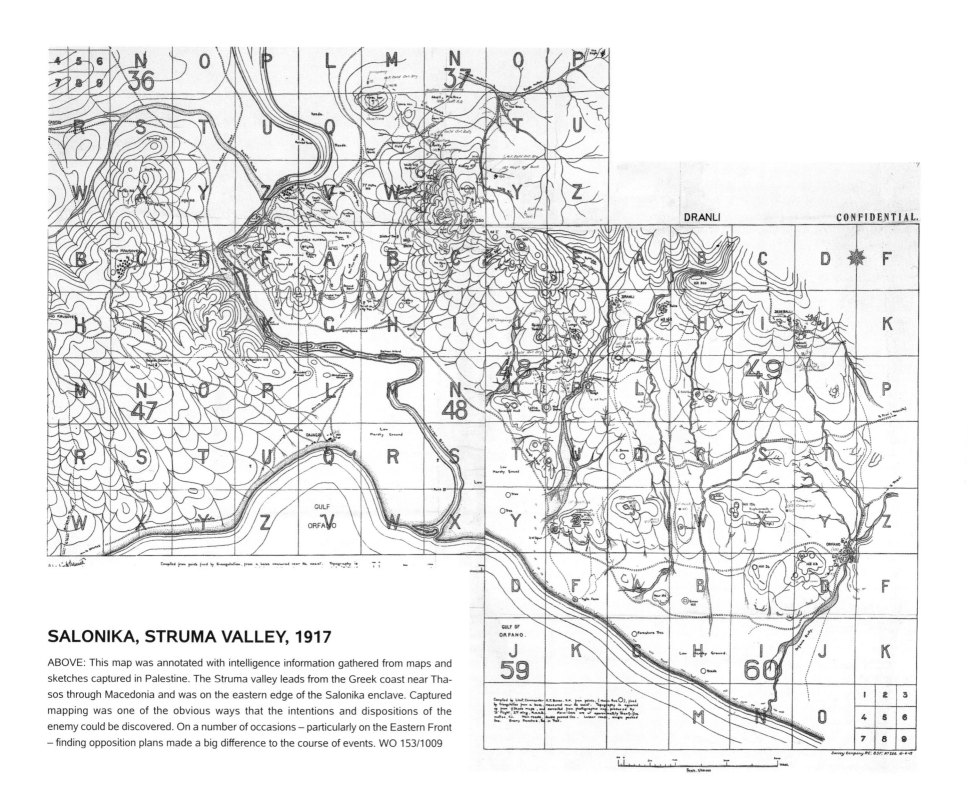

SALONIKA, STRUMA VALLEY, 1917

ABOVE: This map was annotated with intelligence information gathered from maps and sketches captured in Palestine. The Struma valley leads from the Greek coast near Thasos through Macedonia and was on the eastern edge of the Salonika enclave. Captured mapping was one of the obvious ways that the intentions and dispositions of the enemy could be discovered. On a number of occasions – particularly on the Eastern Front – finding opposition plans made a big difference to the course of events. WO 153/1009

RABEGH HARBOUR, 1917

RIGHT: The Arab Revolt was proclaimed on June 5, 1916, by Ali and Feisal Ibn Hussein, the sons of Sherif Hussein Ibn Ali, the senior religious figure and tribal leader of the central Arabian Red Sea coastal area that included the holy cities of Mecca and Medina. They quickly attracted 30,000 men and attacked the Turkish garrisons in the holy cities. Rabegh is a small port roughly half way between the holy cities and was taken by tribesmen from the Turkish garrison by late July that year. Rabegh was seen as the key to Mecca by the British, because the main road passed nearby and it provided the only sweet water for miles around. The port was surveyed by Lawrence to assess its strategic importance, and he stayed there for some time in 1917 to train the Arab tribesmen. Lawrence and Feisal proved an excellent combination, and the Arab Revolt gained strength from British assistance. However, despite Lawrence's best intentions, British and French political self-interest led the Paris Peace Conference to confer mandate status – in other words, colonial administrations – on the new Arab states of Syria, Transjordan, and Lebanon. The Turks would hold out in some areas until 1919 in defence of territory they held for so many years – see pages 142–43. WO 153/1048

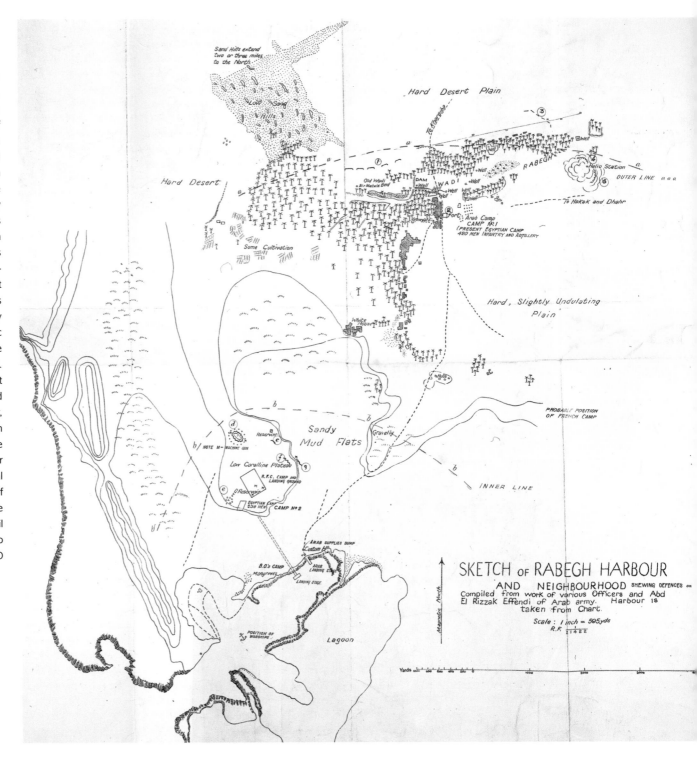

ITALY AND EASTERN EUROPE IN 1917

LEFT: This map of Italy, the Aegean, and Balkans shows another view of way that the Austro-Hungarian Empire was to be split up at war's end. It shows the areas that would be ceded to Greece, Italy, Romania, and Bulgaria, and the creation of Yugoslav and Czechoslavak states after the war. This may have seemed a sensible solution to the problems of nationalism and ethnicity, but as we know it did little more than put a lid on a problem that would continue to rumble on into the 21st century. It would not be until 1929 that the name of Yugoslavia was adopted, but even then there were territorial claims by Albania, Bulgaria, and Hungary to take the problem into the 1930s. The creation of the Czechoslovak state was more straightforward in that the United States and Great Britain recognized a Czech state in 1918, and the Slovak and Ruthene National Councils voted for unification in 1919. MPI 397 (10)

RAILROAD SYSTEMS IN BELGIUM, FRANCE, AND GERMANY, JANUARY 9, 1918

RIGHT: The railroads provided the easiest means of transporting men and munitions to the front. The German system in occupied territory – in spite of Allied air attacks – proved essential to its operations on the Western Front. This map shows a situation report on the railroads of Belgium, dated January 9, 1918, before the 'St Michael' offensive. The key identifies new railroads under construction and supply dumps. MPI 517 (4)

MAIN RAILROAD ROUTES ON THE WESTERN FRONT, 1918

FAR RIGHT: Another Allied map of railroads on the Western Front, this identifies the main routes from Germany and the lateral routes that enabled men and munitions to be taken to important points on the front. WO 153/1

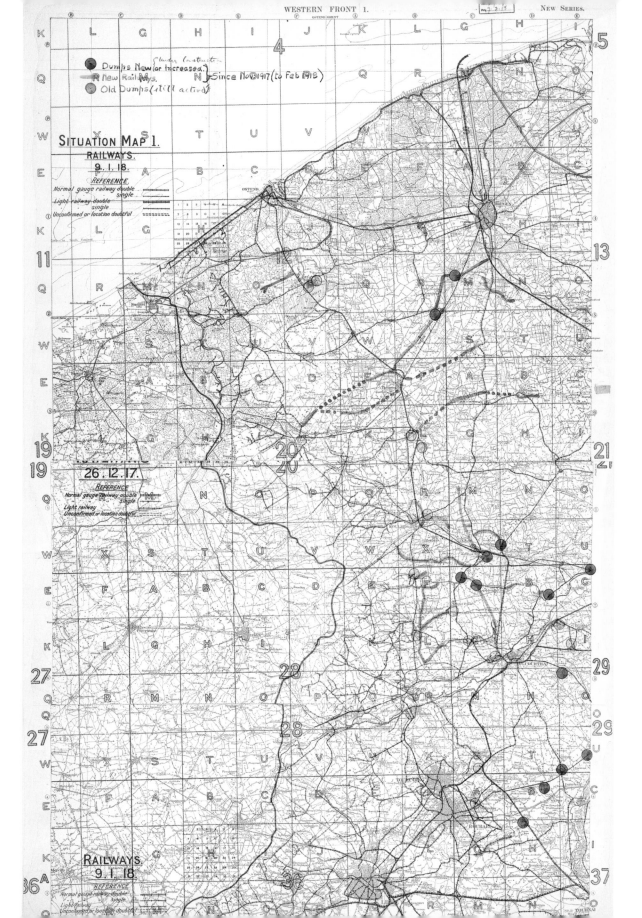

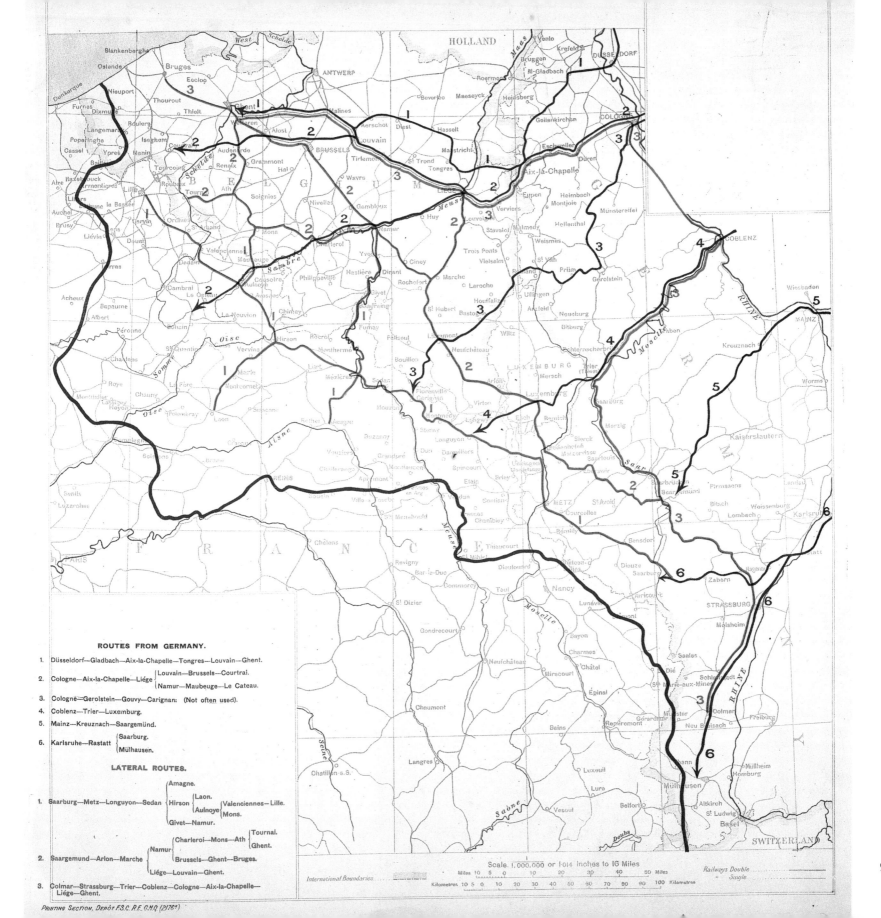

ROUTES FROM GERMANY.

1. Düsseldorf—Gladbach—Aix-la-Chapelle—Tongres—Louvain—Ghent.

2. Cologne—Aix-la-Chapelle—Liége { Louvain—Brussels—Courtrai. / Namur—Maubeuge—Le Cateau.

3. Cologne—Gerolstein—Gouvy—Carignan: (Not often used).

4. Coblenz—Trier—Luxemburg.

5. Mainz—Kreuznach—Saargemünd.

6. Karlsruhe—Rastatt { Saarburg. / Mülhausen.

LATERAL ROUTES.

1. Saarburg—Metz—Longuyon—Sedan { Amagne. / Hirson { Laon. / Aulnoye / Valenciennes—Lille. / Mons. / Givet—Namur.

2. Saargemund—Arlon—Marche { Namur { Charleroi—Mons—Ath { Tournai. / Ghent. / Brussels—Ghent—Bruges. / Liége—Louvain—Ghent.

3. Colmar—Strassburg—Trier—Coblenz—Cologne—Aix-la-Chapelle—Liége—Ghent.

PRINTING SECTION, DEPÔT F.S.C. R.E. G.H.Q. (2176*)

Scale. 1,000,000 or 1·014 Inches to 16 Miles

Miles 10 5 0   10   20   30   40   50 Miles

Kilometres 10 5 0   10   20   30   40   50   60   70   80   90   100 Kilometres

International Boundaries

Railways Double / Single

99

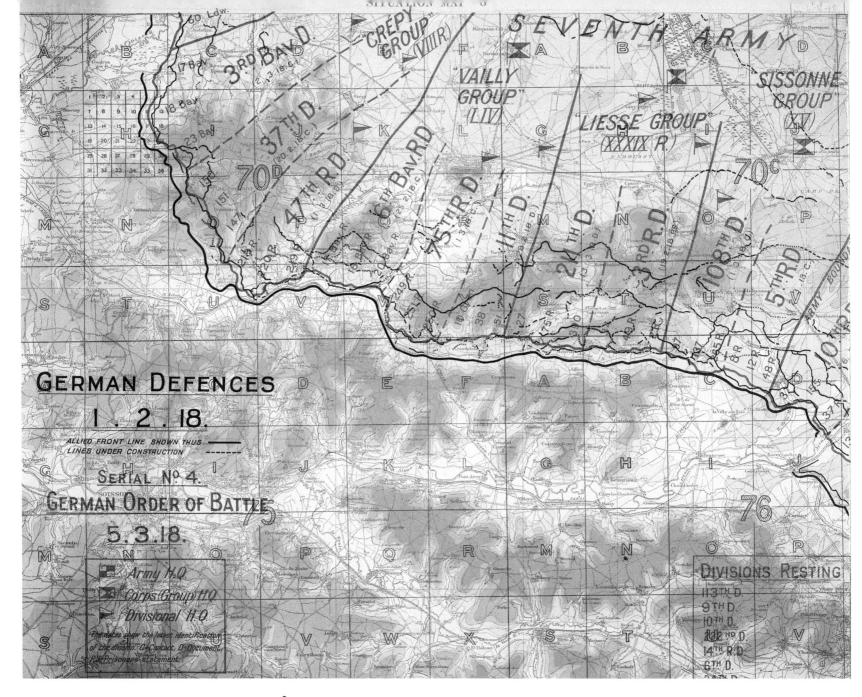

GERMAN DEFENSES ON THE LÂON FRONT, FEBRUARY 1918

ABOVE: This map shows German defenses in the Lâon area just before the start of the *Kaiserschlacht* —the great German offensive launched to end the war before American troops and resources could arrive to support the Allies. Between November 1917 and March 1918 the Germans moved huge numbers of men from the Eastern Fronts to northern France, increasing German strength on the Western Front by a massive 30 percent by the time the *Kaiserschlacht* began. Meanwhile, during much the same period, Allied manpower had dropped by 25 percent. The German Front stretched 56 miles from Arras to La Fère and contained a total of 63 divisions from Second and 18th Armies plus divisions from the 17th. Opposing them were only 14 divisions of the British Third Army, 12 divisions of the Fifth Army and the majority of the British reserves. WO 153/105

BOMBING RAIDS OVER GERMANY, 1918

Two photographs showing Allied strategic bombing of Germany, particularly against railroad targets. The aerial reconnaissance photograph (**right**) shows direct hits on railroad lines at Freiburg on March 13, 1918. The photograph of a burning munitions train (**above**) is at Thionville on July 16, following a bombing raid. Strategic bombing was a concept taken up by the British and United States' air forces and stood them in good stead in World War II. AIR 10/1214

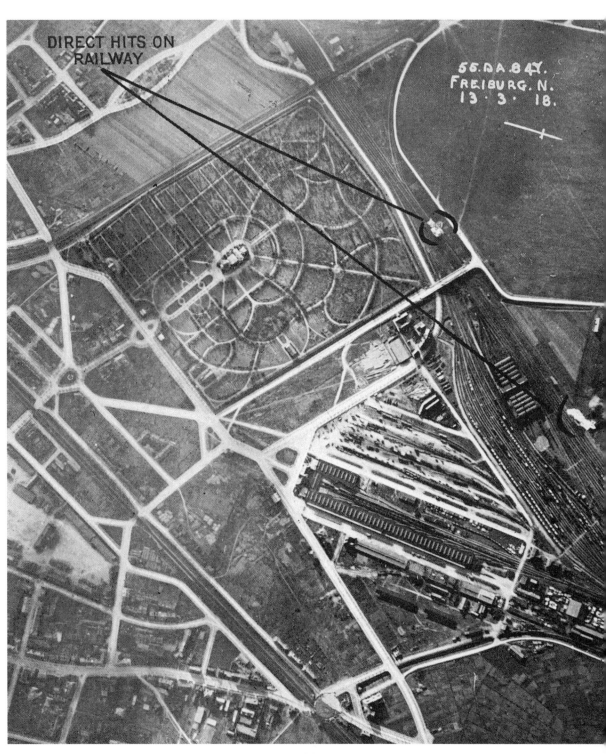

DIRECT HITS ON RAILWAY

55.DA.84Y. FREIBURG. N. 13·3·18.

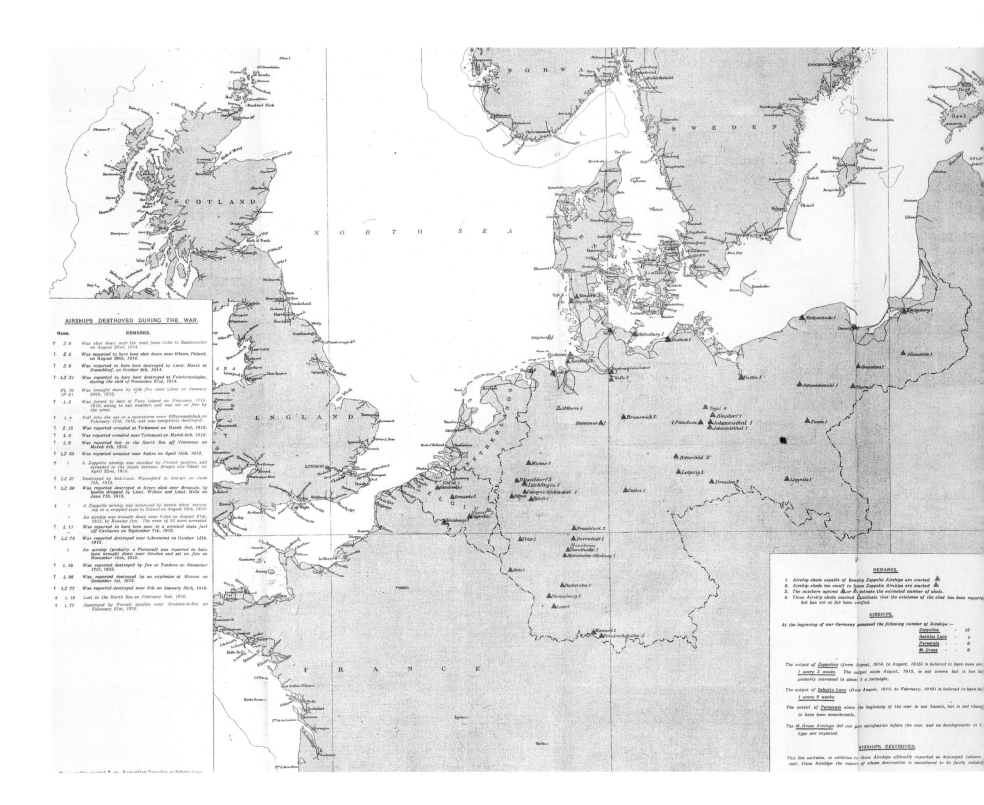

AIRSHIPS DESTROYED DURING THE WAR.

NAME.	REMARKS.
† Z 8	Was shot down over the road from Celle to Badenweiler on August 23rd, 1914.
† Z 5	Was reported to have been shot down near Mlawa, Poland, on August 29th, 1914.
† Z 6	Was reported to have been destroyed by Lieut. Marix at Dusseldorf, on October 8th, 1914.
† LZ 31	Was reported to have been destroyed at Friederieshafen, during the raid of November 21st, 1914.
PL 19 (P 5)	Was brought down by rifle fire near Libau on January 24th, 1915.
† L 3	Was forced to land at Fano Island on February 17th, 1915, owing to bad weather, and was set on fire by the crew.
† L 4	Fell into the sea in a snowstorm near Bilhavaandshuk on February 17th, 1915, and was completely destroyed.
† Z 18	Was reported wrecked at Tirlemont on March 3rd, 1915.
† L 8	Was reported wrecked near Tirlemont on March 5th, 1915.
† L 9	Was reported lost in the North Sea off Vimereux on March 5th, 1915.
† LZ 35	Was reported wrecked near Aeltre on April 13th, 1915.
† ?	A Zeppelin airship was disabled by French gunfire, and stranded in the woods between Bruges and Ghent on April 23rd, 1915.
† LZ 37	Destroyed by Sub-Lieut. Warneford in mid-air on June 7th, 1915.
† LZ 38	Was reported destroyed in Evere shed near Brussels, by bombs dropped by Lieut. Wilson and Lieut. Mills on June 7th, 1915.
† ?	A Zeppelin airship was destroyed by bombs when returning in a crippled state to Ostend on August 10th, 1915.
?	An airship was brought down near Vilna on August 21st, 1915, by Russian fire. The crew of 10 were arrested.
† L 11	Was reported to have been seen in a wrecked state just off Caxhaven on September 7th, 1915.
† LZ 74	Was reported destroyed near Libramont on October 15th, 1915.
?	An airship (probably a Parseval) was reported to have been brought down near Grodno and set on fire on November 15th, 1915.
† L 10	Was reported destroyed by fire at Tondern on November 17th, 1915.
† L 28	Was reported destroyed by an explosion at Husum on December 1st, 1915.
† LZ 77	Was reported destroyed near Ath on January 30th, 1916.
† L 19	Lost in the North Sea on February 2nd, 1916.
† L 77	Destroyed by French gunfire near Brabant-le-Roi on February 21st, 1916.

REMARKS.

1. Airship sheds capable of housing Zeppelin Airships are marked ▲
2. Airship sheds too small to house Zeppelin Airships are marked ▲
3. The numbers against ▲ or ▲ indicate the estimated number of sheds.
4. These Airship sheds marked △ indicate that the existence of the shed has been reported but has not as far been verified.

AIRSHIPS.

At the beginning of war Germany possessed the following number of Airships :—

Zeppelins	12
Schütte Lanz	1
Parsevals	6
M. Gross	2

The output of Zeppelins (from August, 1914, to August, 1915) is believed to have been abo[ut] 1 every 3 weeks. The output since August, 1915, is not known but it has be[en] probably increased to about 1 a fortnight.

The output of Schütte Lanz (from August, 1914, to February, 1916) is believed to have be[en] 1 every 9 weeks.

The output of Parsevals since the beginning of the war is not known, but is not thoug[ht] to have been considerable.

The M. Gross Airships did not give satisfaction before the war, and no developments in th[is] type are expected.

AIRSHIPS DESTROYED.

This list contains, in addition to those Airships officially reported as destroyed (shown [in] red), those Airships the report of whose destruction is considered to be fairly reliab[le]

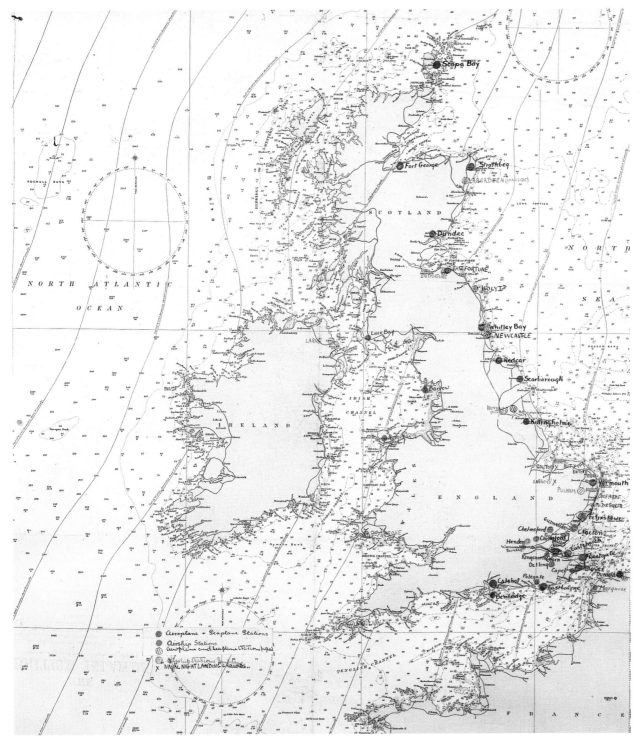

AIRSHIPS AND AIR STATIONS, 1918

LEFT: This map shows airplane and seaplane stations as a blue dot, airship stations as a red dot, proposed airplane and seaplane station as a blue-hatched dot, and airship stations under construction as a red-hatched dot. The blue crosses are naval night landing grounds and the red dots with yellow circle are lights (lighthouses/lightships). The base map is dated 1915 but the annotations are later.

Aerial power was the great new area of discovery in the early years of the 20th century and the ability to dominate airspace, partic-ularly over a battlefield, was quickly perceived as crucial. Early airplanes were still very vulnerable to anti-aircraft fire but airships could fly above the gunfire, and until 1917 could soar to a higher altitude than an airplane could reach. Airships were pioneered in France but the Germans developed them for military purposes with the most famous designer being Count Graf Zeppelin. They were mostly useful for reconnaissance purposes but were also used to drop bombs—albeit indiscriminately from a great height.

The map (**far left**) shows the airship sheds capable of housing Zeppelins, and those reported to be able to house Zeppelins. (In this case airships and Zeppelins are synonymous.) The list at the left of the map shows the airships lost up to February 21, 1916.

Britain, however, did not put as much faith in airships as Germany, although they were used successfully as convoy escorts. Seaplanes, too, proved disappointing because they could only operate in calm conditions, and it wasn't long before it became obvious that the aircraft carrier – basically as we know it today – and ship-borne aircraft were the answer. Pioneering work by the RNAS would see the first flush-deck carrier, *Argus*, in trials, and over 50 wheeled aircraft carried by the Grand Fleet by war's end. **Left:** MR 1/1918 (3), **Far Left:** MR 1/1918 (4)

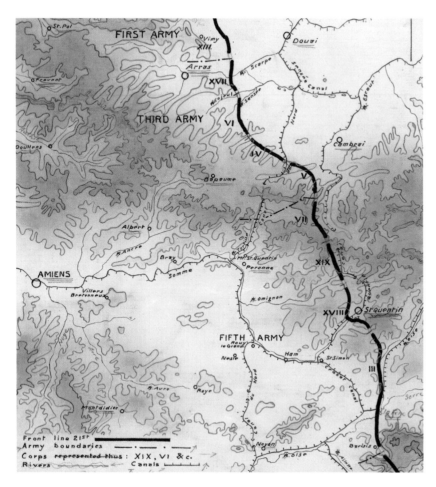

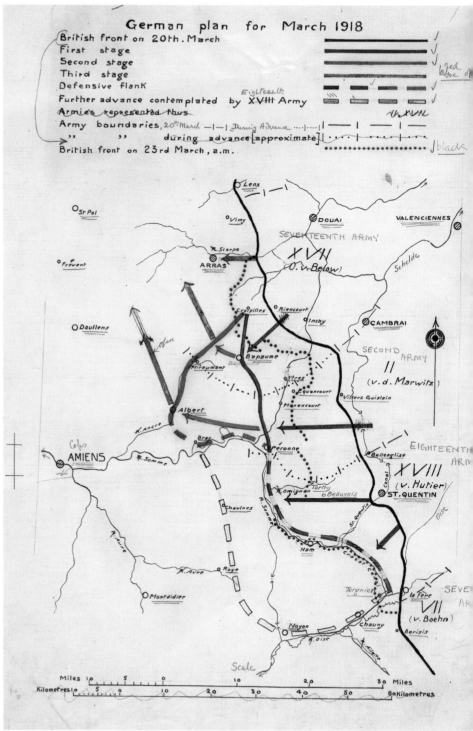

THE GERMAN ADVANCE IN 1918

In spring 1918 the Germans planned to end the war with an offensive before the full weight of the overwhelming numbers and resources of the American forces could play a decisive part. Ludendorff saw immediate defeat of the British and French as Germany's only hope of victory. Using resources freed up from the reduction of hostilities in the east, Ludendorff planned a massive offensive, better known as the 'Kaiser's battle' or *Kaiserschlacht*. These three maps show the code names and planned directions of attack (**far right**), the terrain of the northern battle area (**above**), and the attack stages planned over this area (**right**). The initial assault was to be at the weak junction point between the British and French armies where misunderstandings could occur, then the second phase was to be a frontal attack from Ypres to Champagne. The assault began on March 21 with 65 divisions belonging to the Army Groups of Crown Prince Wilhelm and Rupprecht of Bavaria hitting a 60-mile front between Arras and La Fère. The British Fifth Army quickly collapsed under the assault, but the Third Army, with French reinforcements, just managed to hold out. WO 153/1298 (5/6/7)

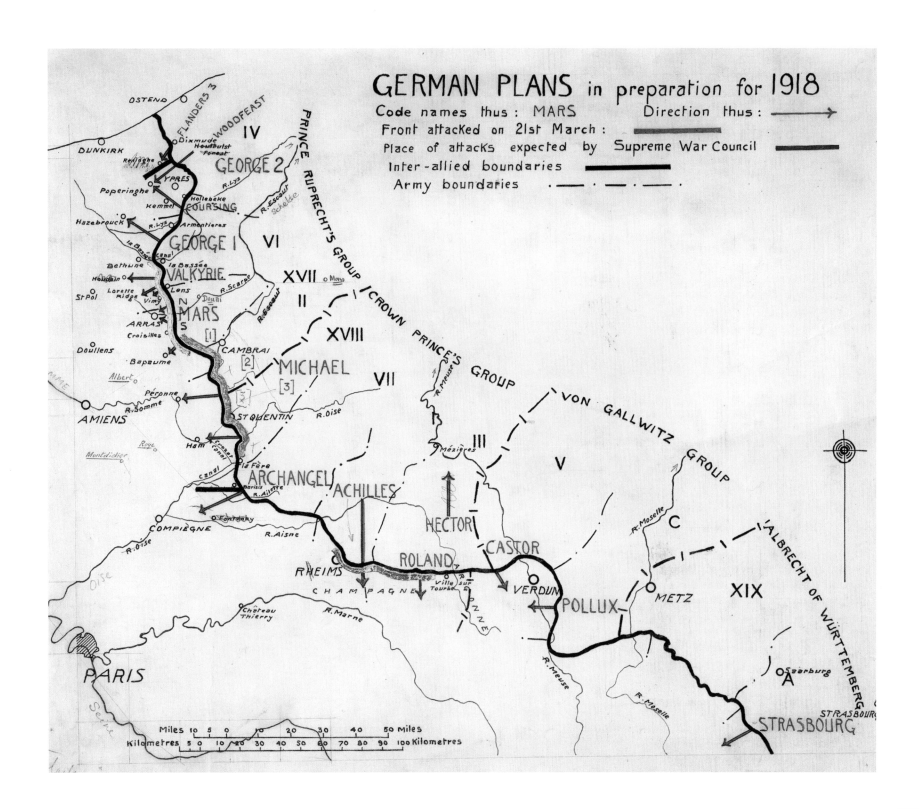

GERMAN PLANS in preparation for 1918

Code names thus: MARS   Direction thus: →

Front attacked on 21st March: ▬▬▬▬

Place of attacks expected by Supreme War Council ▬▬▬▬

Inter-allied boundaries ▬▬▬▬

Army boundaries ·—·—·—·—·

OSTEND
FLANDERS 3
WOODFEAST
DUNKIRK
Dixmude
Houthurst Forest
IV
GEORGE 2
Redinghe
YPRES
R.Lys
R.Escaut Schelde
Poperinghe
Hollebeke
Kemmel
COURSING
VI
Hazebrouck
R.Lys
Armentières
GEORGE I
la Bassée Canal
Bethune
la Bassée
VALKYRIE
XVII
o Mons
Houdain
Lens
R.Scarpe
St.Pol
Lorette Ridge
Vimy
Douai
II
N
MARS
S
[1]
ARRAS
Croisilles
CAMBRAI
XVIII
Doullens
Bapaume
[2]
Albert
MICHAEL
[3]
VII
CROWN PRINCE'S GROUP
Péronne
R.Somme
[3]
St.QUENTIN
R.Oise
AMIENS
R.Meuse
Roye
Montdidier
Ham
Crozat Canal
III
Mézières
Canal
la Fère
Barisis
ARCHANGEL
R.Ailette
VON GALLWITZ GROUP
V
COMPIÈGNE
Fontenoy
ACHILLES
R.Oise
R.Aisne
HECTOR
R.Moselle
C
CASTOR
RHEIMS
ROLAND
VERDUN
METZ
POLLUX
XIX
Château Thierry
CHAMPAGNE
Ville sur Tourbe
R.Marne
R.Meuse
PRINCE RUPRECHT'S GROUP
PARIS
Oise
R.Meuse
Saarburg
A
R.Moselle
Seine
STRASBOURG
STRASBOURG

Miles 10 5 0   10   20   30   40   50 Miles
Kilometres 5 0 10 20 30 40 50 60 70 80 90 100 Kilometres

MIDDLE EAST, 1918

Two rough sketch maps by Lt Col T E Lawrence (better known as 'Lawrence of Arabia') of the Hedjaz Railway and the terrain between Kasrel Azrak. Below is a transcript of the notes that went with the illustrations. WO 158/640B

Secret

Notes on Kasr el Azrak and the country lying between that place and the Hejaz Railway

The country between the Hejaz Railway and Azrak is practically featureless. It consists of quite barren desert, in which the valleys first run SW but after about 20 miles E of the Railway, NE, among rounded hills of limestone and brown flint. Some of the higher hills have rude cairns on the top, but none rise more than 200ft above the surrounding country, and a few of them will be distinguishable from the air. It would be possible to land in most of this area, but very difficult to get off again.

Near Azrak the country flattens out. About Kharaneh, about Amrut, and about Kasrel Weinid, the valleys are sometimes several miles in breadth, with low banks, and scrub-filled bottoms, through which the winter floods have cut treacherous little channels a yard or two wide, and perhaps two feet deep. Whenever possible a forced landing should be made on a patch of bare mud, or on the back of a flint slope, in preference to a wadi. Kharaneh, Amruh and Weinid are large ruined hunting-palaces of the Ghassanide kings.

Lava fields, usually raised 20ft above the ordinary level of the country, and appearing in color either grey or blue or black according to the weather conditions, lie to the north of Amruh and flank the west bank of the great group of valleys that come up from the south – the Ghadaf – into Azrak. Lava fields resemble shingle beaches, with the pebbles made angular, and enlarged to a foot or two in length. Landing in lava fields is impossible. Their tops, however, frequently contain bright yellow mud flats, where the driven sand and dust have settled and been watered out by floods into areasas flat as tennis courts, and harder. If large enough these make ideal landing grounds, (and if possible one of these lying SW of Azrak will be chosen as such when required).

Azrak itself is fairly obvious when reached, for it is marked by a lagoon of fresh water, which, according to season, is an open stretch a mile long fringed with green lawns, or a dense

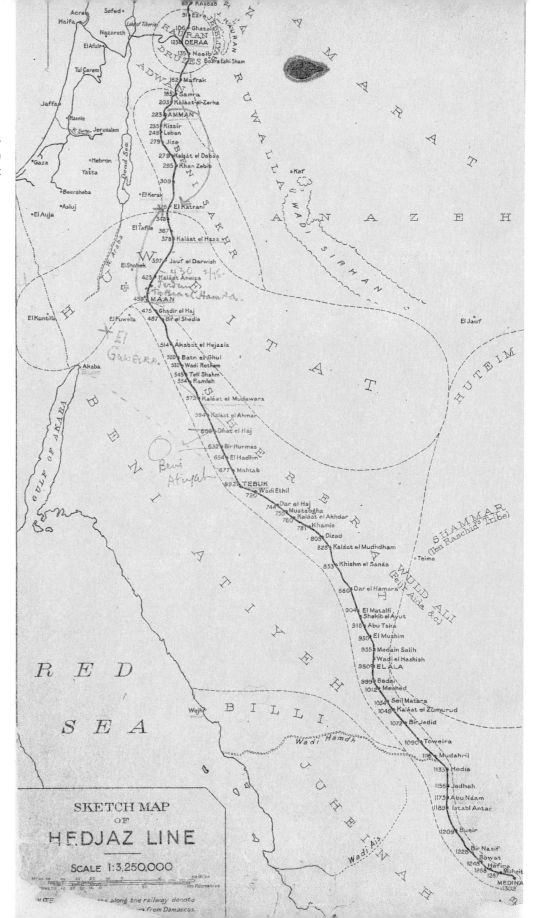

SKETCH MAP
OF
HEDJAZ LINE

SCALE 1:3,250,000

brake of bullrushes and water-cranes. From its brilliant greenness it will stand out for many miles and should make Azrak unmistakable. The place itself is a grove of 60 palm trees, with the square courtyard and corner towers of a fort that began as Roman, was adapted by the Ghassanide kings as a desert outpost, restored by the first Mohammedans and garrisoned by successive Sultans of Damascus as a protection against the Bedouin. It lies a stone's throw from the lake, is built of black basalt, and is about 100 yards square. Behind it, to West and North, is a belt of jagged lava, from a mile to two miles wide, and North of that, rolling flint plains to the outlying spurs of Jebel Druse 12 miles away. To the NE the lava bed is narrower, and beyond it lie the waste of sand-heaps, grown with Tamarisk, that the Arabs call Wadi Sirhan.

Azrak has no other house, and only one permanent inhabitant, but, owing to its unceasing water supply, it is much frequented by Bedouin, who usually camp to the South towards El Weinid, between the lava fields and the branches of the Ghadaf.

In the attached sketch map, the immediate neighborhood of the Kasr – the fort – is shown not inaccurately. The complex of valleys between Amruh and Azrak is not attempted, nor are the areas or extent of the lava fields correctly shown.

(Sgd) *T E Lawrence*
Lieut-Colonel

Lawrence has become a legendary figure since his death near Wareham in 1935. His writings, particularly his autobiographical history of the Arab Campaign, *Seven Pillars of Wisdom*, account for some of this. There is no doubt that he was a charismatic leader who did much to promote Arab nationalism, liaising effectively with the Arab military leader Feisal Ibn Hussein.

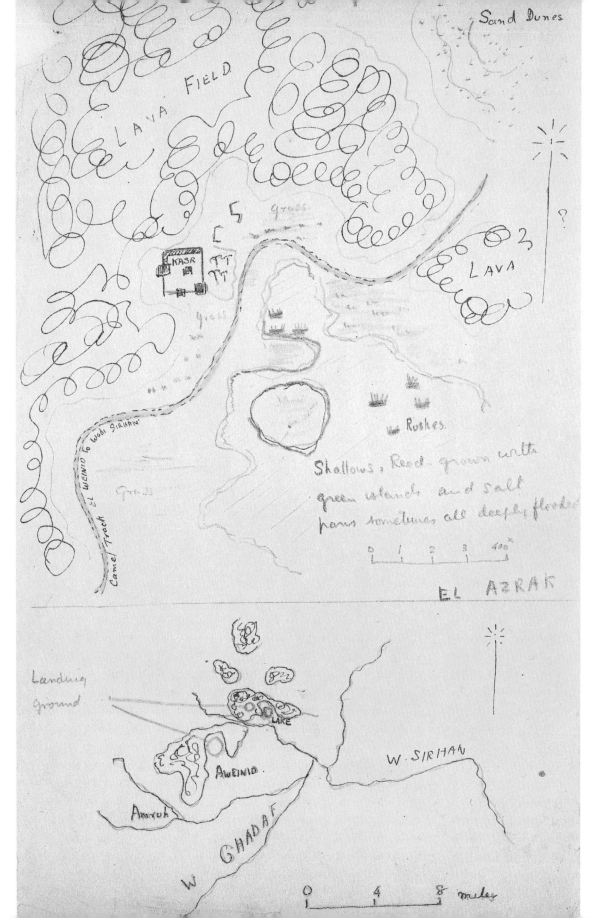

BATTLE OF THE AISNE, APRIL 11, 1918

RIGHT: The Third Battle of the Aisne was the final phase of the spring offensive by the German Army to win the war on the Western Front before the United States forces could arrive in strength. Ludendorff, the German commander, launched this third phase of the offensive with its first objective the Chemin des Dames Ridge held by the French Sixth Army. The Germans prevailed, but at heavy cost. Artillery bombarded the trenches before gas attacks, and eventually 17 divisions of the Southern Army Group advanced through a 25-mile gap in Allied lines. French troops were forced to retreat beyond the Aisne so rapidly that they had no time to destroy the bridges behind them. By day's end the Germans had advanced nine miles and within 21 days were only 56 miles from Paris – having captured 800 guns and some 50,000 prisoners. However, by June 6, with victory virtually in sight, the German offensive ground to a halt. German troops were exhausted by the rapid fighting and the advance had stretched their supply lines to breaking point. In the process of the battle the French Army lost 98,000 men, the BEF 29,000. WO 153/720

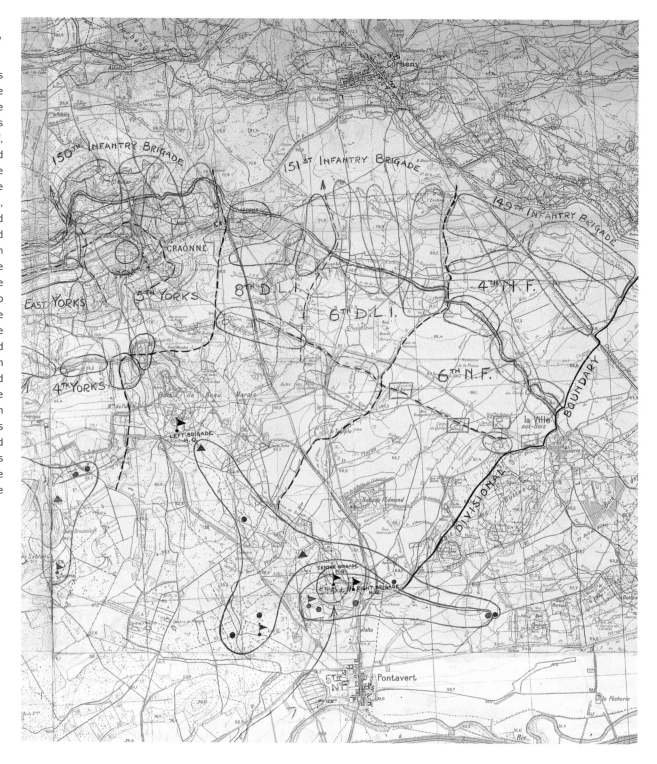

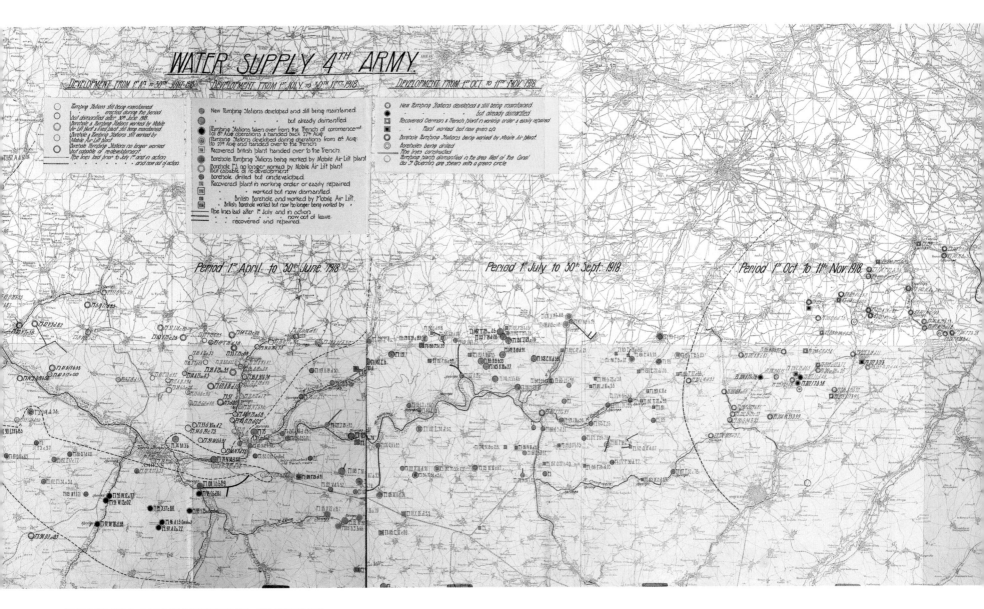

FOURTH ARMY WATER SUPPLY, APRIL 1–NOVEMBER 11, 1918

ABOVE: An area of logistics rarely discussed are the essential supply lines of food and water, without which any army will struggle. This map shows British Fourth Army water supply positions during 1918 centered on Amiens and the courses of the rivers Somme and Ancre. Some of the positions are existing pumping stations in various states of repair. The key gives a highly detailed explanation of the type of water supply – bore holes, pipeline, airlift plant, and mobile units – which ones worked, which had been dismantled or destroyed, and which could be reinstated. These are presented in three keys for three different periods: April 1–June 30, 1918; July 1–September 30, 1918; and October 1–November 11, 1918. WO 153/580

NOT TO BE REPRODUCED.

German Order of Battle
Western Front
1. 5. 18.

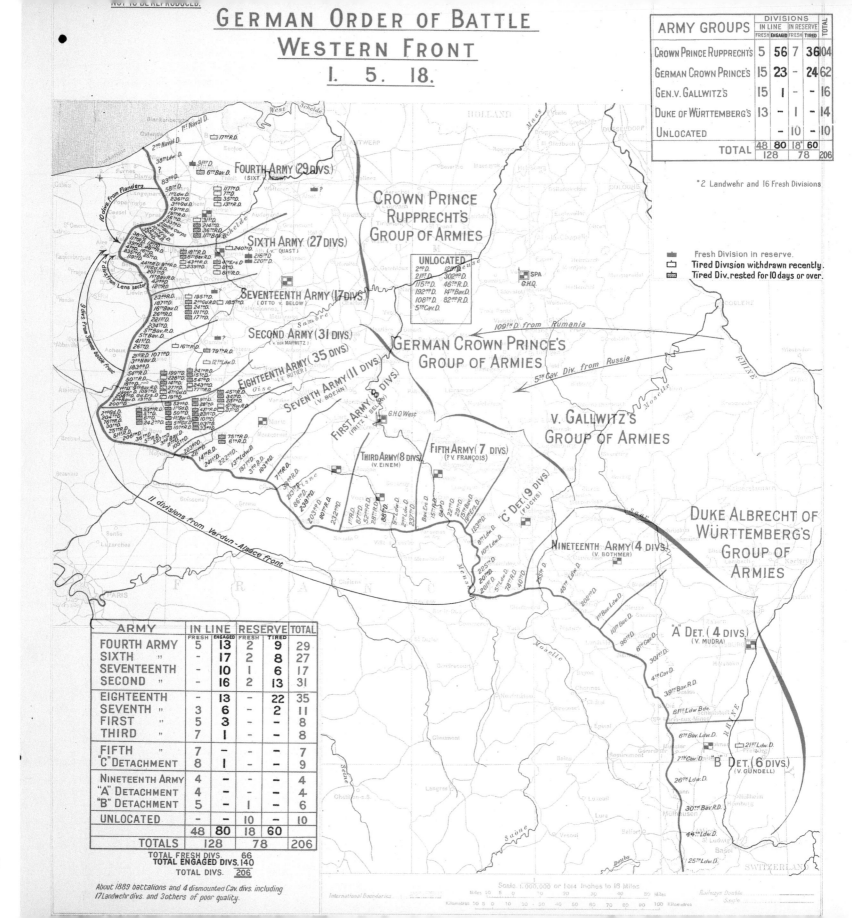

ARMY GROUPS	IN LINE		IN RESERVE		TOTAL
	FRESH	ENGAGED	FRESH	TIRED	
Crown Prince Rupprecht's	5	56	7	36	104
German Crown Prince's	15	23	–	24	62
Gen. v. Gallwitz's	15	1	–	–	16
Duke of Württemberg's	13	–	1	–	14
Unlocated	–	–	10	–	10
TOTAL	48	80	18*	60	206
	128		78		

*2 Landwehr and 16 Fresh Divisions

Fresh Division in reserve.
Tired Division withdrawn recently.
Tired Div. rested for 10 days or over.

UNLOCATED
2ⁿᵈ D.   121ᵗʰ D.
21ˢᵗ D.   302ⁿᵈ D.
115ᵗʰ R.D.   46ᵗʰ R.D.
192ⁿᵈ D.   14ᵗʰ Bav. D.
108ᵗʰ D.   82ⁿᵈ R.D.
5ᵗʰ Cav. D.

CROWN PRINCE RUPPRECHT'S GROUP OF ARMIES

GERMAN CROWN PRINCE'S GROUP OF ARMIES

v. GALLWITZ'S GROUP OF ARMIES

DUKE ALBRECHT OF WÜRTTEMBERG'S GROUP OF ARMIES

FOURTH ARMY (29 DIVS.) (SIXT. v. ARNIM)
SIXTH ARMY (27 DIVS.) (v. QUAST)
SEVENTEENTH ARMY (17 DIVS.) (OTTO v. BELOW)
SECOND ARMY (31 DIVS.) (v. der MARWITZ)
EIGHTEENTH ARMY (35 DIVS.) (v. HUTIER)
SEVENTH ARMY (11 DIVS.) (v. BOEHN)
FIRST ARMY (8 DIVS.) (FRITZ v. BELOW)
THIRD ARMY (8 DIVS.) (v. EINEM)
FIFTH ARMY (7 DIVS.) (v. FRANÇOIS)
"C" DET. (9 DIVS.) (FUCHS)
NINETEENTH ARMY (4 DIVS.) (v. BOTHMER)
"A" DET. (4 DIVS.) (v. MUDRA)
"B" DET. (6 DIVS.) (v. GÜNDELL)

109ᵗʰ D. from Rumania
5ᵗʰ Cav. Div. from Russia
10 divs. from Flanders
7 divs. from Lens sector
9 divs. from Somme battle Front.
11 divisions from Verdun - Alsace front.

G.H.Q West
SPA G.H.Q.

ARMY	IN LINE		RESERVE		TOTAL
	FRESH	ENGAGED	FRESH	TIRED	
FOURTH ARMY	5	13	2	9	29
SIXTH "	–	17	2	8	27
SEVENTEENTH "	–	10	1	6	17
SECOND "	–	16	2	13	31
EIGHTEENTH	–	13	–	22	35
SEVENTH "	3	6	–	2	11
FIRST "	5	3	–	–	8
THIRD "	7	1	–	–	8
FIFTH "	7	–	–	–	7
"C" DETACHMENT	8	1	–	–	9
NINETEENTH ARMY	4	–	–	–	4
"A" DETACHMENT	4	–	–	–	4
"B" DETACHMENT	5	–	1	–	6
UNLOCATED	–	–	10	–	10
	48	80	18	60	206
TOTALS	128		78		206

TOTAL FRESH DIVS. 66
TOTAL ENGAGED DIVS. 140
TOTAL DIVS. 206

About 1889 battalions and 4 dismounted Cav. divs. including 17 Landwehr divs. and 3 others of poor quality.

Scale 1,000,000 or 1·014 Inches to 16 Miles

International Boundaries
Railways Double
Single

HOLLAND

FRANCE

SWITZERLAND

GERMAN ORDER OF BATTLE, 1918

LEFT: This map shows how the German troops were disposed during the middle phase of the *Kaiserschlacht* on May 1, 1918.

Ludendorff's second thrust 'Georgette' had started on April 9, but against stiff fighting only managed to advance 10 miles before the assault was suspended. The third thrusts, 'Blücher' and 'Yorck,' started on May 27, against the French Sixth Army positioned along the Aisne. The French position quickly collapsed and by May 30, Ludendorff had reached the Marne at which point this map explains the German troop dispositions. WO 153/16

BRITISH RESERVES AS AT MAY 24, 1918

RIGHT: On the Western Front in March 1918 the British mustered 14 divisions between the Third Army under General Sir Julian Byng and the Fifth Army under General Gough, plus all available British reserves. In desperate fighting during the second phase of the *Kaiserschlacht*, the British lost almost 100,000 men around Arras. However, despite the greatest German endeavors, by late May they had failed to break the Allied lines and had lost 250,000 men in the process. This map shows British reserves before the renewed German attacks on May 27. MPH 898 (1)

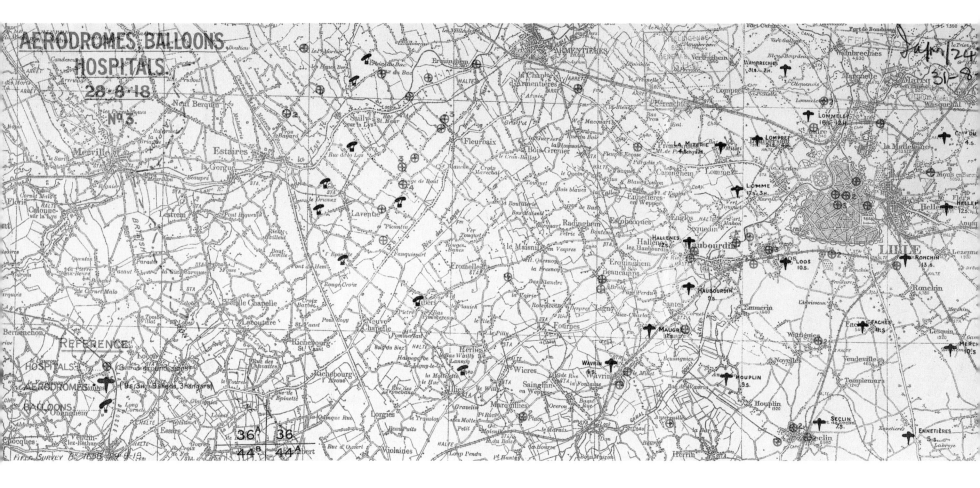

FIFTH ARMY: ENEMY AERODROMES, BALLOONS, AND HOSPITALS, AUGUST 28, 1918

ABOVE: This map shows an area of the Western Front with Armentières to the north and Lille to the east. From Fifth Army intelligence gathering it plots the positions of German army hospitals and aerodromes where balloons and aircraft were based. Balloons were commonly used as observation points for calling in artillery fire along the static battlefronts throughout the war. A ground crew of two or three men would winch the hot air or gas-filled balloon into position to crossreference enemy positions. These they would convey to the ground by means of flag signals or radio transmission; the British crew were the only flying personnel permitted to wear a parachute (it was considered too easy to bail out of combat for aircraft flying crew). The vulnerable ground crew would often be protected by anti-aircraft guns, but the balloons themselves were surprisingly difficult to destroy as bullets simply passed straight through the fabric. Repeated gunfire was needed to ground a balloon with the continual danger of the aircraft getting caught up in the anchor wire. By 1917 incendiary and explosive bullets were accounting for most balloon 'kills.' WO 153/615

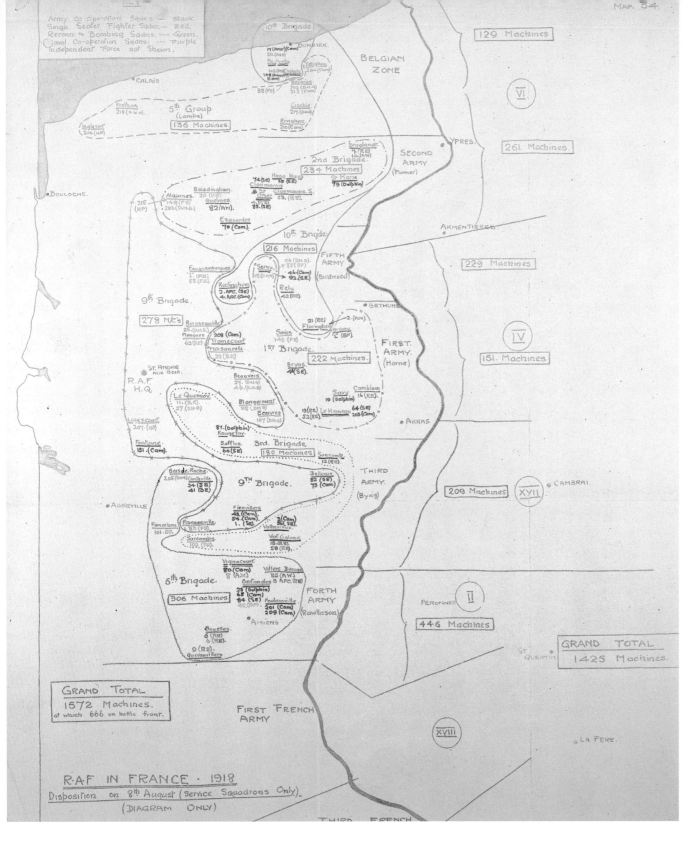

RFC IN FRANCE, AUGUST 8, 1918

LEFT: A diagram showing the number of Royal Flying Corps machines in northern France and Belgium towards the end of the war. It enumerates the numbers of aircraft based in each brigade and gives a grand total of 1,425 machines. Throughout World War I the Royal Flying Corps was the air arm of the British Army. Its brief on the Western Front was mostly reconnaissance of enemy positions, patrols, forward movement, and light bombing missions. For most of the war pilots operated obsolete and inferior machines, so much so that heavy losses prompted a national scandal. As war progressed the importance of air superiority became increasingly clear and as aero technology improved, aircraft were used for ground support and command-liaison operations. By January 1918 the RFC had expanded enormously to operate almost 4,000 combat aircraft (most of them on the Western Front) with 114,000 personnel. By then the RFC was flying technologically superior aircraft – Sopwith Camels, Bristol Fighters, SE5s, Handley Page bombers, Airco DH4s, and Sopwith Triplanes. MPI 647 pt 2 (19)

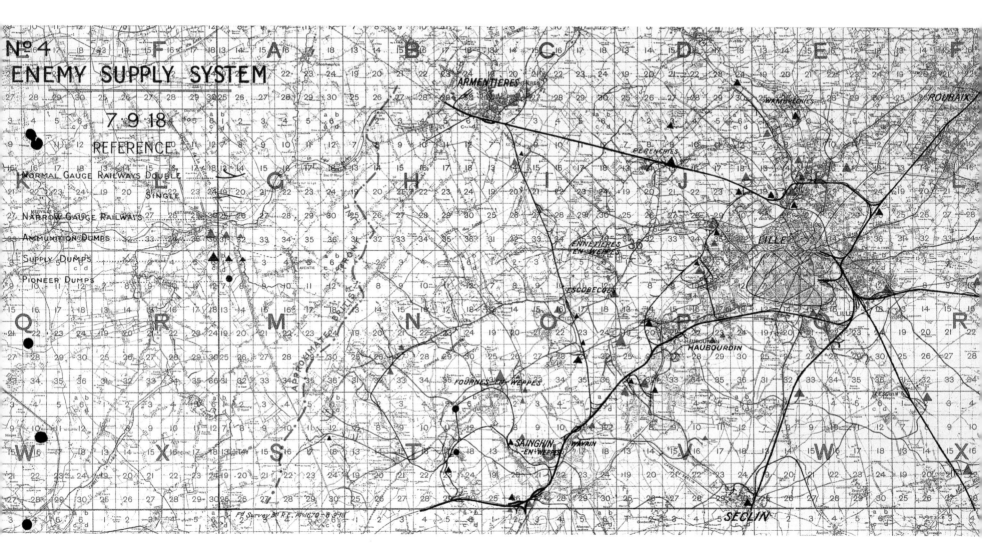

GERMAN SUPPLY SYSTEM AROUND LILLE, SEPTEMBER 7, 1918

ABOVE: This Fifth Army document shows the same area as the map on page 112, but this time depicts enemy railroad lines – both normal and narrow gauge – ammunition dumps, supply dumps, and Pioneer dumps. WO 153/615 (2)

GERMAN COMMUNICATIONS SYSTEM, 1918

RIGHT: A German schematic plan of *Armee Fernsprech Abteilung 2* (Army Telephone Battalion 2) showing their communication network across the Western Front from Douai and Valenciennes in the north, to Mons and Bray in the south. Most communication along the Western Front was via telephone. The cables were very vulnerable to bomb damage and so were buried as securely as possible, in some cases many feet deep. Dedicated signals unit personnel constantly risked their lives to repair the lines. The cables transmitted voice or Morse code in the form of a buzzer. When troops were moving they often carried portable handsets and cables. WO 153/1081 (2)

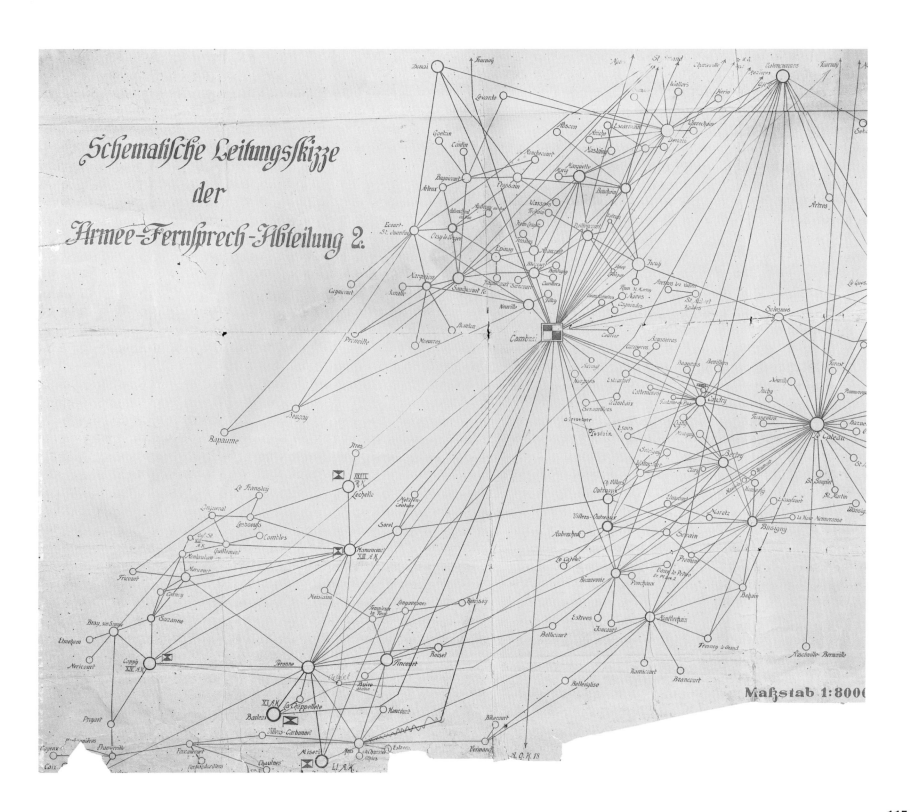

Schematische Leitungsskizze
der
Armee-Fernsprech-Abteilung 2.

Maßstab 1:8000

BATTLE OF ST MIHIEL, SEPTEMBER 12–14, 1918

RIGHT: This battle was the first major engagement for American troops on the Western Front. German troops held the St Mihiel salient (south of Verdun) and this was chosen as the target by US tacticians in mid-1917. By the time US troops arrived in sufficient numbers almost a year later the importance of the salient had declined but General Pershing wanted the position. On August 30 the US First Army, with some French colonial support, occupied a 40-mile front around St Mihiel. By September 16, the salient had been won. WO 153/23

USE OF TANKS, AUGUST 8– NOVEMBER 8, 1918

FAR RIGHT: Use of tanks by British First, Third, and Fourth Armies between August 8, and November 8, 1918. As the key explains, the blue lines indicate front lines and the red washes show the areas in which the tanks operated, with the numbers of tanks and date. The red lines indicate the gains made by the tank operations. The tank was still in a very early stage of development and was used primarily as an offensive weapon – albeit more prone to mechanical breakdown than enemy destruction. The Amiens Offensive was the Anglo-French counter offensive in fall 1918. The action was supported by 342 Mark V heavy tanks and 72 Whippet medium tanks which enabled the breakthrough; however, by August 12 there were only six working tanks left. WO 153/24

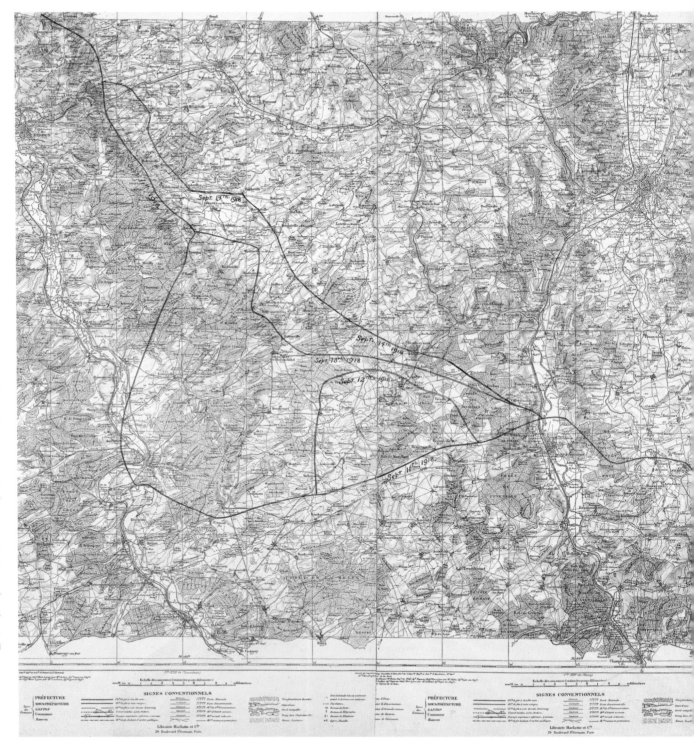

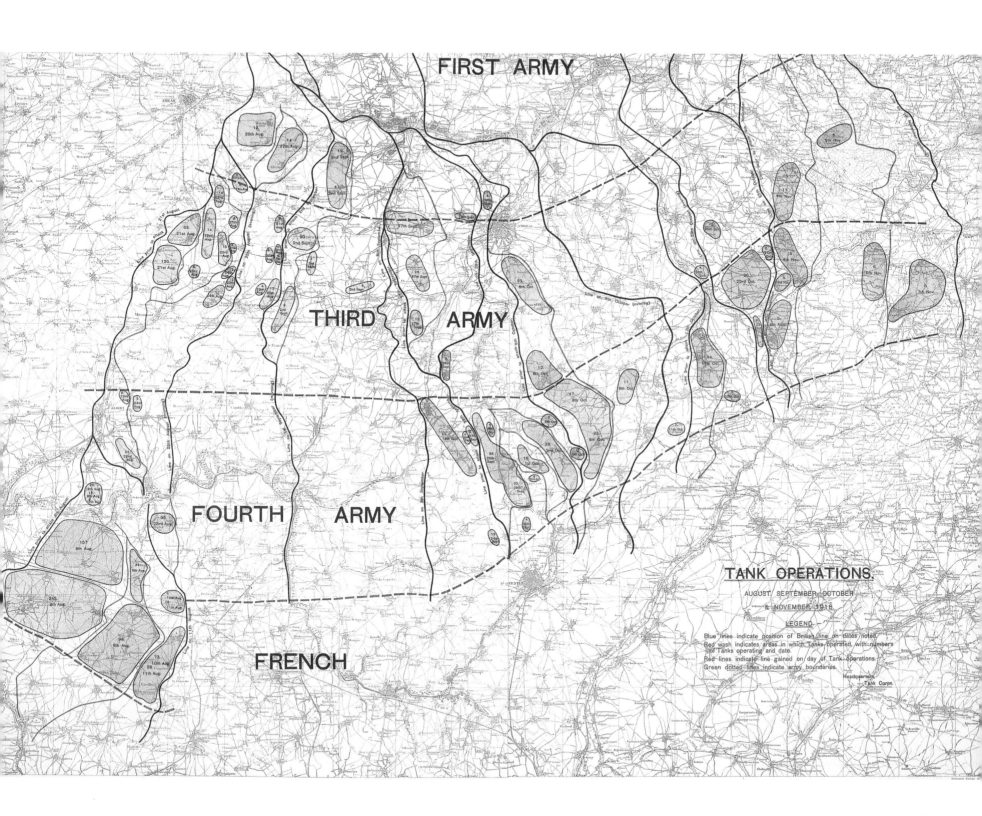

FIRST ARMY

THIRD ARMY

FOURTH ARMY

FRENCH

TANK OPERATIONS.

AUGUST, SEPTEMBER, OCTOBER
& NOVEMBER, 1918

LEGEND.

Blue lines indicate position of British line on dates noted.
Red wash indicates areas in which Tanks operated, with numbers of Tanks operating and date.
Red lines indicate line gained on day of Tank operations.
Green dotted lines indicate army boundaries.

Headquarters,
Tank Corps.

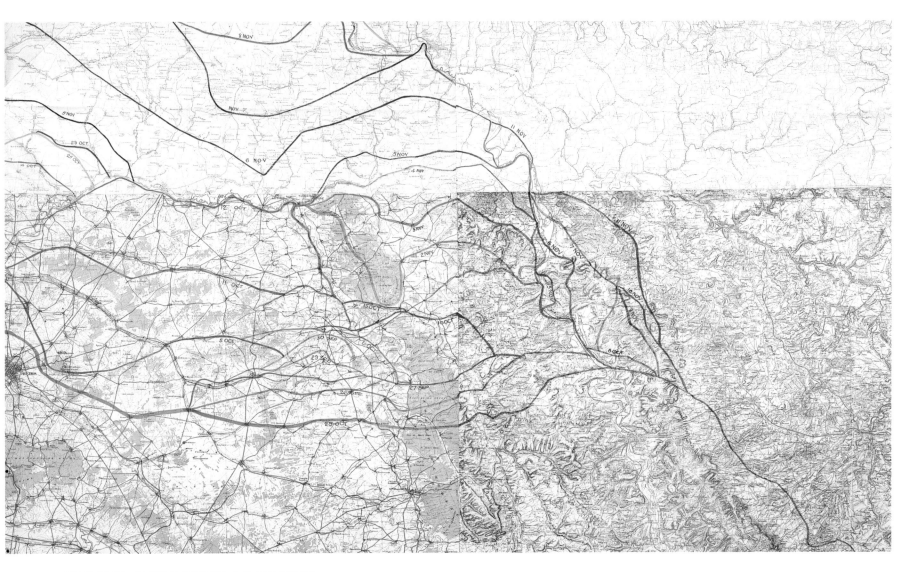

MEUSE-OFFENSIVE ARGONNE, SEPTEMBER–NOVEMBER 1918

LEFT AND ABOVE: The Meuse-Argonne Offensive was a joint AEF-French Army advance on the Western Front in fall 1918. The action started in September east of Verdun at Argonne Forest and drove northward up the west bank of the Meuse to reach Belgium by November. General Pershing insisted on carrying out the attack on the St Mihiel salient before the offensive started, consequently 400,000 troops had to be moved from there to Argonne before the fighting could start on schedule on September 26. The brunt of the assault was taken by fresh American troops belonging to the US First Army, whose 5,000 guns and 500 aircraft were supported by 300 French tanks. Their progress was slowed by weary French and inexperienced American troops and hindered by minefields and well-entrenched German soldiers. After the first day's fighting less than two miles of ground had been made along a 40-mile front. The battlefronts quickly became congested, and confused, and the assault logjammed on September 30 by which time it had made about 10 miles. The offensive resumed on October 4, but the problems remained the same. US troops eventually made ground to Sedan by November 9, and were there when the Armistice was declared. These images show the lines of advance by US troops during the period. WO 153/866 WO 153/22

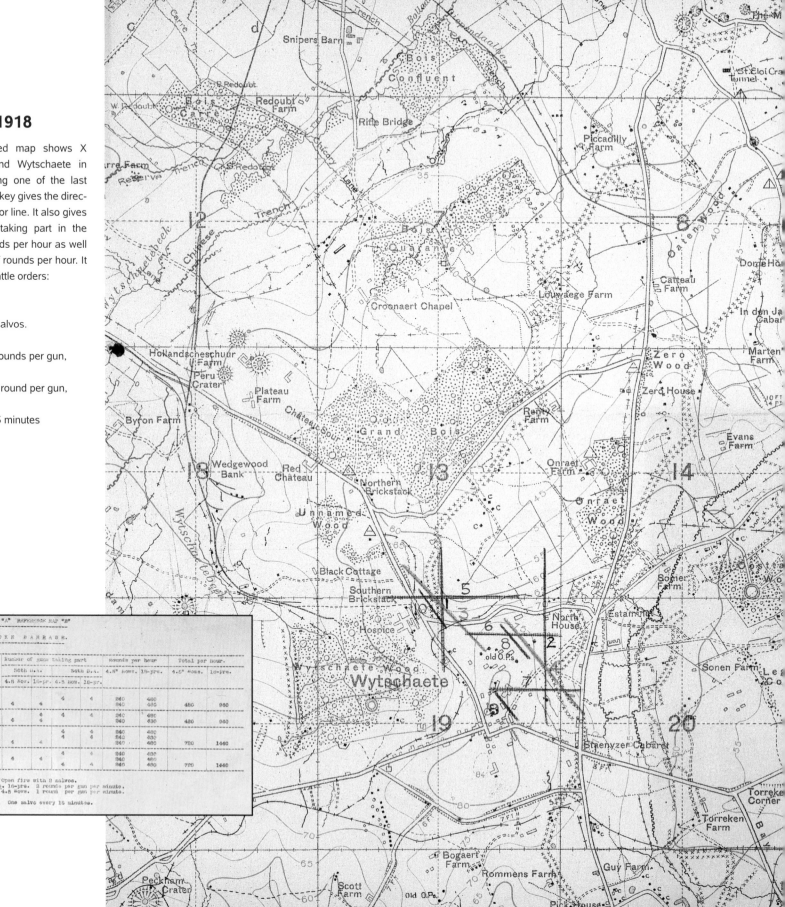

BATTLE OF FLANDERS, 1918

RIGHT: This annotated map shows X Corps barrages around Wytschaete in September 1918 during one of the last phases of the war. The key gives the direction of the wind in a color line. It also gives the number of guns taking part in the action, how many rounds per hour as well as the total numbers of rounds per hour. It also enumerates the battle orders:

At zero hour:
    open fire with two salvos.
Zero onward:
    18-pounders, two rounds per gun, per minute.
    4.5 Howitzers, one round per gun, per minute
    One salvo every 15 minutes

WO 153/1110

BRITISH BATTLES, AUGUST–NOVEMBER 1918

LEFT: 'The advance to victory.' At last the Allies were on the offensive and starting to gain ground. The map shows much of Northern France and parts of Belgium and shows how the ground changed hands.

The key (below right) shows the numbers of prisoners and guns captured by the British and Allied Armies from July 18 to November 11, 1918. It reads:

	Prisoners	Guns
British armies	188,700	2,840
French Armies	139,000	1,880
US Armies	43,300	1,421
Belgian Armies	14,500	474

WO 153/15

Map labels:

AREA OF FRANCO-BELGIAN ATTACKS

YPRES SECOND ARMY 28TH–29TH SEP. 4,800 PRISONERS 100 GUNS

COURTRAI 2ND ARMY 14TH–31ST OCT. 6000 PRISONERS, 200 GUNS.

AREA OF GERMAN WITHDRAWALS 15TH AUG.–20TH SEPT. (CONSEQUENT ON BRITISH ADVANCES TO HINDENBURG LINE)

AREA OF GERMAN WITHDRAWALS NOV. 8TH–11TH (CONSEQUENT ON BATTLE OF MAUBEUGE)

AREA OF GERMAN WITHDRAWALS OCT. 14TH–31ST. (CONSEQUENT ON BRITISH ATTACKS, NORTH & SOUTH)

ARRAS 1ST ARMY 26TH AUG.–3RD SEP. 18,850 PRISONERS 200 GUNS

SELLE RIVER 1ST, 3RD & 4TH ARMIES 17TH–25TH OCT. 21,000 PRISONERS 450 GUNS

VALENCIENNES–MAUBEUGE–MONS 1ST 3RD & 4TH ARMIES 1ST–11TH NOV. 19,000 PRISONERS 460 GUNS

CAMBRAI–ST QUENTIN PHASES 1 & 2 1ST, 3RD & 4TH ARMIES 27TH–30TH SEP. 36,500 PRISONERS 380 GUNS

CAMBRAI–ST QUENTIN PHASE 3 1ST, 3RD & 4TH ARMIES 8TH–10TH OCT. 12,000 PRISONERS 250 GUNS

EPEHY 3RD & 4TH ARMIES 18TH–19TH SEP. 11,750 PRISONERS 100 GUNS

BAPAUME THIRD & FOURTH ARMIES 21ST–31ST AUG. (& SUBSEQUENT DAYS) 34,250 PRISONERS 270 GUNS

AMIENS FOURTH ARMY 8TH–12TH AUG. 21,850 PRISONERS 400 GUNS

AREA OF FRENCH ATTACKS

Captures by British and Allied Armies from July 18th to Nov. 11th, 1918.

	Prisoners	Guns
British Armies	188,700	2,840
French Armies	139,000	1,880
American Armies	43,300	1,421
Belgian Armies	14,500	474

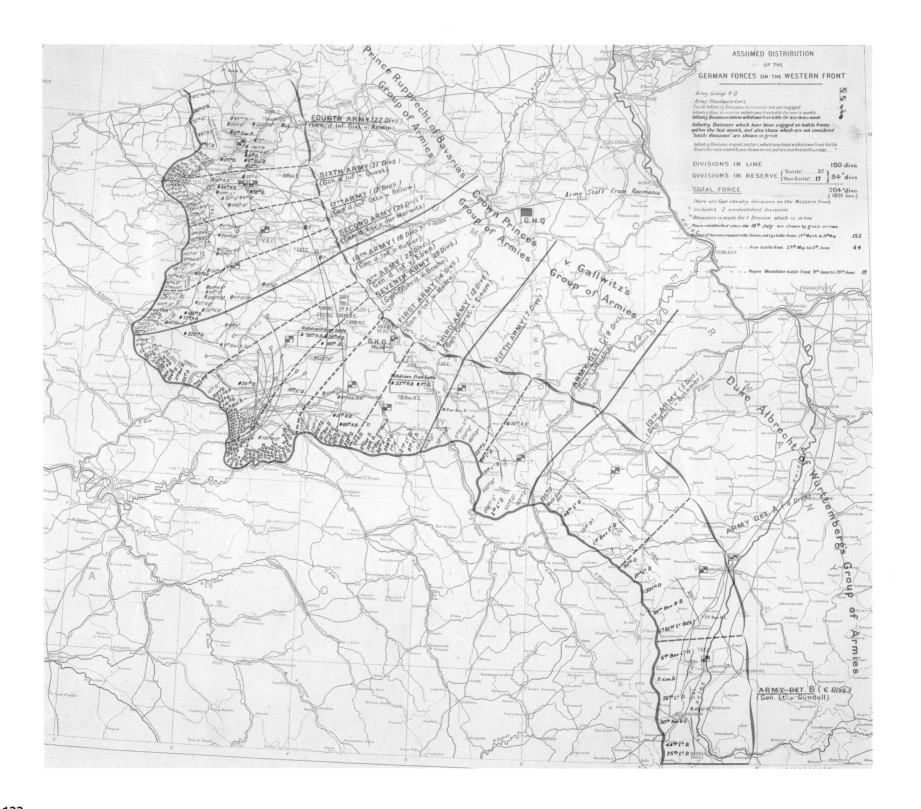

ASSUMED DISTRIBUTION
OF THE
GERMAN FORCES ON THE WESTERN FRONT

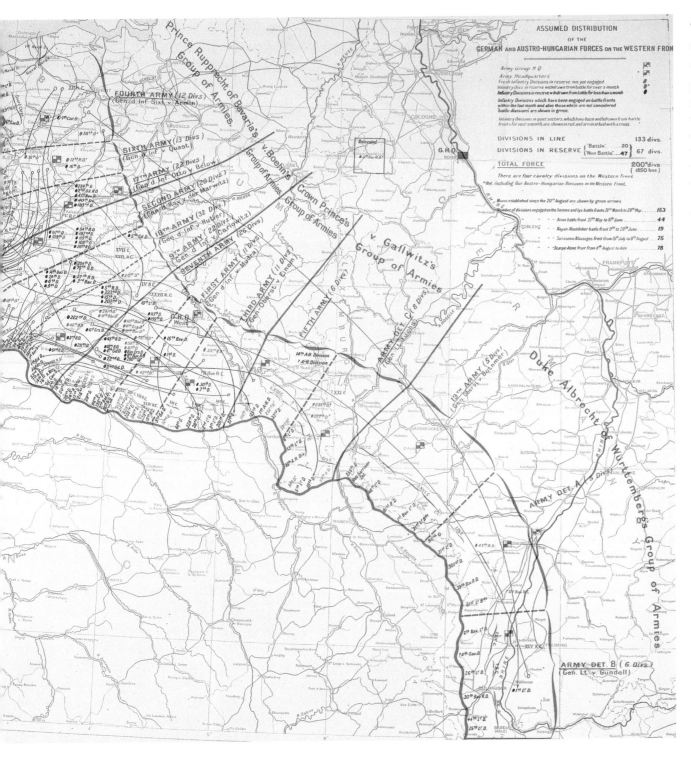

ASSUMED DISTRIBUTION
OF THE
GERMAN AND AUSTRO-HUNGARIAN FORCES ON THE WESTERN FRONT

THE RETREATING GERMAN ARMY, JULY–AUGUST 1918

FAR LEFT: By mid-1918 the Germans were in retreat, but the Allies still needed to know where they were and the strength and distribution of their troops and assets. This was the assumed distribution of German forces gathered from intelligence during the period from July 23, 1918. The key describes the assumed distribution of the German Forces as being 150 divisions in line, 54 divisions in reserve (37 battle, 17 non-battle). This gives a total force of 204 divisions—1,891 battalions. The map also speculates that there are four cavalry divisions on the Western Front, plus two unidentified divisions. WO 153/19 (1)

LEFT: This map is dated a month later than that on page 122, August 27, 1918. It proposes that there were 133 divisions in line, 67 divisions in reserve (20 'battle,' 47 'non-battle'). Giving a total force of 200 divisions (1,850 battalions). It also says that there are four cavalry divisions on the Western Front, but mentions that it does not include four Austro-Hungarian divisions stationed somewhere else on the Western Front. WO 153/19 (4)

SUCCESSIVE FRONTS ON THE WESTERN FRONT IN 1918

RIGHT: In 1918 the war moved at a faster rate than at any time since the beginning in 1914. The Allies advanced as the Germans slowly retreated northward with every yard of territory bitterly contested. This map shows the successive fronts in March, May, and November 1918, from a field survey carried out by Royal Engineers dated December 1, 1918. WO 153/26 (1)

AMERICAN CORPS, WESTERN FRONT, OCTOBER 15, 1918

FAR RIGHT: This annotated map shows an area of France with St Souplet in center; Le Cateau-Cambrais lies due north, just off the map. The map was issued by II American Corps as Artillery instructions No 3 and is dated October 15, 1918. It shows the field artillery barrage areas giving distances and vectors. WO 153/1161

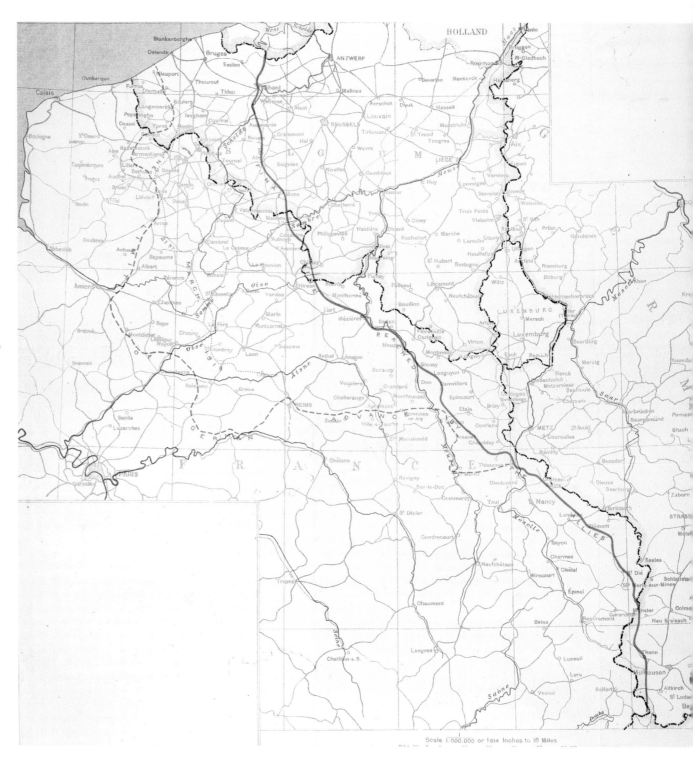

FRENCH ORDER OF BATTLE, AS AT NOVEMBER 1, 1918

RIGHT: The diagram shows the French order of battle just before the Armistice in November 1918. It shows how the troops are distributed along the Allied front (including US troops) in a line that generally follows the prevailing river courses. It also describes in the key the state of the French troops: red circles indicate tired troops, green show fresh troops, and blue circles show which troops have been reconstituted and are ready to return to action. WO 153/81 (1)

FRENCH ORDER OF BATTLE, AS AT NOVEMBER 6, 1918

FAR RIGHT: This diagram shows the French Order of Battle as before, but dated at November 6, 1918. By this time French soldiers were battle weary and badly depleted after four years of hard fighting. American troops were fresh to the war and eager, if inexperienced, for combat. Their overwhelming numbers and freshness gave them the edge against equally battle-weary German troops. WO 153/81 (5)

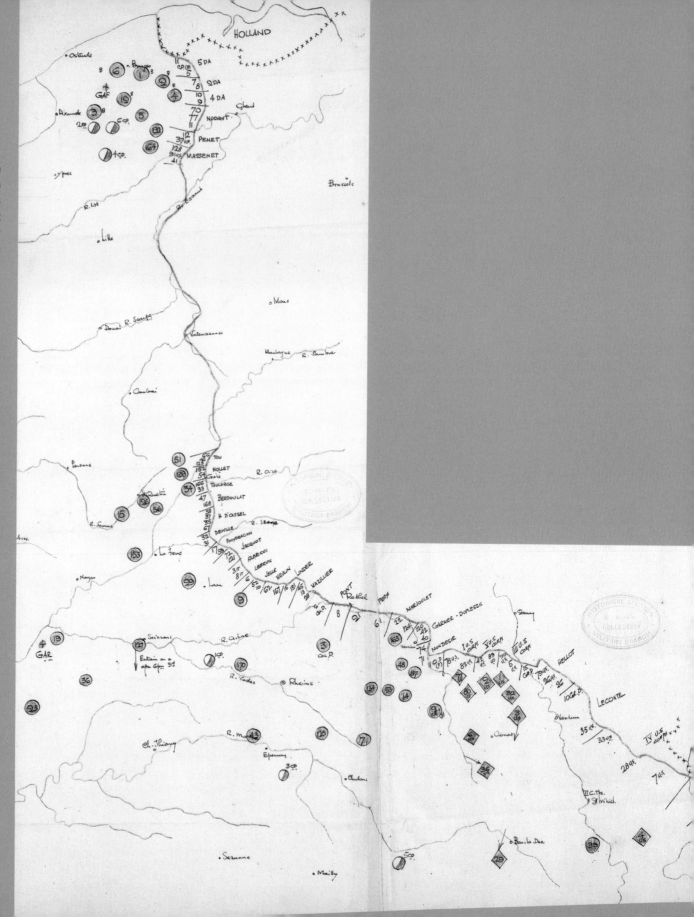

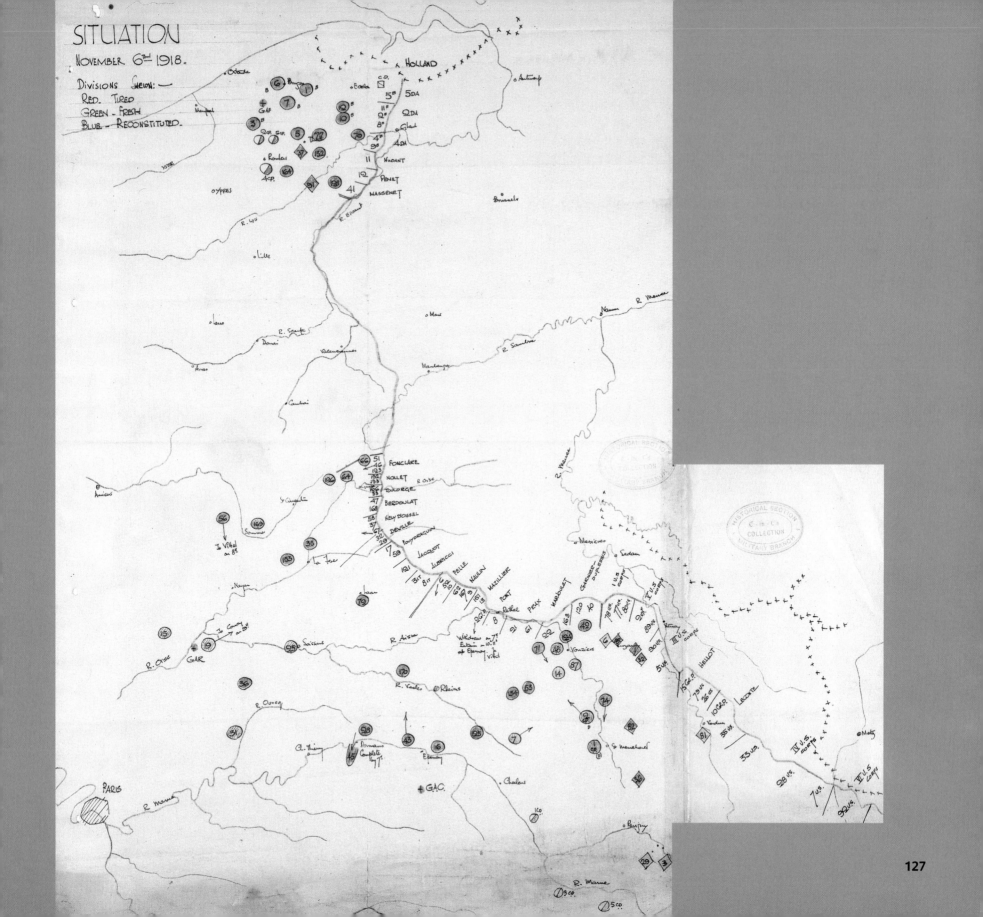

SITUATION

NOVEMBER 6TH 1918.

DIVISIONS SHEWN:—
RED. TIRED
GREEN - FRESH
BLUE - RECONSTITUTED.

VITTORIO VENETO, OCTOBER 30, 1918

RIGHT: The first phase of the last battle of the Italian Campaign opened on October 23 when Italian Army Chief of Staff Diaz pushed his Allied troops northwest into the Austrian Army in the Monte Grappa sector. The town of Vittorio Veneto was besieged on October 30.

The map gives Allied strength as:

Divisions	57
Battalions	709
Combatants	912,000
Guns and mortars	8,929

The Austrian strength was:

Divisions	63
Battalions	827
Combatants	1,070,000
Guns and mortars	7,000
MR 1/764 (1)	

BELOW RIGHT: The second phase was launched on October 31 (arrows show movements ordered). With enemy resistance rapidly crumbling, a ceasefire was called on November 2, by which time Allied forces had reached Trento in the west and Tagliamento in the east. The dotted line shows the positions reached by 1500hrs on November 4. MR 1/764 (2)

FAR RIGHT: Lines reached by the Italian army during the battle. MR 1/764 (3)

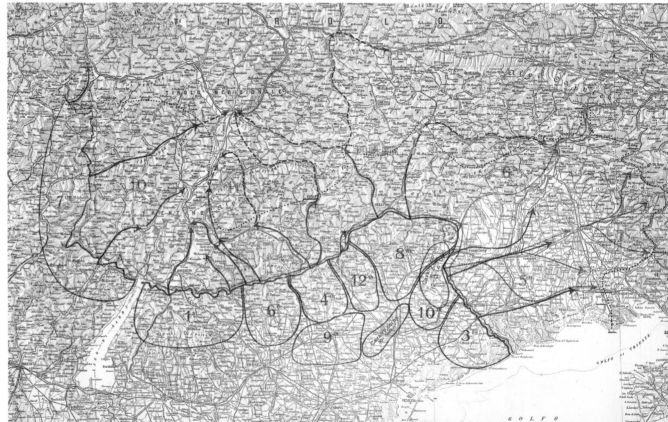

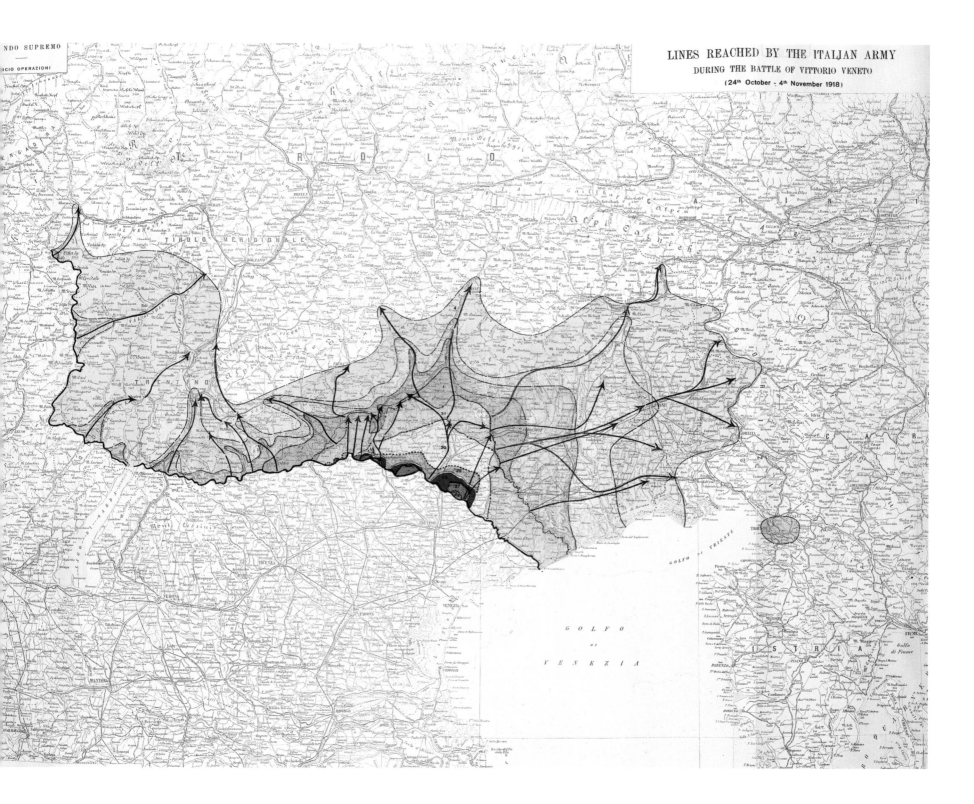

LINES REACHED BY THE ITALIAN ARMY
DURING THE BATTLE OF VITTORIO VENETO
(24th October - 4th November 1918)

VITTORIO VENETO CAMPAIGN, OCTOBER– NOVEMBER 1918

RIGHT: An annotated summary of the positions reached and the divisions involved between October 24, and November 4. The map gives the statistics and positions of the Army Groups belonging to General Oberst Archduke Ferdinand's 10th and 11th Armies and those of Field Marshall Boroevic von Bojna's Fifth and Sixth Armies. In 10 days of fighting the Italian Army captured 300,000 prisoners and suffered 38,000 casualties. WO 153/780 (12)

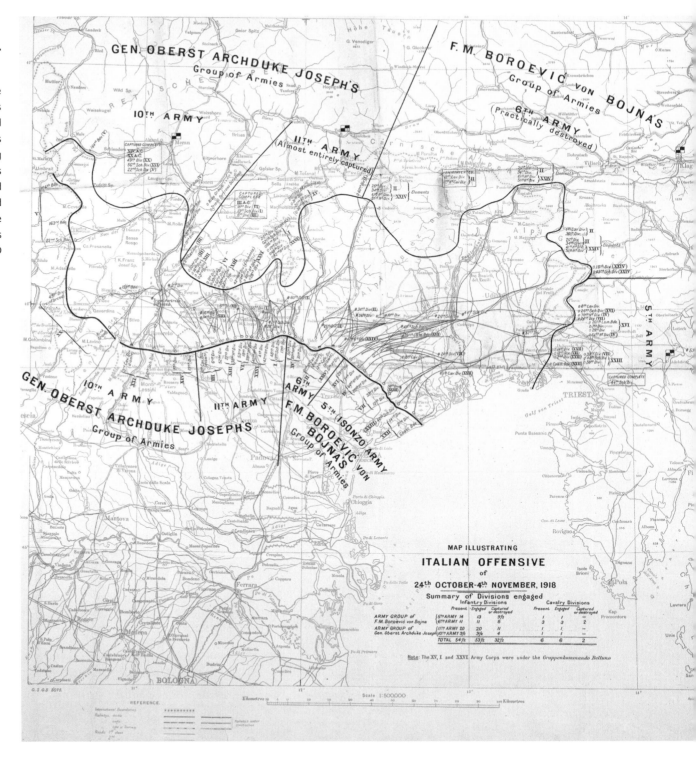

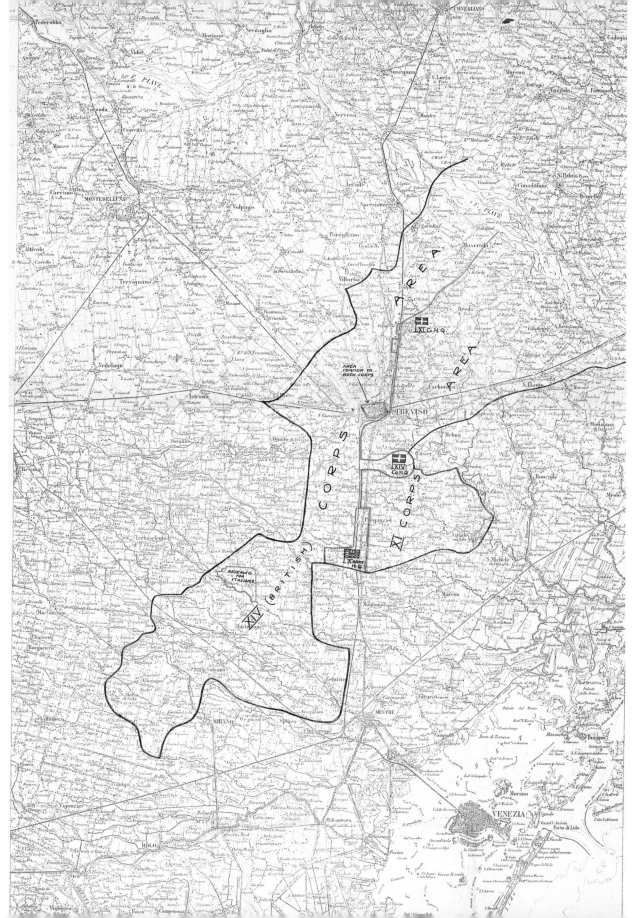

XIV CORPS IN ITALY, OCTOBER 1918

LEFT: An annotated Italian map giving the position of British XIV Corps based around the Treviso area. French, British, and latterly, American troops moved into Italy to assist the Italian Army in the final, successful, operations of the war. The Piave was finally crossed by units of French 12th and British Tenth Armies breaking Austro-Hungarian resistance completely. WO 153/734 (1)

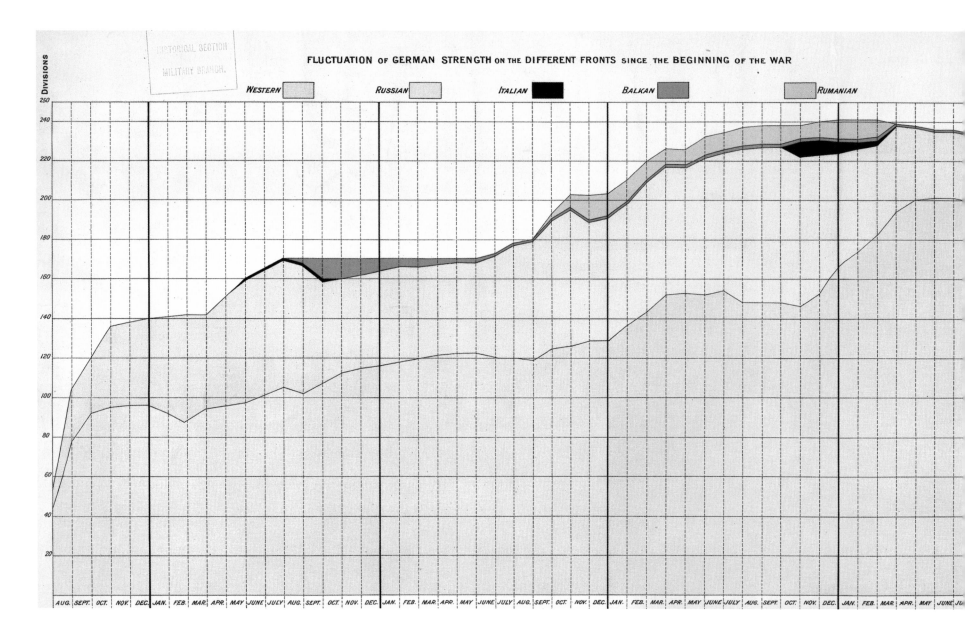

HISTORICAL SECTION
MILITARY BRANCH.

FLUCTUATION OF GERMAN STRENGTH ON THE DIFFERENT FRONTS SINCE THE BEGINNING OF THE WAR

WESTERN   RUSSIAN   ITALIAN   BALKAN   RUMANIAN

DIVISIONS

GERMAN STRENGTH ALL FRONTS,
AUGUST 1914–AUGUST 1918

ABOVE: This graph shows the fluctuations of German strengths on different fronts throughout the war. It very clearly shows the numerical weight of troops concentrated in Western Front – over twice the number committed at any one time to the Russian Front. Initial strengths were easier to calculate than after-battle totals. Estimates of the numbers of dead are harder to collate than perhaps expected due to the movement of peoples during wartime, recovered casualties returning to the front line, and the survivors not necessarily returning to their original units or even to their homes. It has been estimated that Germany lost over 1.8 million men in battle fighting on five main fronts. WO 153/1261 (20)

GERMAN MILITARY CALL-UPS, 1914–18

RIGHT: The chart shows the ages and time period of men called-up to serve Germany throughout the war. Before the war, servicemen were conscripted for short-term military service which was then followed by a longer period in the reserve. This gave the German Army a large pool of well-trained men to call-up as the demands of war required. German Army training was impressive and was generally regarded as being the best for producing well-disciplined and efficient troops. The army could mobilize, maneuver, and operate quicker, better, and more efficiently than any other army in the world. At the beginning of the war in August 1914 the German Army mustered 700,000 men split between 25 corps with reserves of 3.8 million men who could be mobilized and in uniform within a week. No other army in the world could even begin to match German Army's efficiency and preparedness for action. WO 153/1261 (21)

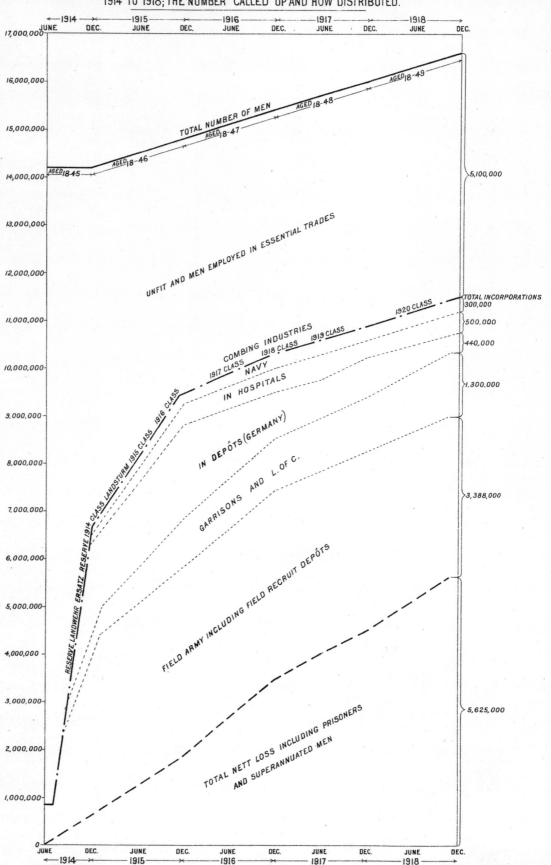

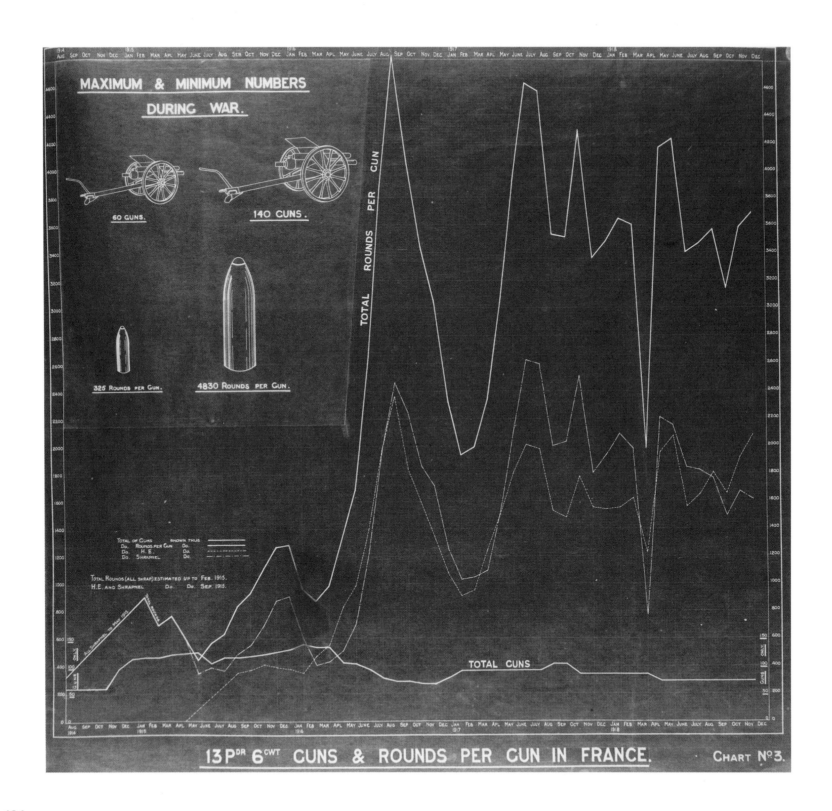

MAXIMUM & MINIMUM NUMBERS
DURING WAR.

60 GUNS.

140 GUNS.

325 ROUNDS PER GUN.

4830 ROUNDS PER GUN.

TOTAL ROUNDS PER GUN

TOTAL OF GUNS   SHOWN THUS
Do.   ROUNDS PER GUN   Do.
Do.   H.E   Do.
Do.   SHRAPNEL   Do.

TOTAL ROUNDS (ALL SHRAP) ESTIMATED UP TO FEB. 1915.
H.E. AND SHRAPNEL   Do.   Do.   SEP. 1915.

TOTAL GUNS

13 P^DR 6^CWT GUNS & ROUNDS PER GUN IN FRANCE.   CHART N°3.

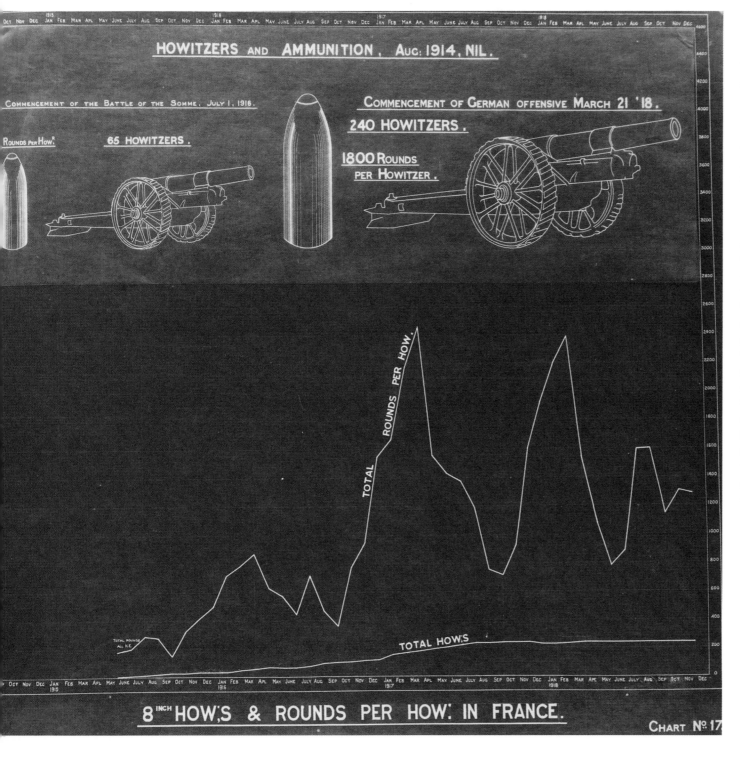

HOWITZERS AND AMMUNITION, Aug: 1914, NIL.

COMMENCEMENT OF THE BATTLE OF THE SOMME, JULY 1, 1916.

ROUNDS PER HOW:

65 HOWITZERS.

COMMENCEMENT OF GERMAN OFFENSIVE MARCH 21 '18.

240 HOWITZERS.

1800 ROUNDS PER HOWITZER.

TOTAL ROUNDS PER HOW.

TOTAL ROUNDS ALL H.E.

TOTAL HOW;S

8 INCH HOW;S & ROUNDS PER HOW: IN FRANCE.

CHART N.° 17

CHARTS SHOWING AMMUNITION EXPENDED IN WORLD WAR I

The charts on these pages are taken from a remarkable set of documents that show the amount of ammunition and artillery available and numbers of rounds per piece for guns and howitzers in France during 1914–18. These charts show (**far left**) the number of guns and rounds expended by 13-pdr 6-cwt guns, and (**left**) the same for 8-in howitzers. Vast quantities of munitions were expended on the Western Front during the war and the efficiency of the weapons improved throughout the conflict. The use of artillery became increasingly important for the successful culmination of battle as opposed to the work of the infantry. This was particularly relevant during such a static and prolonged conflict as the battles around the trenches on the Western Front. The Germans later calculated that in the first year of the war there were 49 casualties caused by artillery to every 22 by infantry. But for the period 1916–18 the figures had altered to 85 casualties caused by artillery for every six caused by infantry. WO 153/1225 (3, 17)

135

ROYAL ENGINEERS CHART, WESTERN FRONT, 1916

RIGHT: Defenses against artillery became more sophisticated as the war continued and Allied techniques began to match the Germans'. This diagram was drawn up by Royal Engineers to show how to sink a cupola under a sand dune. This detailed plan was produced for 10th Division battle headquarters. The scale is 1in to 10ft. WO 153/1253

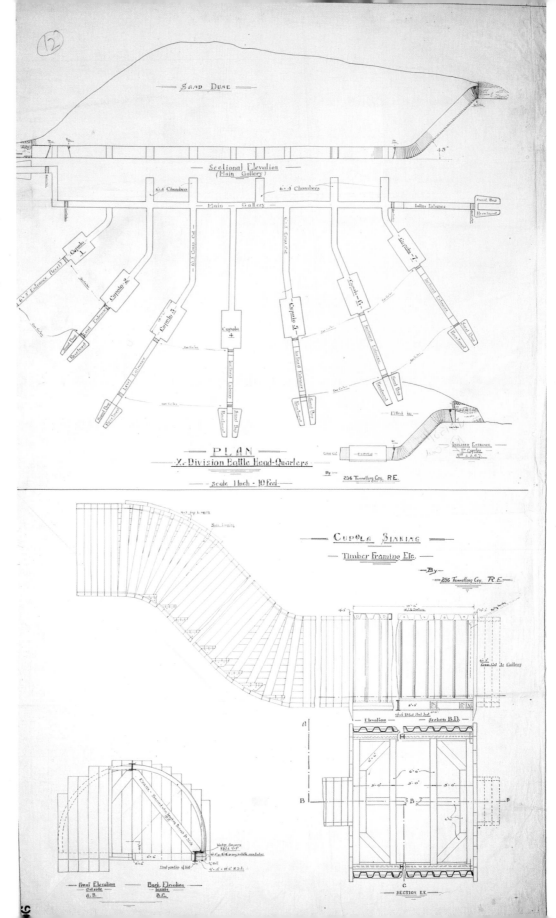

GUNS AND HOWITZERS: ROUNDS PER PIECE IN FRANCE 1914–18

LEFT: A set of charts showing guns and howitzers in France during the war. The graph (**left**) shows the total number of all guns and howitzers in France at the beginning and the end of the war. The second chart (**below left**) shows the number of rounds fired by each type of gun and howitzer. The final diagram (**below right**) shows weight of metal thrown, energy developed, and the life of guns or howitzers before becoming unserviceable. WO 153/1225 (21, 22)

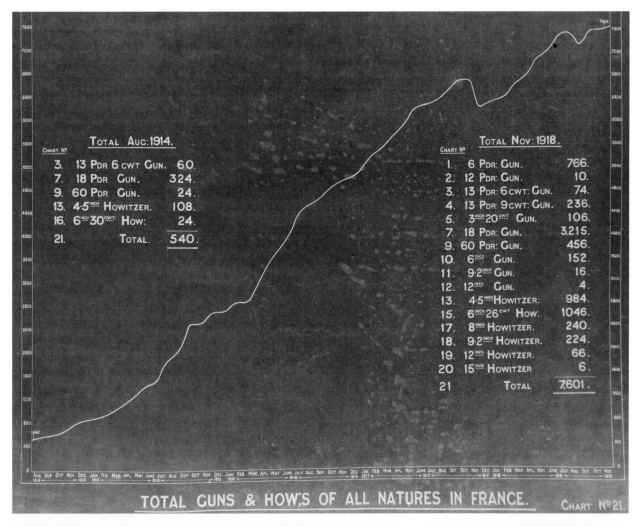

TOTAL AUG: 1914.

CHART Nº		
3.	13 PDR 6 CWT GUN.	60.
7.	18 PDR GUN.	324.
9.	60 PDR GUN.	24.
13.	4·5 INCH HOWITZER.	108.
16.	6 INCH 30 CWT HOW:	24.
21.	TOTAL.	540.

TOTAL NOV: 1918.

CHART Nº		
1.	6 PDR: GUN.	766.
2.	12 PDR: GUN.	10.
3.	13 PDR: 6 CWT: GUN.	74.
4.	13 PDR: 9 CWT: GUN.	236.
5.	3 INCH 20 CWT GUN.	106.
7.	18 PDR: GUN.	3,215.
9.	60 PDR: GUN.	456.
10.	6 INCH GUN.	152.
11.	9·2 INCH GUN.	16.
12.	12 INCH GUN.	4.
13.	4·5 INCH HOWITZER:	984.
15.	6 INCH 26 CWT HOW:	1046.
17.	8 INCH HOWITZER.	240.
18.	9·2 INCH HOWITZER.	224.
19.	12 INCH HOWITZER.	66.
20.	15 INCH HOWITZER	6.
21	TOTAL	7,601.

TOTAL GUNS & HOW'S OF ALL NATURES IN FRANCE. CHART Nº 21.

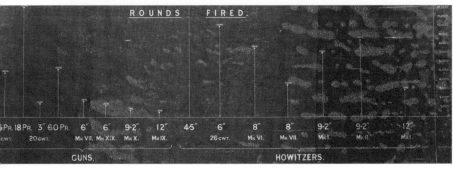

ROUNDS FIRED.

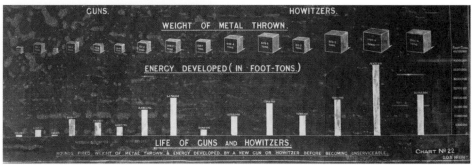

GUNS. HOWITZERS.
WEIGHT OF METAL THROWN.
ENERGY DEVELOPED (IN FOOT-TONS.)
LIFE OF GUNS AND HOWITZERS.
ROUNDS FIRED, WEIGHT OF METAL THROWN, & ENERGY DEVELOPED, BY A NEW GUN OR HOWITZER BEFORE BECOMING UNSERVICEABLE. CHART Nº 22

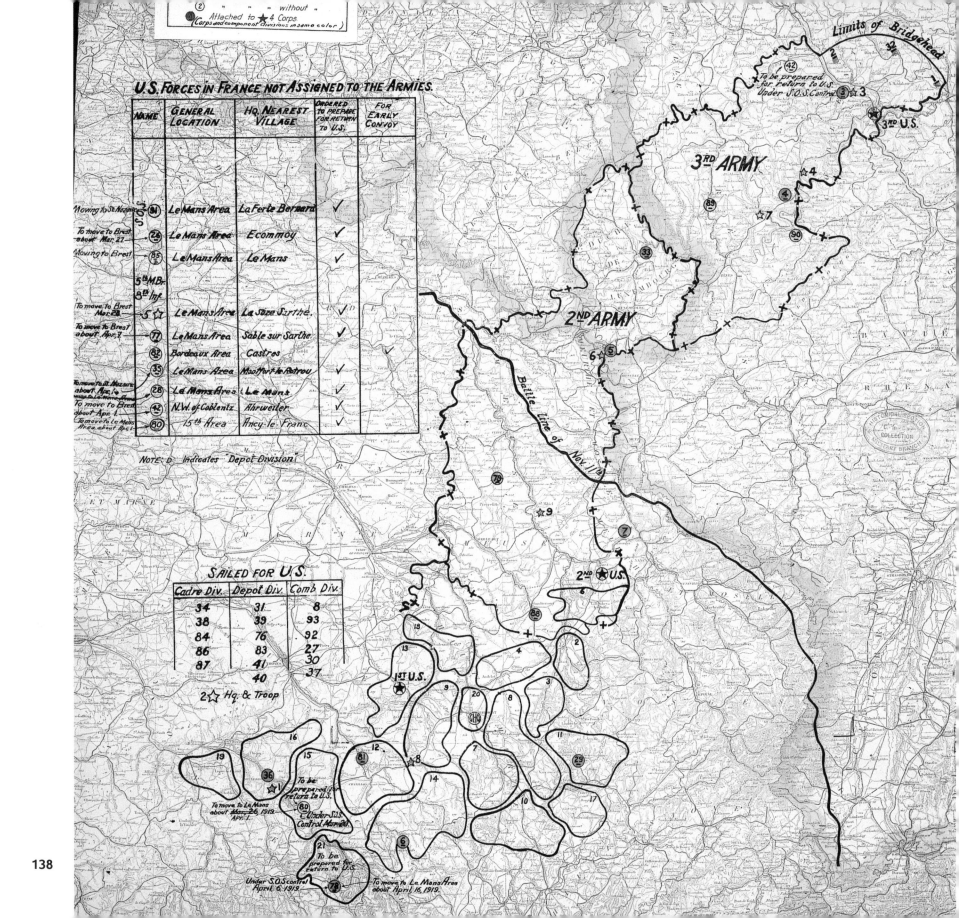

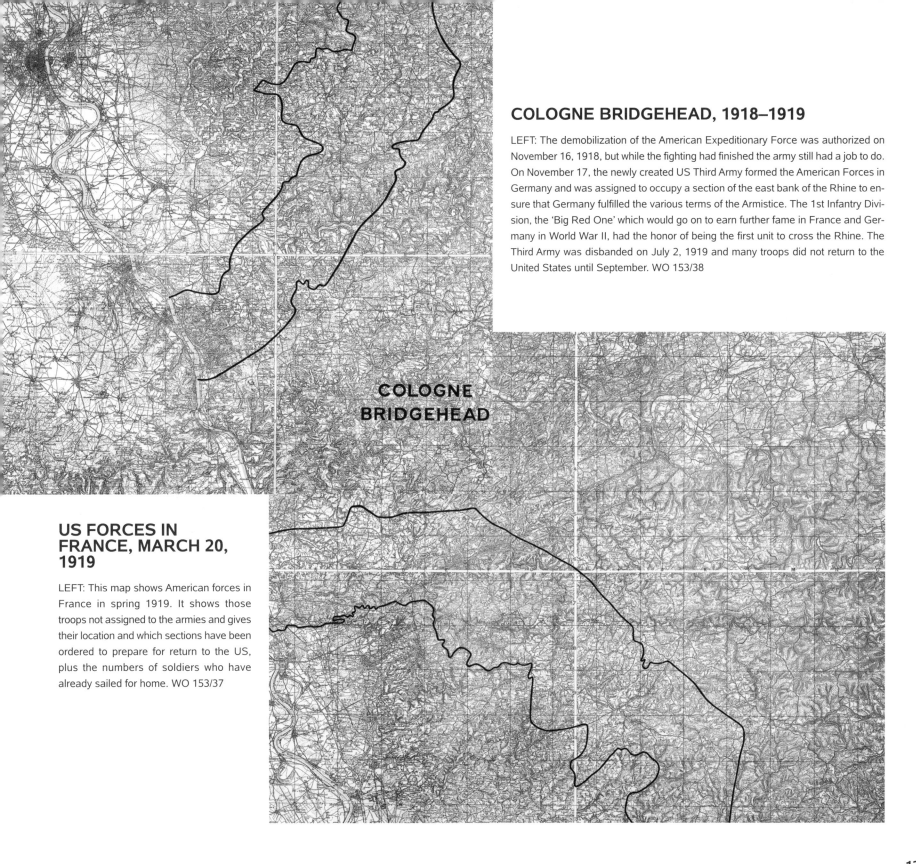

COLOGNE BRIDGEHEAD, 1918–1919

LEFT: The demobilization of the American Expeditionary Force was authorized on November 16, 1918, but while the fighting had finished the army still had a job to do. On November 17, the newly created US Third Army formed the American Forces in Germany and was assigned to occupy a section of the east bank of the Rhine to ensure that Germany fulfilled the various terms of the Armistice. The 1st Infantry Division, the 'Big Red One' which would go on to earn further fame in France and Germany in World War II, had the honor of being the first unit to cross the Rhine. The Third Army was disbanded on July 2, 1919 and many troops did not return to the United States until September. WO 153/38

COLOGNE BRIDGEHEAD

US FORCES IN FRANCE, MARCH 20, 1919

LEFT: This map shows American forces in France in spring 1919. It shows those troops not assigned to the armies and gives their location and which sections have been ordered to prepare for return to the US, plus the numbers of soldiers who have already sailed for home. WO 153/37

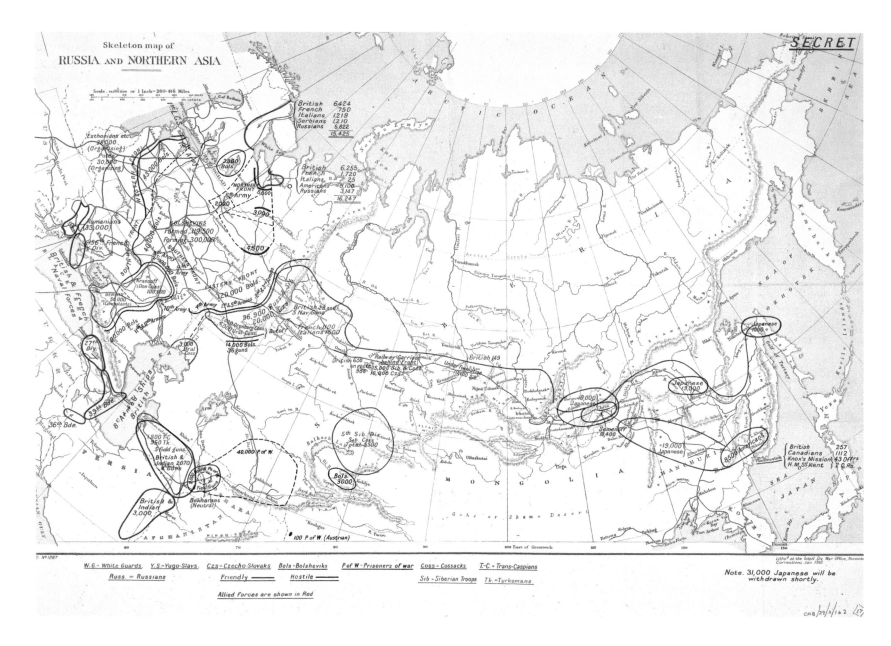

The map image contains the following labels and annotations:

Skeleton map of
RUSSIA AND NORTHERN ASIA

SECRET

Scale 1:11,000,000 or 1 Inch = 260·416 Miles

British	6,424
French	750
Italians	1,219
Serbians	1,210
Russians	5,822
	15,425

British	6,255
French	1,720
Italians	25
Americans	5,100
Russians	3,147
	16,247

British	257
Canadians	1,112
Knox's Mission	43 Offrs
H.M.S. Kent	} 2 O.Rs.

Note. 31,000 Japanese will be withdrawn shortly.

W.G. = White Guards.   Y.S = Yugo-Slavs.   Czs = Czecho-Slovaks   Bols = Bolsheviks   P of W = Prisoners of war   Coss = Cossacks   T-C = Trans-Caspians

Russ. = Russians   Friendly ——   Hostile ——   Sib = Siberian Troops   Tk. = Turkomans

Allied forces are shown in Red

RUSSIA AND NORTHERN ASIA, 1919

ABOVE: The war in Russia continued but not against the Germans. The Russian Revolution led to Civil War as Communists and Royalists clashed for control. This map of Russia and Northern Asia is annotated to show the numbers and nationalities of troops in different areas. The Allied forces are shown in red, with friendly nationalities in green and hostile nationalities (including prisoners of war) in blue. MPI 1/397 (17)

RUSSIAN CIVIL WAR, 1919

Right and **Far Right:** Two maps showing the situation in Russia between January 1 (**far right**) and March 20 (**right**) during the Russian Civil War. The first map shows the high tide for the White Russians. The anti-Bolshevik fronts are illustrated in red and the Bolshevik fronts in blue. Comparison with the map far right shows that by March the tide had turned in favor of the Communists. MPI 1/397, WO 153/803

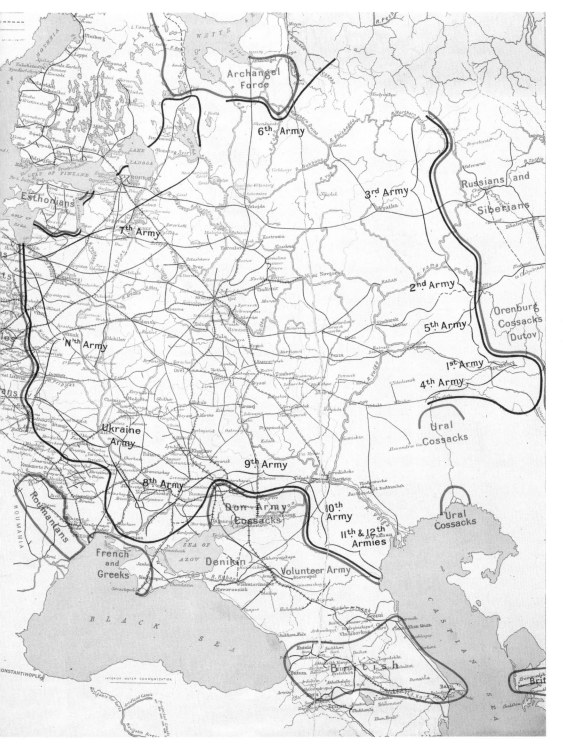

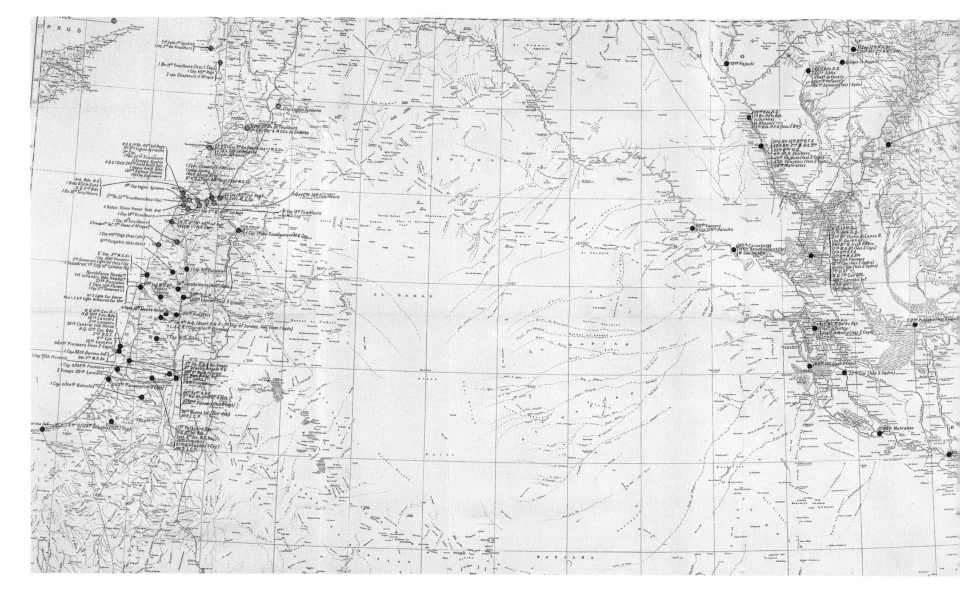

BALANCE OF POWER IN THE MIDDLE EAST, 1920

ABOVE: French and British troops in Palestine, Syria, and Mesopotamia as at March 17, 1920. The map shows the postwar occupation of this area that had been controlled by the Ottoman Empire for centuries. Allied forces occupied the former territories as part of the Armistice terms. Colonial involvement in these countries would continue until after World War II, and contribute greatly to their instability. MPK 1/310 (1)

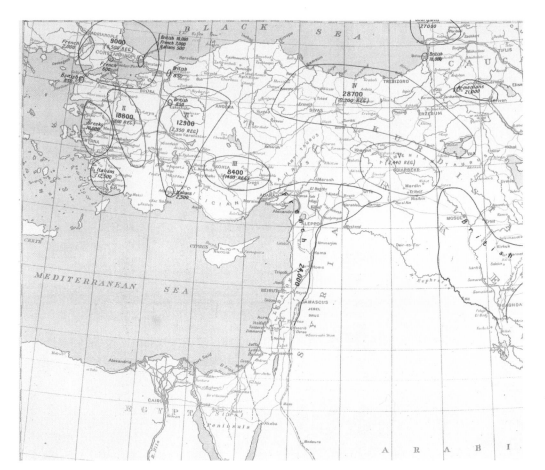

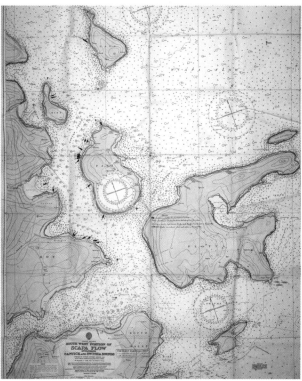

BALANCE OF POWER IN THE MIDDLE EAST, 1920

ABOVE LEFT: Turkish and Allied troops in Asia and the Middle East as at March 17, 1920. Seen in conjunction with map left, it shows the level of military commitment that existed in the area after the war. A mixture of self-interest and the wish to ensure that the terms of the Armistice were met saw Allied forces involved until well into the 1930s. MPK 1/310 (5)

GERMAN FLEET, SCAPA FLOW, 1919

ABOVE RIGHT: The German High Seas Fleet formally surrendered in the Forth of Firth on November 21. The modern ships were steamed to Scapa Flow where the skeleton German crews scuttled their vessels on June 21, 1919, afraid that the ships would be commandeered by the Royal Navy. This Admiralty map shows the location of the German High Seas Fleet under the waters at Scapa Flow. ADM 116/2074

INDEX OF MAPS